The Trouble with Spain

Martin Lloyd

Queen Anne's Fan

The Trouble with Spain

First published in 2005 by Queen Anne's Fan
PO Box 883 • Canterbury • Kent • CT1 3WJ

Reprinted 2013, 2018

ISBN 9780 8547 1501 4

All personages and characters portrayed in this book, whether corporate or particular, are real life. Following the established convention in travel writing, only the facts, primordial, substantive and trivial may have been altered out of all recognition in order to preserve the integrity of the narrative.

A complete catalogue record of this book can be obtained from the British Library on request.

This book is sold subject to the following utterly unenforcable condition: it shall not be resold, lent, hired or loaned to a third party. If they ask to borrow it, tell them to buy their own copy. This book will sulk if sent to a charity shop.

Cover photographs by Alan Nicoll and Andrew Cook

Printed in England
Set in New Baskerville 11pt
www.queenannesfan.com

Queen Anne's Fan

The Trouble with Spain . . .

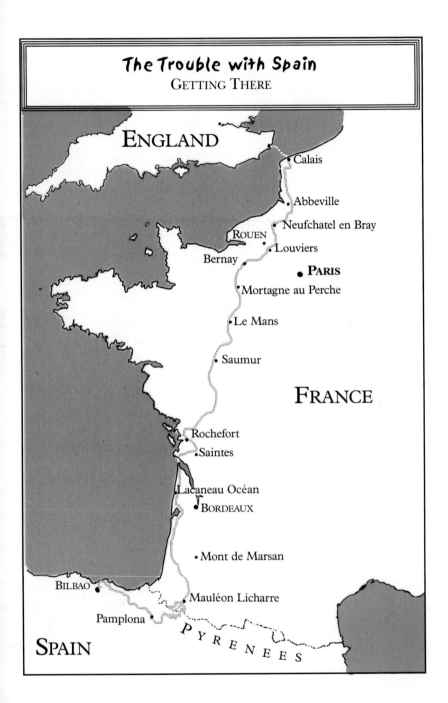

The Trouble with Spain
GETTING THERE

ENGLAND

Calais

Abbeville

Neufchatel en Bray

ROUEN

Louviers

Bernay

PARIS

Mortagne au Perche

Le Mans

Saumur

FRANCE

Rochefort

Saintes

Lacaneau Océan

BORDEAUX

Mont de Marsan

BILBAO

Mauléon Licharre

Pamplona

SPAIN

PYRENEES

chapter one

The trouble with Spain...

The trouble with Spain, I suddenly realised, was that I had to go through France to get there. I stopped spinning my wet sock above my head and draped it over my handlebar. And the problem with going through France was that it still had a score to settle with me. I pulled my other wet sock from my jacket pocket and hoisted it to the helicopter rotor position ready to start the drying process.

A quick survey of the cloud layer suggested that the rain would hold off for another hour or so. The impetus for my expedition to Spain was a desire to cycle in a country where the sun shone whilst I was on my bicycle and not just for the ten minutes that I spent in the supermarket. The damp sock whirring above me was a dizzy reminder of the French unreliability in matters meteorological and it hardened my resolve to reach Spain despite the impediments before me.

One of the latter was of my own making. I had taken the utterly daft decision to try to cross the nine hundred miles of France without going on any main roads. What was the point of that? Did I think that by sneaking through Gaul by the back alleys I would escape detection? Vain hope!

I was nearing a town. A car rollicked around the corner and the two ladies inside pointed and screamed derision as they roared towards me. Much too late did I remember that I had stretched my underpants across my front light so that they would dry in the breeze of my travelling. Something had to be done. If I was to be faced with a perpetual set of damp clothes I needed a system for drying them on the bike that did not offend the locals or frighten the horses.

So I stop at the ironmongers. I wait whilst a woman in a navy blue gabardine raincoat conducts her business with Mrs. Ironmonger, who is saying, 'But it shows you on the tin what colour the paint is. Look, it's pale blue.'

'Oh I can see what colour the tin is,' says Mrs. Raincoat. 'I want to know what colour the paint inside is.'

Mrs. Ironmonger gropes under the counter and pulls out the broken-bladed knife which should be a shopkeeper's favourite tool. With a hiss and a thud she prises the lid from the can.

'See, it's pale blue.'

'Oh that's no good.' Mrs. Raincoat takes another can from the shelf. 'Try this one.'

'This is peach,' Mrs. Ironmonger says and, faltering

before the woman's eyes she adds, 'At least, that is what it says on the tin.' *Hiss, thud.* They look in. 'Yes, peach,' she confirms.

'That's no good. What about this one?'
'That's red. But what colour are you looking for?'
'The tin's red.'
Hiss, thud.
'So is the paint.'
'Don't want red.'
'What colour are you looking for?'
'Pink.'

I reach up and silently hand a tin of coral pink paint to Mrs. Ironmonger. Mrs. Raincoat turns her whole body around to look at me and then swivels back to the counter where the broken knife blade is already feeling the rim.

'Coral pink. That'll do,' she says.
'Don't you want me to open it?'
'No don't trouble yourself. It's got the colour on the tin.'

I secretly pray that the contents are canary yellow. I purchase a plastic string bag. Green to match my bike. With my washing arranged in this, I can hang it from the handlebars in all decency and the breeze can dry my clothes even when travelling through towns.

The sun emerged from a patchy cloud sky when I stopped to eat my lunch at Senarpont. I sat by the old ford where the Bresle tinkled its route to the sea at Le Tréport. I watched the fish squirming sinuously in the river whilst, a little further upstream, the traffic to Beauvais thundered over the concrete span which had been built to avoid the narrow bridge and ford which were now my picnic stop.

The day now began to get quite hot, reminding me that with every day's travel I would be moving further from the moderating influence of the sea.

I saw two other touring cyclists, probably English, having their lunch in the shade of the trees by the church. I tried waving to them but they stared stone-faced at me. This reminded me of a story which was recounted to me by a Frenchman purporting to illustrate differing national characteristics. A woman, her husband and her lover are all shipwrecked on a desert island. All they possess is a bed and a revolver. What happens? If they are French, the lover shoots the husband; if they are Dutch, the husband shoots the lover; if they are Spanish, the husband shoots his wife; if they are German, the husband shoots himself; if they are Italian, the wife shoots her husband; if they are Belgian, they throw the gun into the sea and if they are English? Nothing happens because they have not been introduced.

It had been a short, sharp descent into Senarpont from the north; the southerly road out was a long climb towards the forest of Guimerville. In the elbow of the wood nestled a factory. It appeared to be a glass factory. All along the verge of the road and impressed into the tar metalling itself, glass splinters of all colours reflected and refracted the sunlight in a riot of rainbows and jewel-like beams. The lorries which were bringing to the factory the glass for recycling were obviously not quite as secure as they should be. Whilst enjoying the colours I nevertheless gave the margin of the road a respectfully wide berth. I did not want to be picking psychedelic splinters from my inner tubes for the rest of the day.

The landscape was now characterized by a series of short steep valleys and hilltops crowned by forests. I had arranged my route so as to take advantage of this and traverse as many of these forests as I could legitimately put in my way. I had time in hand so when I saw the next wooded ridge appear on the horizon I decided to do a little exploring. I knew what I would find. I had studied the subject so many times that I had become a little blasé about what I now realise to be an unusual knowledge that I have of the woods of northern France. On various journeys in company I have pointed out dumb shapes lurking in leafy shade and thrown bald explanations to my companions and I have been astonished by their deference to my apparent erudition.

From a distance of a quarter of a mile I surveyed the silent, dark mass of trees. I needed the north west edge of the wood, just where the trees gave way to the fields of maize. Or where they would have done in 1944. There should be a small road. Studying the exit from the village through my spyglass I could just distinguish a hedge leading up to the wood. That would do. As I plunged into the green shade of forest, escaping the harsh sun for the first time, I realised what a jolly good idea I had had. I also noticed the overgrown concrete track and before I could stop myself the bike had swerved down it. I was on German concrete.

Twenty yards into the wood the track forked and I knew that the branch would go to the motor transport store. I continued on the unbroken rib of concrete which was beginning to disappear beneath a scattering of twigs and leaves until I reached a low rectangular brick and concrete building. This would have been the final preparation area. The road ran through it and further on I stopped before the characteristic wide open arch of the non-magnetic building. A wider entrance than the other buildings because at this stage extra clearance would have been needed for the wings. In the floor there would have been a bronze azimuth ring to enable the staff to set the compass. I could see the groove where it had been fixed but the valuable metal itself had long gone. Only the shell of the building remained, the interior invaded by the trees and shrubs pushing up through the bombed concrete floor.

I checked on my compass. The bearing was about 280 degrees. It was just right for London. The non-magnetic building, of course, would have been built in the same alignment as the launching ramp. I peered through the unyielding greenery. I parked my bike and stumbled on through undergrowth that had been churned and tussocked by five-hundred pounders. All that remained of the ramp was a low, moss-covered wall of the grey concrete blocks that they always used for the blast wall. I continued through the site, past the long storage building built with a curved end to avoid bomb blast from detonating its contents. These were the buildings which from the air looked like skis and gave the name of 'ski site' to the 'targets for tonight' of Bomber Command.

Regaining the unassuming country lane I looked at the peaceful wood. The tall, heavily foliaged trees would continue to withold the secret from all but the most curious of investigators. The casual rambler would never know that he was walking past a V1 launch site of the Second World War. A place from which the doodlebugs or flying bombs of 1944 were hurled roaring into the night sky in a cloud of steam and jet fumes to fall thirty minutes later and redesign a portion of Kent or London with their load of Amatol explosive. And I had found scores of such sites in northern France. But then, that does not interest many people.

In the next village I discovered that the road that I wanted to take was closed by a makeshift barrier. Knowing that these barriers never really applied to bicycles, I swerved around it and carried on.

The verges on both sides of the road were flattened as if by the passage of many feet, and mud had been spread everywhere. As I pedalled away from the village, the road sunk between the hedgeless fields and there I could see evidence of works of some sort. A great scar had been gouged out of the field on one side, the unbordered earth sculpted like blancmange. At the next corner it was the opposite side of the road where the earth had been moved.

There was something bizarre about this. The work was obviously unfinished – the road surface was in a terrible state, covered with mud and shingle and yet I could see no diggers, nor any of the other paraphernalia that one usually finds at road works. And why had they dug the outside of the curves – why widen the road there? It was the opposite of straightening it and those curves were somehow too artistic. What was going on?

When I came to the bridge carrying, over my track, the fast main road which I had taken the trouble to avoid, the mystery resolved itself. At the foot of the bridge had been excavated a lagoon to take the rain shed from the carriageway above. It was deep, well-fenced and utterly empty. It had contained water, a lot of water probably, indeed, sufficient water to breach the downhill bank and thunder down the road, slicing great chunks from the fields and flattening the verges with mud before charging down the village street to dissipate in the broader, flatter fields beyond. It must have given the villagers something to talk about.

The old main road into Neufchatel en Bray had been declassified and its *route nationale* soubriquet switched to the bypass which stalked long legged across the valley. This meant that I could legitimately claim that I had cycled the day's miles solely on secondary roads. As I rode into the town a man hailed me from the opposite pavement. I stopped and crossed the road to him.

'Which road do I take for St. Valéry?' he asked. 'Do you know?'

'No, but I can work it out.' I pulled my map from my cycle bag.

'Is it that one?' he asked.

'Just a minute. Let me get my bearings.' I turned the map to the correct quadrant. 'St. Valéry is on the coast isn't it?'

'They say it is.' I found his answer to be rather mysterious. He continued, 'Or do you think it is that road over there?'

'No. It's that road there. Look...' I showed him my map. 'I've just come down from the north. To get to the coast I would have to turn right, which makes it that road by the side of–'

Without a word, he turned from my map and slowly walked across the road to look in the window of the pharmacy. I stared after him for a while, expecting him to come back to me but when he had finished his study of the display of pill boxes he began to stroll along the opposite pavement, idly window shopping, ignoring me completely. I refolded my map and reminded myself not to drink the tap water in Neufchatel.

I checked in at the Hotel du Lion d'Or, musing that it was probably possible to cross all of France and sleep only in hotels of that name.* Once my bike was safely locked in the vast hotel garage, I thrust my hands into my pockets and mingled with the holiday crowds which were sunning themselves on the afternoon pavements. A happy, relaxed atmosphere infused the town.

When you are carrying three sets of cycling clothes to last you a thousand miles, you have to work out a fine procedure to ensure that you always have something to wear. Mine is this. Having reached the hotel by about four in the afternoon, I go straight to my room, strip off and wash the clothes I am wearing. I then wring them in my magic towel and peg them out on my washing line which I will have previously attached to any process or protuberance which will support it. I then take a shower and put on my evening wear which consists of a pair of crease-proof black trousers and a short sleeved open necked shirt made from a sort of artificial seersucker which is meant to look creased and so does not need ironing. If it is chilly in the evening, I slip on my thin vee-necked sweater.

Sometimes I can hang the damp clothes across my open window, having closed the shutters. This allows them to dry in a breeze without offending the passers by, or the hotel manager. You become quite astute at recognising opportunities to dry clothes. One night I leapt out of bed

---

* I came to regret this fatuous claim when later I was challenged to prove that such a journey was feasible. *Hunting the Golden Lion* was the result.

suddenly at three in the morning because my subconscious had heard the radiator click as it heated up and I was thus able to take down my damp clothes from the line and steam them dry on the radiator. On another occasion, feeling the heat radiating from my bedhead reading lamp, I had laid out a pair of soggy socks and bent the flexible lamp down so that it gently basted them whilst I ate my dinner. It is when I can find no system to work for me, that I end up cycling along, spinning my laundry above my head. But now, with my latest acquisition – a plastic string bag – all these difficulties would be banished.

When I came downstairs to dinner, the town had changed dramatically. The bustling crowds, the hooting cars, the skipping children, the shopwares spilling out onto the street; these were all gone, to be replaced by... well, nothing really. Indeed, it seemed to me from listening to the conversations throughout the very ordinary meal, that the natives' requirements in evening entertainment were being amply furnished by the burglar alarm on a car parked opposite the church which kept spontaneously playing a one-note fanfare.

At breakfast I realised that I had been in France forty eight hours and I was already half way across the second of my fifteen large scale maps of France which would relay me in dog-leg fashion across the Seine and the Loire, down the Atlantic coast of France and over the Pyrenees to Bilbao.

I can hear you laughing at the ridiculous amount of luggage that I must have been carrying. You forget that after ten years of lugging a loaded bike around the countryside anybody can think up tricks to lighten their load. I am not talking about expedition gimmicks like cutting the labels from clothes or drilling holes in spanners but practical and sensible ideas like preparing stamped addressed envelopes so that as I used the maps I could mail them home; or metering out the disposable razors to correspond with the projected number of days' journey;

taking only three changes of clothing but a bar of soap and a washing line and pegs. My retinue was designed to lighten itself the longer I travelled so that by the time I reached the Pyrenees I would be on my last map, my last razor and my last scraping of soap. If I ever reached there I would be on my last legs as well.

Buchy is a sweet little town but for some reason, perhaps because it is the weekend of Ascension, the street lamps are garnished with loudspeakers which are emitting a strident mixture of tin-pot music and brain-rot babble. The screeching noise doggedly follows me into the small supermarket where I buy my lunch.

Today is the day that I am to cross the River Seine. My secret roads take me direct south to an overgrown track that snakes down through a wood to the narrow valley of the Andelle just upstream of its confluence with the Seine. To avoid the main road I remain on the north bank till I reach Pont St. Pierre. In a yard attached to what I assume to be a recycling depot of some sort, slumbers the biggest mound of empty plastic water bottles that I have ever seen. It is the size and shape of a long low bungalow, built of bluey-greeney-grey cylindrical plastic bricks.

Crossing now to the south bank of the valley I round a bluff and catch my first sight of the Seine as it winds its way down to the sea. Here, I am only one and a half meanders upstream from Rouen.

The sun is now unequivocally shining and so I remove my fluorescent yellow cycling shirt. It had already caught a few amazed looks. Two minutes later I nearly fall from my bike in surprise as a young lady cycles past me in the opposite direction, also without a shirt; indeed, wearing nothing above the belt of her shorts. I stare after her, although the view from the rear is not so stunning. Remembering the contours of her chest I cannot help thinking that she would surely be better streamlined with a shirt over them.

The Seine valley at this point is about three miles across and is the home to two rivers. The Seine runs just below me; alongside the road and close under the opposite bank of the valley flows the Eure. The space between is full of lakes and clumps of trees. It is difficult to distinguish lake from river.

I cross the Seine at St. Pierre du Vauvray. Alongside the level crossing there is laid out a diverse assembly of colourful and bizarre items, offered for sale by an equally heterogeneous squad of amateur vendors. It is the *Brocante de l'Ascension*. A young lady with long blond hair and dressed in a short PVC skirt presides over her display of the entrails of motor cars – shock absorbers, dashboards, steering wheels – all, one must presume, having been obtained legally. A tired-faced elderly man, strapped up in some equally tired and elderly corduroys, has arranged his stock of plastic dolls and fluffy animals in a wedding cake meringue of vivid pinks and yellows. Someone is trying to sell broken cardboard boxes full of empty glass jars, another, some off-cuts of carpet and a kitchen stove. Satisfied, smiling customers are hurrying away, bundles tucked enthusiastically under their arms and others are arriving, bright-eyed and expectant.

As I wheel my bike carefully between the stalls, I eventually identify the atmosphere which infuses the meadow. Holiday. Everybody is on holiday.

Over the ridge in Louviers the holiday spirit is foremost. The hotel recommended by the tourist office is shut. The lady tut tuts at the unprofessionalism of the hoteliers on her manor and sends me to the only hotel staying open that weekend.

'One hundred and thirty francs for the room. Pay me now, I can't leave the bar.' The patron flicks the froth from a pair of beer glasses with a wooden spatula. 'Hotel entrance is up the pavement, first door along from the end of the terrace. Put your bike at the bottom of the stairs.'

I cast my eye around the noisy, bubbling bar, the youth of Louviers in relaxed mood: the shrieking, the giggling, the juke box playing, the cars revving and squealing as they circuit the roundabout. This is life!

'Breakfast is down here in the bar tomorrow?' I enquire.

He shakes his head as he folds my money into his shirt pocket with one hand and with the other, slides a cup of coffee towards a freckly youth who sports a toothbrush moustache.

'The bar closes tonight at eleven and opens again on Tuesday. Don't you know it's Ascension Day? I'm going away for the holiday.'

'How nice for you.' My voice is hollow. 'Will there be anywhere in the hotel for breakfast?'

'No there won't. I run the hotel as well. When you leave in the morning, put the street door key back in through the letter box.'

'And... breakfast?'

'Oh, there will be cafés open tomorrow.'

He was lying of course.

chapter two

One midnight, in the month of July, in a year long ago, I could have been seen clutching my British Visitor's Passport on the deck of a Dieppe-bound cross Channel steamer which was loaded chock-a-block with English exchange students. It was my first time abroad and I was essentially on my own as I watched the coloured flashing lights in the Channel with a deal more apprehension than excitement.

The family I was to visit owned a flat in Paris and an old country house south of Rouen. There were six children. Of course, the only one with whom I had nothing in common was the one who was destined to be my exchange buddy.

For the first two days I only said *oui* and *non*. At the end of the first week I told a joke. At the end of the second week I was haggling with the lady at the post office. At the end of the third week I was thinking in French. Although the exchange did not flourish and I never saw nor contacted the family again, those three weeks in France were to exert a persistent influence on the rest of my life.

I returned to school and within a year rose to fifth overall in the class and third in French. My success made me belatedly interested in studies. I went on several school trips to France where strangers would approach our teacher and compliment him on my accent. My years of obsessive mimicry ensured that once I had heard real French people speaking, then my accent would always be better than the teacher's. Of course, my knowledge did not match my accent and I spent many conversations nodding with feigned interest whilst understanding only one word in ten.

When I reached polytechnic, I was introduced to that antithesis of everything that language was designed for – the language laboratory. It was a room full of perspex cubicles where you clamped headphones over your ears and gazed, mesmerised, for hours on end at the rotating tape reels before you. No faces to look at, no expressions to accompany the language, no waving arms nor shrugging shoulders, just pure sound. I hated it. The only incidents to look forward to were when the girls would occasionally get a bolt of static electricity up their tights or the tape head would pick up the local police radio frequency. When I had finished college I went to work in Paris. I stayed there for three years. Everything of note that I have done since the age of thirteen has been influenced by those three weeks in St. Aubin.

Why am I telling you this? Because thirty years later I am cycling through the fine Ascension Sunday mist towards the village of St. Aubin.

Never go back.

Do they still own the ancient house? Will they be there? The parents will be dead by now of course. Madame Barral, petite, neat, smart and authoritative. Madame Barral, standing on the doorstep of the flat in Paris, wringing her hands in anxious relief to see me making my own way back home after Christophe had 'accidentally' given me the slip. Monsieur Barral, dignified, upright, serious and a little frightening, accompanying us discreetly on family outings.

The children might be there, if they still own the house.

Christophe, my exchange student – I could laugh and tell him what a revolting specimen I must have been at that time. Hopefully he would admit that he was too. Jerome, his broody younger brother, taller and a better fighter than Christophe. Pascal, the youngest boy, pedalling barefoot round and around the garden on his tricycle. I cannot remember any other names. Yes I can. Sophie. Dark-eyed Sophie who was frightened of the enormous, forbidding snake-cage tree which crouched on the back lawn and so she had to hold my hand. Sophie who always tried to stay up later than her bedtime so that she could carry on playing with the 'boys'. Sophie, sitting cross legged in the front garden, pale blue dress, olive skin, no socks, saying, '*Je t'aime, tu sais*' and obfuscating forever in my English mind the real meaning of the verb.

And the water... There was no piped water in the village. The pipes were stacked up outside the village hall but the trenches and connections had not yet been made. The water we used was pumped up from a frog-speckled tank at the bottom of the garden. It spat from the bathroom tap, pale green, mixed with minute twigs and leaves. We were strictly forbidden to drink from the taps – I needed no second instruction. Water was only drunk from bottles, taken from the wooden crates in the cellar.

The breakfast table; an enormous grey saucepan of boiling milk surrounded by bowls of coffee and chicory and *tartines* of bread, butter and jam. Lunchtime; eating everything from the same plate with the same knife and fork, swabbing the plate clean with bread between each course. Tea time; rushing in to the kitchen, grabbing a *tartine* and chasing out again and up the garden, shrieking like a Red Indian.

Tall bedroom windows which opened strangely inwards. Squeaking stiff shutters clasped to crumbling stonework. Eerie nocturnal rasping of crickets in the garden, the glow worms in the bushes.

Sitting in four inches of water in an oval turquoise plastic basin on the floor of the bathroom whilst watching a lone French mosquito droning around and around like a spotter plane for the artillery. The toilet. Oh the toilet, perched on a wooden platform in its own little room like the throne of an Eastern potentate. And the ammonia fumes which knocked me backwards from the dais when, with ignorant curiosity, I peered into the black hole which appeared in the pan when I pulled up the flush lever.

Cycle rides on unfamiliar bikes to collect the eggs and milk from the farm. Sunny, singing outings in the Panhard, wallowing along country lanes or sliding about on the unattached armchairs in the back of the Renault Estafette van. I wonder if they remember any of that.

Bacquepuis. Quitteboeuf. It is unnerving how one can remember village names thirty years later. I can see the spire of the church. St Aubin is about a mile away now. There is no point in going to the village. All this happened thirty years ago, nearly two generations ago. People move on, villages metamorphose, memories tarnish.

Never go back.

This house at the cross roads used to be the post office where I argued with the old postmistress. The letter box is still there. I don't remember the church being that way around, I thought the door was on the other side. There is the grass where the water pipes were stacked up. I suppose they are hidden beneath it now.

Fundamentally, the village has not changed at all. If I were to see a goggle-eyed, fair-haired boy come pedalling precariously down that road opposite and scoot off past the bread shop to their house, I would not bat an eyelid. It would be me.

It would be me but here I am. A thirty year time warp later, but still wearing shorts and still on a bike.

Seeing the bread shop reminds me that I have not eaten breakfast yet. I shall buy my breakfast in St. Aubin to commemorate the breakfasts of my past. The shop is really the converted front room of a cottage.

'Monsieur?'

'A demi-baguette please and a couple of croissants.'

'Those are the last two.'

'Thank you. Tell me, do you remember a Monsieur and Madame Barral living here?'

'Oh I don't know whether they are back. They went out this morning. Gloria!' She called into the back room. 'Have Monsieur and Madame Barral come back?'

'Yes mum. About half an hour ago.'

'They are still in the big house just up the road on the left?' I ask.

'Yes, that's right.'

'I didn't know whether they would have moved. It's a long time since I have been here.'

'Well, we bought the business twelve years ago and they were living there then.'

The Monsieur Barral that I knew would be quite old by now – or is it one of the children who lives there?'

'The children are due down for the weekend. They are expected this afternoon.'

'Thank you for the information. I've been out of touch. Last time I bought bread here was over thirty years ago.'

'*En effet,*' was all she could reply.

I knew now that I was going to visit the Barrals. I had know it all along, really. And now that Fate had assembled the family for the very day that I would be cycling past their house, we would all be together again for one more time. It just had to be. What a superb surprise it would be for them!

This is the gate. A lot smarter than it was. The sheet of rusty corrugated iron which used to block up the hole in the hedge is no longer there and the hedge has grown over the wound. There is no bell that I can ring, no name plate to confirm that this is the correct house. It must be. Peering over the gate, I can see the scrap of grass where

Sophie had sat cross-legged in her blue dress, I can see the gravelly drive leading to the side door which everybody used. The snake-cage tree is almost certainly still around the back of the house, out of sight.

I shall muster up my courage, go in and knock on the side door. I cannot. The gate is locked and with no bell I do not know quite how I can summon their attendance. I think I can see someone moving around in the kitchen... perhaps if I wait. I wait. I lean my bike up against the wall and fiddle with it to legitimise my loitering. I hear a door bang. A stooping lady with straight white hair is coming down the steps from the kitchen door into the garden.

'Madame!' I shout.

She continues, turns away from me and, showing no signs of having heard me, walks gently out of sight around the back of the house. Perhaps she is deaf. There is no doubt in my mind that this is Madame Barral.

I wait.

About five minutes later she reappears, carrying a trug with some green leaves laid in it. She is walking towards me now so even if she cannot hear me she will see me.

'Madame!' I shout louder, trying not to sound too brutal, and wave a fluorescent yellow arm above the gate in greeting. She climbs the steps and disappears into the kitchen without a glance.

I am completely nonplussed. Perhaps she cannot see very well. Whilst I am reflecting upon my attainment of complete invisibility, she comes out of the kitchen and–

'Madame Barral!'

–walks across to the garden shed, opens the door and disappears inside.

I remember there being a shed there. It is probably not the same one, these structures do not last that long. Funny that I have only just noticed it.

The door swings and she emerges, leaving the door open. I half-heartedly wave my arm.

'Madame, *s'il vous plait*,' I call to the back of her flowered apron as it wafts up the steps into the house.

After a time I notice a movement at the shed door and I realise that I can just see the blade of a tool of some sort, waving rhythmically to the sharpening strokes of an unseen person standing behind the door. Eventually the honing stops and the gardener appears, dressed in blue overalls and a check shirt. I am sure that if I asked the gardener to get Madame Barral, he would do so. Just a minute, that is no gardener, it is Monsieur Barral, even after thirty years I can recognise that upright stance.

'Monsieur Barral!' I now spare no effort in my arm-waving and calling.

He stops inspecting the blade and looks at me.

Success at last! It has taken me nearly half an hour to get them to–

He turns and walks away from me, up the gravel drive into the back garden. Up to where the snake-cage tree is lurking to frighten Sophie with the dark eyes, up to the water tank where we threw stones at the frogs, up to the lean-to garage where we played many a boisterous game of ping-pong. All the people who played in that summer of thirty years ago will be assembled again at the reunion. All except one.

Never go back.

All that afternoon I cycled to Bernay in the pouring rain. My stomach felt hollow; my life, empty; my journey, pointless.

There was a lad called Perrée who went to school in Bernay. He went away to study and then came back in the 1930's as an architect and built an art deco house called *Le Paquebot*. As I stand sketching it in the morning light, I cannot but admire the sheer guts of someone who has the strength of their convictions; to do what they believe to be right in the face of ridicule born of ignorance and opposition born of fear.

Le Paquebot, its rendering is traced by cheaply repaired stress cracks, some of the window frames are disintegrating, the deck railings at each level need a lick of paint but *Le Paquebot* is undeniably a transatlantic liner safely moored in the high street of Bernay. Next door to it squats a supermarket which looks like a brick shoe box. It probably won an architectural award.

Whilst I was sketching, the two ladies in the boulangerie opposite must have been watching me with their beady, avaricious eyes and plotting my ambush. There is nothing in the world to surpass the slyness of a French *commerçante* when she applies herself.

'A demi-baguette please madame.'

She looked at my bicycle propped up outside the shop.

'Is this your breakfast monsieur?'

'Lunch. I always buy it first so that I can do thirty kilometres knowing that I have the food with me.'

'That's very wise,' she flattered me and with a natural smoothness produced a half a baguette from the drawer below the counter. 'One already cut? That will do?'

Very clever. Obtain the customer's agreement before cheating him.

'Of course,' I assured her.

She slid it across to her partner in crime and turned to the lady behind me. I moved up the counter where her, presumably deaf, assistant was wrapping my bread.

'One demi-baguette and two croissants,' she declared as a challenge.

Well, why not? I had not asked for two croissants but I could easily eat them and my attempts to make the deaf assistant understand that I only wanted the demi-baguette were met with the impatient repetition of, 'One demi-baguette and two croissants.'

I paid and departed. Three hours later I discovered the bread to be as hard as leather and the croissants, fossilised. In a country where bread is considered old if it has cooled for more than four hours and stale by the end of the day, to manage to sell yesterday's bread is an achievement on a par with the one concerning fridges and Eskimos. But they had seen me coming a century ago.

I was due for something to cheer me up and Providence came up with the goods. I was ambling along a nondescript minor road two miles from the town of Aigle when that epitome of every cyclist's nightmare: a brainless yappy dog, lurched out of a garden in front of me

'Gnaff gnaff,' he said in French.

(This is pronounced *nyaff nyaff*. It is a French onomatopoeic representation of the noise that yappy dogs make. Bigger dogs say, '*Ouah ouah*' pronounced, *wah wah*.)

I can imagine you scratching your heads and wondering why cyclists should have nightmares about such silly creatures. I will tell you why. Brainless yappy dogs run alongside you and try to bite your feet at each turn of the pedals. If that fails they simply stick their head into your front wheel, throwing you smartly over the handlebars. Being brainless, of course, they do not hurt themselves one smidgen and whilst you are lying in the road nursing a broken leg, multiple contusions and a wheel the shape of a coathanger they are able to continue snapping and yapping at you, thus convincing all bystanders that you were a menace that needed immediately felling.

Each cyclist has his own particular technique for dealing with brainless yappy dogs. I secretly envied the American Marine I met in Bangladesh who, when worried by a dog, used to draw an air pistol from his holster and shoot it.

Not possessing a firearm, I use the sly psychological approach. To the yapper's opening salvo of, '*Gnaff gnaff*' I usually shout something inordinately witty like, 'Clear off!' then snatch my cycle pump from the frame and fetch him a hefty blow behind his ear. You may have wondered where, in such a brutal pre-emptive strike, is the psychology employed? It is the psychology of perception. When the yapper sees my arm raised he thinks, 'no need to move, he can't reach me with that,' little realising that when I bring my arm smartly downwards, the pump doubles in length as it slides out. Whack! By the time he has recovered his surprise, I am miles away.

One of the bicycle modifications I made for this voyage was to replace my full length pump with a short stubby one. The reason being that when I stretch my arms apart and apply pressure to a big pump, my joints come adrift, which is a nuisance. With a small pump, this does not happen. Unfortunately, the small pump is only suitable for close combat and is, in any case, safely packed in my pannier. Time for Plan B. I grab my water bottle and, squeezing it hard, hit Gnaf Gnaf in the eye with a stream of *'Marguerite'* which, as you all know, is a slightly sparkling water from the Vosges.

The dog shakes his head, trips over his paws and rolls down the verge like a hedgehog in a bowling alley. Laughing gleefully whilst I mutter, 'cyclists one, yappy dogs, nil,' I pedal off victoriously into the distance.

I notice nothing amiss until a quarter of a mile further on when a car coming towards me swerves at the last moment, blowing its horn furiously as it sweeps past. Unusual behaviour for French drivers who, as a rule, show no antagonism towards cyclists. A few hundred yards later the next car to approach me zig-zags erratically and then skids to a halt.

'Can't you keep your dog off the road?' the driver shouts angrily through the window at me as I breeze gaily past him.

Keep my dog off the road? What is he talking about? I glance behind me.

'Ha! You squirted water in my eye. I'm gonna get you for that. *Gnaff gnaff.'*

'Oh for goodness' sake, you stupid little dog, have you been chasing me for the last half mile?'

'I'm gonna get you. *Gnaff gnaff!'*

'We'll soon see about that. Have you any idea how fast I can pedal?'

At that point the road began to climb perceptibly and, try as I might, I could not prevent my slowing down. The dog began to catch up, slowly at first and then as the weight of my baggage began to make itself felt, more quickly until I could hear the pattering of its paws on the road and the slapping of its stupid ears.

'I'm gonna get you. *Gnaff!*'

'You don't scare me.'

'Oh yes I do.'

For every uphill, there is a downhill, I consoled myself. When I get around the next corner I shall be on the descent where I can easily wind the bike up to thirty five m.p.h. That will sort him out.

'And don't think you're gonna get away from me on the downhill, cos there isn't one. *Gnaff!* I know this road.'

He was right. Around the corner the road ran dead level through a small settlement of a half a dozen houses. I looked at my cycle computer. This one-member canine revenge force had now been chasing me for three quarters of a mile and to my consternation, showed less signs of flagging than I did.

I rattled through the houses with the ridiculous dog panting in hot pursuit. A lady in a navy blue headscarf and heavy-rimmed spectacles called out in a scandalised tone, 'That's too cruel, monsieur, making your dog run like that.'

My dog? My dog! I glanced back. It was putting on the full works by rolling the whites of its eyes and swinging its tongue around its neck like a scarf. It knew all the tricks.

'Gonna get you!'

'What no *'Gnaff'*? Could we be getting tired my canine friend with the brain of a spirogyra?'

'I've... got... friends... where... you're... going. You... watch... out!'

'You haven't, by any chance, got a cousin in Hesdin

called Max, have you?'

'So... you... know... cousin... Max?'

After one and a quarter miles I established sufficient lead to begin to obscure him from sight at each corner although he always eventually appeared, pattering gamely behind, a little smaller with each corner till, at one and a half miles, I finally lost sight of him altogether. This was providential because a half a mile ahead was a road junction where I knew I would have to stop to look at the map to take the correct road leading to Mortagne au Perche.

The obvious road, the signposted road to Mortagne, was busy with serious travellers but I could see from my map that this was a modern road. The old road lay opposite. I threaded my way across the traffic, but before pushing off I glanced back. Around the corner trotted the stupid dog as if it did not have a care in the world.

Mortagne au Perche is a compact little town and, parenthetically, it is perched on top of a steep-sided hill. If you believe the signposts, all the hotels are two and three star establishments situated without the precincts at the bottom of the hill. I do not believe them and find the one star Hotel de la Poste in the square in the town centre. It turns out to be the friendliest and consequently the best hotel of the entire journey. After I have checked in and lodged my bike in the back garden, I wander into the square, buy a local newspaper and sit on a bench in the sunshine. This is a trick I discovered a couple of years back. Not only do you merge into the surroundings since you are reading a local paper and so are not a stranger, but you pick up an indication and superficial knowledge of the concerns of the region which enables you to eventually eavesdrop intelligently upon conversations in bars and restaurants.

I started off on the following morning with the intention of reaching Le Mans by early afternoon but before I left Mortagne I was to have a couple of encounters to put me in good humour. First, a local cyclist stopped me as I wheeled my bike through the square and chatted to me for a while. He thought that I was Dutch because of the shape of my bike. He was able to understand the technical excellence of it and when I told him that I had come from England and was going to Spain on the minor roads, he displayed a decent amount of respect. He added even more weight to this respect when he went on to explain that every year he did a *diagonale* Brest-Nice or Biarritz-Strasbourg, so he knew exactly what I was tackling and clearly did not relish the idea of doing it himself.

The second encounter was a remark a girl made to one of her schoolfriends as I pedalled past. 'What a funny little man!' she said. It should have upset me, but it did not. I thought it was rather gentle.

At last the sun came out. It became so hot at midday that I stopped cycling and I sat in a square under some trees and ate my lunch. I was aware that the bench that I was slumped on was dangerously low for me, but I could not tear myself away from watching the old lady in the town hall. She was cleaning the windows. These windows were high six-paned affairs, easily twelve feet tall, and were ranged along the first floor of the imposing municipal building to provide light to what was probably an important committee room. For each window, she first fully opened both casements inwards, thus creating a void through which a medium sized, suicidally depressed elephant could have launched itself without tucking in its ears. Into this cavernous aperture she dragged a ten-rung step ladder, shaped like a witch's hat. Then up she clambered with her bucket and cloths. One slip on the parquet and she would have been catapulted through that window with no hope of arresting her fall till she met the gravel a long way below. Wincing at the reckless energy she expended whilst vigorously polishing the glass, I wondered whether there was some factor that I had overlooked. Had she a safety harness? Perhaps she was blind? Perhaps she could fly?

Well, I can't sit here theorising all day. I have to get to Bilbao. The road to Le Mans from Mortagne au Perche is a former *route nationale* demoted to *départementale* so I can faithfully take it without defeating my goal of riding across France on the minor roads.

In Mamers I stop in the town square and lounge under the trees for a short respite. All is quiet. The shops are closed, the schoolchildren have gone home for lunch. I am intrigued by a poster advertising a railway bicycle. The abandoned branch line from Mamers to La Ferté St Bernard has been taken over by a band of railway enthusiasts. They have converted some old gangers' trolleys to cycle operation. The gangers' trolley was the funny little truck with the see-saw handles that Buster Keaton always seemed to end up driving. In its present incarnation, a bicycle frame has replaced the see-saw and the locomotion is provided by the pedaller's legs. I would love to have a go but... I am cycling to Spain.

By dint of some really crafty map reading, I manage to penetrate right to the centre of Le Mans on a B road. It leads to a square on one corner of which squats a small hotel. The patronne is well into her sixties but dresses in the glamour and sparkle of a film star of half her age. She swirls up the staircase before me in her expensive gown and sweeps down the corridor to show me my room.

On my short journey across the square to the steak house where I was to eat my dinner I discovered in a quite disagreeable manner that Le Mans was obviously a propserous town for I was accosted three times by East European beggars. They employ none of the whining and suppliance of the Far Eastern mendiant, hoping to appeal to your better self. No, intimidation and aggression are their tools. They pull at your clothes, the children kick your ankles and pinch you. They all but pick your pockets. This procedure had the opposite effect upon me. Feeling threatened, there was no way that I was going to reveal where on my body I kept my money and so they were left empty handed. And I did not like the experience.

When I checked out of the hotel in the morning, the film star's husband tried to add twenty five francs to my bill, being the charge for parking my car in their courtyard. Standing patiently there in my black tailored cycling shorts, fluorescent yellow cycling shirt, my cycle cap on my head and my cycle bags in my hands, I pointed out with what I thought was remarkable self restraint that the only means of transport to which I would admit proprietorship was the bicycle which I had been obliged to leave outside overnight, leaning against their dustbins. He apologised profusely and reduced the charge to fifteen francs. In circumstances such as these, I always think that it is worth proffering the money just to see whether they will take it. He did. He has an expensive wife.

Pedalling southwards from Le Mans, which, as I am sure you know, is the birthplace of Henry II, the first of the English Plantagenet kings, I am aiming for a highway which will irrevocably prejudice my daft attempt to cross France on the minor roads. I am positively seeking out the Route Nationale 138. It will be a broad, busy, fast main road and I want to cycle along it. Am I losing my marbles? It is inescapable that at some time in a journey of nine hundred miles I will have to negotiate the odd main road or two. If I stuck doggedly to my farm tracks, canal towpaths and forest trails I would become a grandfather before ever reaching the Pyrenees. So, accepting that an occasional lapse is permissible, why not do it with style? This short section of the Route Nationale 138 is better known as the Mulsanne Straight on the Le Mans 24 hour race track. Formula One racing cars rip down this tarmac at speeds which force their makers to introduce negative aerodynamics into their design in order to prevent the darn cars from becoming airborne. I pedal down it with the wind behind me at a creditable twenty five miles per hour, utterly unworried by such pressures. Half way along the Straight, the traffic is forced to negotiate a round-about of straw bales and plastic cones. This is to prevent drivers from emulating their race-track heroes. Judging by the tangle of interlaced black tyre marks charcoaled onto the quarter of a mile of road approaching the obstruction, some had been embarrassed by their attempts.

Everybody knows of Le Mans for its race track and its affiliation with the motor car. Ironically, the town is plum in the middle of a prosperous horse rearing region. Bernay, through which I passed yesterday, has an annual horse fair and Mortagne au Perche is the centre for breeding the famous Percheron working horse.

The soil around here is notably sandier and drier. I take this as proof of a clement climate. When I stop for a rest at Pontvallon, five motor lorries towing caravans bounce off the road and onto the hard, barren grass of the picnic site. In a tumult of shouting and loud colour, the passengers tumble out and, men and women alike, start to urinate and argue. One party wants to continue to the next town, another wants to camp here whilst the third just cannot understand why they left the previous place.

I pack up my food and, giving them a cheery wave which they acknowledge, I continue on my road. Fifty yards away I can still hear them shouting at each other. I wonder if I shall still hear them when I reach the Loire.

By half past four I am five miles from Saumur and stuck. This idea of cycling only on small roads is very worthy but introduces several difficulties. One, quite naturally, is that you have to possess good maps because the road signs are not designed to tell you where the road goes, but to get you onto the road that the local authority wants you to use to travel to your destination. And it is always the main road. So you have to learn to ignore in greater part what the sign proclaims and read the subtext. Sometimes they let slip a clue. If you can see from your map that you have to go past the big bottling plant to get to your destination then you follow the sign to the bottling plant even though the main sign denies that the road goes nowhere near your goal.

In employing such subterfuges, thanks to my incredible intelligence, I had ignored the *'road closed'* and *'diversion'* signs to get to this point, five miles from Saumur. And that was why I was stuck. This was the third minor road that I had attempted and the third that stopped at the motorway works. Straddling my intended route a ribbon of bare terrain stretched broader than a football pitch. It scarred the countryside and severed all the minor roads. Back and forth across this lunar landscape charged enormous yellow dumper trucks and graders. The air was filled with the monotonous whine of high speed hydraulics and the coarse roaring of diesels. Out of the translucent cloud a leviathan would suddenly lurch at a frightening speed and hammer past me in a flash of saffron to be swallowed up in the cloud of dust and exhaust fumes left swirling in the air by its predecessor. This was a madness of motors. Trucks which burned fuel at the rate of four miles to the gallon were carting giant mouthfuls of France a quarter of a mile across a field and then returning for another bite. In China they would achieve the same result in relative silence by using baskets and a million coolies.

I took out my spyglass and surveyed the untouched fields on the far side of the jaundiced gash. A jolly little farmhouse sat aside the continuation of my lane at the point where it emerged from the scarred earth. The road wound enticingly away through neat green meadows towards the river Loire and the town of Saumur. I gauged the distance. It was about two hundred yards I reckoned. Another truck thundered across the scene before me. The enormous churning tyres were taller than me, the driver's cab was ten rungs up the ladder. It would be a folly bordering on suicide to attempt to cross this site.

But then, I have never claimed to be sane. I gave a kick on my pedals and launched forth. I immediately jumped out of my skin as a strident air horn blasted at me. A truck the size of a semi-detached house had materialised from nowhere and was bearing down upon me at an unstoppable thirty miles per hour. In a panic of terror I pulled my handlebars around and pedalled back the ten yards I had covered. I felt the ground shake as the truck lumbered past, its horn still blaring. I understood what he was saying and it made sense. But I ignored it.

Whilst waiting for my heartbeat to subside, I studied the traffic to discover how it was organised and where it was going. I concluded that if it was ordered, I could not see to what matrix, for the vehicles were travelling in all directions at their individual whims. I decided that the best approach was to start out immediately after a truck had passed so that I would have the maximum time interval before the next.

I watched the truck lumbering up towards me. The driver was wearing a blue checked shirt. He waved his arm across the windscreen at me, telling me to keep away. The moment his truck was past I pushed off. He had imprinted tyremarks in the soft ground that looked like the fortifications of some giant sand castle but they did not crumble as I banged over the ruts. Coming from my right I could already see the next truck. It had a radiator grille like a six foot high cheese grater and there was a saucepan lid hinged to the top of the exhaust pipe. It was blown vertical by the forceful blast of gases.

I put my head down and pedalled hard but I seemed to be still in the intended track of the approaching juggernaut. It was then that I realised that it was not following directly in the wake of its predecessor; it was running parallel to it. Indeed, several more trucks were thundering up towards me. The drivers were presumably paid by the load. The quickest to the other end was the first to unload and return for another load. They were racing, five abreast;

bouncing, snarling, lurching and feinting.

Should I slow up and let the next truck pass before me? No, I would speed up and let it go behind. It was fifty yards away and its windscreen was two blank sheets of white glass, reflecting the sky. Anonymous. I pushed harder but now it seemed to have turned towards me, intent on flattening me into the earth. No, I was wrong, it would pass behind. In a thundering belch of dust and noise it obliterated the puny track left by my cycle tyres with a twin pavement.

To my horror I discovered another truck on its blind side. It had been trying to overhaul the cheesegrater. Before I could decide what to do I was engulfed in a swirling cloud of stinging dust and grit. It blew into my eyes. I was blinded. I stopped and somewhere in that grey-yellow cloud the monster pounded by, utterly unseen by me. I heard it. I felt the ground quiver like jelly but I could not see a thing.

I coarsely rubbed the back of my hand across my eyes and forced them open. Just in time. The next truck was thirty yards away, heaving like a trawler and blowing like a brass band. It was not going to stop. The terror inspired my legs and my back wheel skidded and slithered as I tried to apply the power to the loose surface. The truck bore on and ten seconds later, the piece of ground on which I had been standing was darkened by its earth shaking passage.

I had to keep my head. I shot a searching look across the site to try to fix my bearings on the farmhouse that I was aiming for. I needed to go a little more to the right. A bit of luck, my route was free. My shock reaction to the sudden shriek nearly bent my handlebars. The driver held his hand on the caterwauling whistle as the truck hurtled by from my left. It was empty. It rattled and banged across my intended trajectory at forty miles per hour. The cloud of dust it threw up obliterated the sun. The air went grey. Once again I found myself in a fog of airborne earth, surrounded by klaxons and engines. Something grey moving to my left. No, not grey, just dirty green. I was now in the middle of the empty trucks racing each other back to get another load.

Suddenly, the ground gave way beneath me and I was hurtling down the side of a hollow. I hit the bottom and was pitched into the soft sand on the floor of the crater. For a moment, everything seemed to go quiet. I was below the level of the site and I had dropped out of the noise. What a relief. I felt like one of Bairnsfather's heroes with his, 'If you know of a better 'ole, go to it.'

I took the time of respite to gather up my bicycle. With a black roar, the underside of a gargantuan engine reared above the edge of the crater. I could see a spinning pulley, there were hydraulic rams to steer the wheels, shiny steel knuckle joints as thick as my thigh. And it was coming down onto me. If I could not see the cab, the driver could not see me. In a sobbing frenzy of utter fear I yanked my bicycle up the sliding, shifting sands of the crater. The truck was a grader. A gigantic engine dragging an enormous shovel shaped scoop to level off the ground. Tons of loose sand shifted. The crater disappeared and the grader ground on. The driver had never even known that I had been there.

With terror in my legs I charged through the remaining maelstrom of machines. When I reached the firm ground at the farmhouse it occurred to me, rather belatedly, that it would have been more sensible to have abandoned my bicycle in the crater and to have scrambled out unhindered.

Later that evening, I even considered the novel idea that it would have been more sensible to have followed the first set of diversion signs that I had encountered, but dismissed that idea as being utterly preposterous.

chapter three

The next morning the sun is shining. The sky is blue and cloudless and it will be like this now until I get to Spain because I have crossed the Loire. The Loire is where the weather changes. Any time you listen to the French weather forecasts, which are no more accurate than the British predictions in this field, the meteorologist will divide France simply into 'north of the Loire' and 'south of the Loire.' It would appear that France only gets two versions of the weather. Or three, if you include the temperature of the seawater in Cannes.

I looked over the parapet at the river Loire itself. Considering that it is the longest river in France, I find it quite unimpressive. The river bed is broad but it has substantial trees growing in the middle of it. The shallow strands of water thread around them. The banks are green with vegetation and it seems that every curve forms itself provocatively into a sandy beach.

The water level was low. I was almost tempted to walk across the river. Almost, but not quite. The Loire, I had been told by people who live along its banks, is one of the most treacherous rivers in France. Treacherous because it looks so innocent. But out there, tons of water are moving relentlessly down to meet the Atlantic Ocean at St. Nazaire. They swirl in rapids and whirlpools, shifting sandbanks and quicksand. In autumn it floods. It storms down and rips through these bridges under which, at the moment, it is gently trickling.

In view of the appetising probability of unrestricted sun for the next few weeks, I decide to buy some solar protection. In the pharmacy the young lady customer in front of me chats in a familiar manner with the lady pharmacist whilst the latter swabs at a nasty looking graze on her elbow.

'I will have to pick out some bits of gravel, Marise.'

'OK. That's the trouble with these public gardens,' the wounded customer replied.

'But didn't you see it coming?'

'My umbrella was in the way. Anyway, you don't expect a bishop.'

'Quite. So what happened to the goldfish?'

'The goldfish was alright but I broke my vacuum flask. It was the one I bought in Corsica. Ouch!' she added.

'Sorry. It's all clean now. Do you want a plaster on it?

'Yes please. Can you put it on for me?'

'Certainly. Hold still.'

The plaster was applied. The pharmacist turned to me. Marise chatted with the customer waiting behind me.

'I am going down to Spain and I need something to protect me from the sun,' I explained.

The middle aged lady pushed a wisp of grey hair back under her cap and looked at my legs.

'You've already caught the sun,' she observed. 'This will be what you need.'

'What do I do with it?'

'Just rub some on your skin.'

In an imitation of Marise I said, 'Could you put it on for

me please?' I innocently hitched up the leg of my shorts.

'Certainly.' She automatically bent to my bare thighs and began to open the carton of the suncream. Marise shrieked with laughter and the man she was chatting to started to guffaw before the pharmacist could recover herself.

'Oh. Get on with you!' she straightened up quickly. 'You nearly had me there!'

Still laughing, they all wished me, '*bonne route.*'

The traffic is dawdling behind two officer cadets from the famous Saumur Cavalry School. They are doing a spot of shopping. On horseback. They arrive at the shop they were looking for and park their horses neatly by the kerb. They tie the reins to the lamp post and go in. The horses twist their ears around and blow down their nostrils but stand patiently.

Back in June 1940, the officer cadets of Saumur held off the invading Germans for three days. It earned them the recognition of the enemy and some ungrateful citizens point out that it also resulted in the destruction of the north bank of the town. But here, on the south bank, the mediaeval street layout is apparent.

I quash any burgeoning ideas of tourist visits and push on. I am still only half way through France. I am not having trouble drying my clothes any more but I realise that I am beginning to weary because I am cycling seven days in seven. I should take a rest. Two days later I take a day off. I stay with a friend out in the marshes near the town of Rochefort.

'Since you saw me last I've taken up painting,' the lady declares. Around the dining room, in the salon, all down the hall, every scrap of wall bears a trophy to the victory of acrylic paint over gravity.

'Oh yes?' I say.

Try to be non committal but for heaven's sake think of

something meaningful to say because if you don't proffer an opinion, she will squeeze one out of you.

'It's a class every Tuesday up at the Municipal Hall. We have great fun. Somebody usually brings a couple of bottles of wine.'

'That's lovely. It's a lovely idea,' I correct myself quickly just in case she had thought that my gaze had settled on one of her canvasses.

'I'm developing quite a technique, the prof. says.'

I nod encouragingly.

She also nods.

I smile.

She smiles.

My grin fixes on my face as my heart plummets.

My idea of what constitutes 'art' is perhaps a little too subjective for most people to accept. I work on the basis that as I am not an artist, 'art' has to be something that I cannot do. If I go into a gallery and see a rusty nail pushed into a block of driftwood, I think to myself, 'I could do that' and so as far as I am concerned, that exhibit is not art. If I see an adult painting executed in 'the naive school', it just looks to me like the effort of an average child. Not only could I do that, I could do better. So could the average child.

She is still looking at me. Intently.

To my ignorant eyes, the canvasses are just meaningless daubs executed with no recognisable artistic expertise. Blotches and splotches of primary colours. Had she not even tried mixing up new shades? Did she apply these colours neat from the tube?

'You ought to get some of those brass lights that you hang over paintings,' I suggest. 'You could really make a feature of... er... one or two of them. Nicely illuminated. Bring up the colour. The colours. Really make them stand out.'

She says nothing.

My eyes sweep frantically around the room. Red, blue, yellow. Shapeless blobs. Suddenly one leaps out at me. 'Oh I like that one.' I put a reckless amount of enthusiasm into my voice as I walk towards it. 'It's a cockerel, isn't it?' She makes a funny shrug. 'In a farmyard.' I get nearer. 'Yes, I like the clever way the light falls on the feathers.'

I am standing before it and it really is quite good. It distinguishes itself from the others. A different range of colours, a different approach, a different technique.

A different signature.

There are thirty three paintings in this room and I choose to praise the only one that is not hers.

'Are you staying tomorrow night as well?' she asks.

'If it's no trouble.'

The next day I leave my bicycle in the barn and we ride in her car into Rochefort. We are to celebrate the birthday of a cousin of hers by eating at the restaurant where he is the cook. But first, we have to buy a present. The streets are full of people wearing shorts and not much else. Whilst she is choosing a tee shirt I study a bizarre bonnet. It encases the head and ties under the chin but the peak continues around the face like a funnel.

'Oh that's a *quiche notte*,' she says. She pulls it from the stand and wraps it around her red face. It makes her look like a traffic light. 'It's a traditional costume.'

Most of what is done locally concerns either ships or oysters so I decide that this must be some sort of medieval industrial headgear. Then she astonishes me with a proclamation.

'It's what the women used to wear centuries ago to stop the English invaders from kissing them.'

I laugh in an unkindly manner. To me, her explanation suggested an unhealthy historical level of feminine conceit. I just stop myself from the waspish observation that, given the talent I had seen locally to date, I could understand why the *quiche notte* had fallen into disuse. I wondered which bonnet manufacturer had fabricated the story in order to sell his wares. I decided that the *quiche notte* was the Willow Pattern of the millinery trade. When I got home I found that Larousse did not concur with my views but defaulted to the idea of a French secret weapon against the lecherous intentions of the English Military. It even declared that the name, *quiche notte,* came from the English, 'kiss not'. Preposterous. What next? Give them half a chance and they would assert that the bayonette came from Bayonne.

However, such outlandish claims are not the exclusive prerogative of the French. Whilst undertaking research for a book on an unrelated subject, my eye was caught by the following entry in a genteel work of reference entitled, *Haydn's Dictionary of Dates and Universal Information Relating to all Ages and Nations.*

It went thus:

> '*BLANKETS are said to have been first made at Bristol by Thos Blanket, in the 14th. century. This is doubtful.*'

At least they had the goodness to admit that they were being silly.

The restaurant was on the Ile d'Aix: a miniscule island with a resident population of a couple of hundred persons. It is heavily fortified because it lies opposite the entrance to Rochefort harbour.

They showed me Napoleon's house which he had built here for his intended retirement. Ironically, he had only lived in it during the last week of his life on French territory before surrendering to the British and being carted off to exile.

We ate a long, leisurely, afternoon lunch in a sort of bungalow which looked as if it had been an army hut. Given the size of the former garrison on the island, it probably had been. We ended up with singing and dancing on the tables – the latter was a particularly perilous occupation for me since every time I stood up straight I got scalped by the ceiling fan.

By five o'clock we were waiting for the ferry to take us back to the mainland. The only means of access to the Ile d'Aix is still by ferry and the last boat runs at about eight o'clock in the evening. This is a boon to the only two hotels on the island, for imprudent and unbelieving tourists often find themselves stranded overnight.

But I was worried by something else. Our car.

'Why does your front wheel look smaller than the back wheel?' I asked.

'Because it is. It's the spare.'

'Oh, it's one of those space saving spare wheels is it?'

'Yes. They are a bit of a nuisance. You are supposed to not go above fifty kilometres an hour.' I thought of the high speed journey we had made around the twisting roads in order to arrive at the restaurant in time. 'And only use it to drive to the garage.'

'Is that where the proper wheel is? At the garage?'

'No.'

'Where is it?'

'In the boot.'

'Well shall we put it on then? We've got time before the ferry comes.' My offer was made not entirely from a point of disinterest.

'Not a lot of point.'

'Why?'

'It's still got the puncture. I keep meaning to drop it in to the garage but I always forget.'

'Oh,' I said. 'How long have you been running on that little thing then?'

She blew air from her cheeks and inspected the spindly wheel. 'A couple of months?' She seemed uncertain.

I wondered how much a hotel room would cost.

At breakfast I started totting up the figures in my note-book. The day's break from cycling had done me a lot of good. I came back to my journey with renewed vigour. Especially as I knew that now the topography was flat as far as the Pyrenees.

'Why do you want to go to Spain?' she asked.

'For the sunshine.'

'The sun shines here.'

'But it must shine hotter in Spain.'

She gave another of her non-committal shrugs.

'How long will it take you? You will be going to Bordeaux and then straight down the Nationale 10 to the border won't you?'

'Not likely.' The Route Nationale 10 was the famous road to the south that the French authorities maintained in a purposefully haphazard fashion. Their reasoning was that as it was only used by tourists trying to go somewhere other than France, why should they spend money on it? And in order that the Germans and other holidaymakers would be further dissuaded from entering Spain, as they approached the frontier, they would have to run the gauntlet of French campsites which lined each side of the road. 'I shan't go anywhere near Bordeaux,' I assured her. I checked the calculation in my notebook. 'Today is my twelvth day. I have ridden six hundred and twenty five miles which is exactly one thousand kilometres and only twelve of those kilometres have been on main roads. I shall try to get into Spain without adding to that main road total.'

'Impossible!' she exclaimed. 'For a start, how will you get through Rochefort without going on a main road?'

'I shan't go through Rochefort.'

'But everyone does.'

'That is exactly my point. I want quiet roads. I am very happy that France provides *routes nationales* because they attract most of the traffic.'

I nearly added that I would be especially glad if all this traffic was driving recklessly fast on two-month old thin spare wheels.

'So where do you go from here then?' she asked.

'Turn left at your gate and down through the back lanes to Tonnay Charente.'

'To the *nationale*,' she said triumphantly.

'Across the *nationale* and over the old suspension bridge on the Charente.'

'You can't. It's closed to traffic.' She sounded smug.

'It's closed to motor traffic. It's open to pedestrians and bicycles.' I outsmugged her.

'Oh, I didn't know that. So how do you get around Bordeaux then? Pretty big place.'

'I shan't get anywhere near Bordeaux,' I said. I slid the map across to her. 'Look, I can go to Royan and get the ferry across the mouth of the Gironde.'

'Yes but its *nationale* to Royan,' she protested.

'Just watch this,' I said. I traced my finger down the map keeping to yellow and white roads till I got to Royan. She looked at me as if I had performed some trick of magic.

'Do that again.'

'No, you do it. Go on. It's quite easy. After all, you live here. Just stop thinking like a motorist.'

Hesitantly, her manicured finger wandered across the green shadings of the cartographer. She went wrong once but back tracked to the cross roads and got it right.

'Done it!' she announced, her face beaming. 'This is fun!'

'Yes, that's why I do it.'

She unfolded the map fully.

'You will have to go on *route nationale* to get around the Pyrenees at Bayonne.'

'I am not going around the Pyrenees, I am going through them.'

She frowned at the roads leading to the passes and the

tunnels leading into Spain.

'But they are all main roads. You can't do it.'

'Oh yes I can. I have a secret weapon.'

'What is it?'

'If I told you it wouldn't be a secret.'

'Hmm.' She folded the map and handed it to me. 'Send me a postcard when you get to Spain.'

The bridge at Tonnay-Charente was worth a journey. It had been built towards the end of the nineteenth century to carry the main road over the navigable River Charente. Now, a hundred years later, the main road crossed on a newer, wider bridge a few miles upstream leaving this wooden decked highway to us quiet travellers. The bridge itself was nothing special. It was the view. You only have to be fifty feet up in the air in marshland and you can see to God's eyebrows.

I made a relaxed ride to Royan, arriving in the late afternoon. Royan was too big for me so I decided to cross immediately to the Pointe de Grave and find a hotel on the other side. I discovered that my ride had been almost too leisurely, for the ferry I was awaiting would be the last departure of the day. The water here looked like serious stuff. It was the estuary of the Gironde upon which Bordeaux stands, but it was really the sea. It was grey and choppy and looked deep and judging by the size of the tankers I could see moored across at Le Verdon, it was.

About two dozen cars, a motor caravan and some motor bicycles were in line awaiting embarkation. I was the only bicycle. The unloading and loading of the ferry was the best example of officialdom-induced chaos that I have ever seen.

Just before the ferry's ramp touched the slipway, the marshal ushered forwards the first line of cars awaiting to embark, coaxing them onwards into the neck of the slip. This reduced the width available for the disembarking vehicles to one lane, which was a pity because the ferry carried two lanes of vehicles. Then the tannoy made the nonsensical announcement that for 'security reasons' it was forbidden for cars to embark whilst carrying any passengers so car doors opened everywhere and passengers poured out onto the slipway. The same rule applied for those cars disembarking. The first driver off, therefore, drove about ten yards and then stopped on the slipway to await his passengers who were somewhere behind him amongst the throng, fighting their way through the extraneous bodies now clogging up the passage. No other cars could get past him, of course, because the embarking cars had been pulled forward to block the gap. Whilst everybody waited, his passengers clambered in and he pulled forwards but the car at the front of the left column on the ferry decided that he had as much right to disembark as the others and could not see why the embarking cars were stopping him so he pulled across the lanes. He managed to squeeze in at position three because, of course, the car at position two had pulled forward and then stopped in order to await his passengers. And so it went on. Each driver stopped the moment he touched terra firma in order to re-embark his companions. What should have been achieved in three minutes took twenty. And the astonishing aspect of it all was that nobody seemed to either realise or care.

And when we got to the other side, we did it all over again. I never did work out how the 'security' aspect applied. But why should I care? I had at least three days of flat riding before me.

Those three days took four and were not without incident. On the very first day, just after breakfast, I was pedalling innocently along a superbly surfaced cycle track which ran alongside a high chain-link fence. I knew that several areas of the Landes had been set aside for army firing ranges and so thought no more of this until I remarked a man on the other side of the fence. He was standing arms akimbo, head thrown up, boldly facing me and the road. And he was stark naked.

Hmm. Obviously not a firing range then.

I recovered from the shock and wished him a polite but ironic 'good morning' as I swept past. Why a naturist should want to disport himself alongside the only road within ten miles when he had hundreds of acres of pine woods and dunes to play in, I could not fathom. Perhaps he felt he had a point to make.

From the mouth of the Gironde, southwards to the Pyrenees, the stretch of the coast is called the *Cote d'Argent* – the Silver Coast and indeed the Atlantic Ocean here is as silver as the Mediterranean is blue on the Cote d'Azur. As I sped along silent cycle tracks I caught occasional glimpses of lines of sunlit rollers, glinting and sparkling as they charged towards the beach.

The hinterland has had a tough time of it over the years. Because of the dominant direction of the wind, the sand encroached on the land often by twenty or thirty yards every year. So the inhabitants tried to restrain it with wattle fences. They were not very successful. The effect of this advancing wall of sand was that ports such as Soulac became separated from the sea. It also meant that the rivers could not flow into the ocean. Indeed, I did not see any river which had achieved access to the sea between the Gironde and the Pyrenees but I suppose there must have been one. Not being able to reach the sea, these truncated rivers formed lakes whose level rose as the sand built up their banks. They are now inland lakes, sixty or seventy feet above sea level and are very popular with water sport enthusiasts.

The other problem was the nature of the soil. Waterlogged and boggy, it would not drain and nothing useful would grow in it. The heroes of the region are two valiant engineers called Brémontier and Chambrelent. In the eighteenth century the former built a wall of beams and piles parallel to the shore to stop the sand encroachment. As the sand built up against his wall, he built it higher and *voilà*, the sand dune was invented. On the top, he planted marram grass which was particularly suited to windblown salty sand and its long, water seeking roots bound the dunes together. The dunes then became self regulating – stopping the advance of the sea and sand.

Although the land had been saved, it was still not a lot of use. You may remember those old photographs of country people hobbling about on stilts that often figured in picture books and which were intended, no doubt, to highlight the charm of the French countryside but which simply succeeded in implying that all French peasants were retired circus performers. The reason that the locals stalked about on poles was because the ground was so boggy. Along came the second hero, Chambrelent, who, by a system of deep ploughing, managed in the following century to break the crust of impermeable salts that had formed in the subsoil. He then planted a genus of pine tree that liked the sea side and the forests were born.

My cycle track now left the company of the road and began exploring these forests. The reason why the track suddenly took off in this direction was because it had been laid on the bed of one of the several steam tramways which used to run down to the resorts along the coast. I was now cycling on a pathway of concrete rectangles, roughly the size of paving slabs, which stretched lengthways on the sandy soil. They wound serpent-like amongst the trees. They were all loose. I allowed myself to be mesmerised by the rhythmic *clink clonk clink clonk clink clonk* coming up from my wheels. In this remote wilderness of pine trees and shrubs, it was the only noise to be heard and I realised that it was uncannily similar to the noise that must have been made by the narrow gauge trams over whose ghostly lines I was riding.

I failed to notice the discreet and insidious trap that was being set for me: the ground was gently falling away on both sides of the track so that I was raised on an embankment.

An embankment too narrow for me to put down a foot should I have to stop. But I had no need to stop. The track was flat. When I was about ten feet higher than the surrounding woodland I came to the missing slab. Knowing what was going to happen I just had to let it. My front wheel dropped into the hole and my bicycle came to an abrupt halt. I leaned to put my foot down and encountered free air. With the grace of a collapsing clothes horse I fell sideways and slithered head first down the sandy embankment with my bicycle entangled lovingly on top and around me.

But the day had not finished with me. In the middle afternoon I was making good headway along a hot earthen track through an area of cleared deciduous forest when my back tyre suddenly deflated. For most riders this would be a mere inconvenience. With me, it is a minor catastrophe. The first thing I have to do is to remove all the bags from the bicycle and turn it upside down. And then, of course, my bicycle is not like every other bicycle in France. It has a hub gear made in Germany. This means that the actual gear cogs are not whirring around in the weather, picking up as much gluey sand and grit as they can to slow you down, but revolve sweetly in a bath of grease whilst safely ensconced inside the hub of the wheel. Unfortunately, the mechanisms required to operate the gears and hub brakes mean that in order to remove the wheel, a selection of extra nuts and bolts have to be undone and levers to be manipulated. The most fiddly was a greasy spindle, about four inches long, which was held inside the hollow axle by a red plastic collar. Both these had to be removed and stored somewhere clean before I unbolted the wheel.

I eased the red collar off and with an insolent *twang* the spring loaded rod shot straight over my shoulder into the tangle of ferns and spiky grass which here formed the undergrowth. I just managed to stop myself from charging in after it. I would never find it like that and I did need to find it because if I did not, then my trip to Spain would stop right here and now. Not allowing my gaze to shift one gnat's whisker from the area into which I thought the spindle had impacted, I unzipped my belt pouch and pulled out my spyglass. Working on the assumption that nothing in nature could be absolutely regular, I began to visually quarter the area at my feet for anything that looked man made.

After five minutes, I had whittled the possibilities down to two. One was a silver shaft and the other a grey line. I tossed a mental coin and chose the silver shaft. As I moved my foot in towards it, several things happened. The net of grass, spikes and needles shifted; the light fell differently on my target which I now identified as a bleached blade of grass; and at the same time I saw that the grey line was my gear spindle which was slipping down into the darkness beneath. I swerved and grabbed at it and could not believe my good fortune when I found it in my hand. Had I given in to my first impulse and rushed after it, the dull spindle would have been shaken into the deep undergrowth and I would have had to push my bicycle for the next twenty miles.

Make no mistake about it, this place was remote. I had not seen another living being for the previous three hours. Which made it all the more astonishing when, five minutes later as I was fully engrossed in changing my inner tube, two cyclists pedalled silently past me without a word. Not a syllable did they utter, let alone ask me if I needed help. It's a funny old world.

In accordance with my pre-designed logistical plan, I had posted off my last envelope home. It contained my previous three maps. The map I was starting now took in the rest of the Landes, the belt of the Pyrenees that I intended to cross and reached as far as Pamplona in Spain.

On the evening of my sixteenth day I was in a hotel at Mauléon-Licharre; my last French hotel. It had been the middle of May when I had started my journey and now it was the beginning of June. I had crossed France from the flatlands of the north to the mountains of the south; eight hundred and fifty one miles and I had only used nine miles of main road. To do this I had crept through woods, skirted fields and accompanied canals. On more than one occasion I had found myself asking directions in the middle of a farmyard and now, here I was, ready on the morrow to unleash my secret weapon which would get me across the Pyrenees without spoiling my record.

The question was – would it work?

chapter four

The day was not starting auspiciously. This was quite the most challenging breakfast I had eaten so far. The bread was fighting a guerilla warfare with me and the jam had taken up a retrenched position inside those little tin pots with foil lids. The coffee smiled up at me with a broad innocence, having planned its ambush for later. Happily, when its slow burning fuse reached the powder, I was still within reach of the hotel WC.

Outside, the morning traffic swished down the wet road into the town which was blanketed in a dank mist. There was no sign of the sun. The light was as gloomy inside the stone and timber hotel as it was outside.

As I waited for the receptionist to make up my bill I studied the wall map for any further intelligence that I might glean. It was a modern map of the Basque Country presumably drawn up to serve political ends for it admitted no boundary between France and Spain but showed the Basque regions of the two countries united as one entity. But it did not show the detail necessary to help me deploy my secret weapon.

I will tantalise you no further about my secret weapon.

When I had first dreamed up the project of crossing all France on the minor roads, negotiating the Pyrenees had caused me a great deal of head scratching for, as my friend in the Charente Maritime had pointed out, the passes and tunnels were main roads. So I had set to work to study how far into the mountains I could penetrate without using a main road and the answer always came out to be: 'as far as the road goes.'

The Pyrenees are a simple style of mountain range – a gaggle of untidy ridges stretching from the Mediterranean to the Atlantic. Simple they might be, but they are rugged nonetheless. The roads I traced on the maps would start off southwards from the last French town and march confidently towards Spain but very quickly they would lose heart or confidence and change from yellow to white. Then they would start to wriggle a lot more than appeared strictly necessary. They would split into two, or three or four and each explore a minor valley only to reunite at a common crossroads. And then, when they were certain nobody was looking, they would stop for a quiet smoke, turn around and go home.

I had stretched out the map on the floor and then lain on it. This is the only way to really read a map although it is frowned upon in public libraries. After an hour or two I had found a road which reached nearly into Spain. And looking over the ridge onto the Spanish side, I could see a Spanish road which reached up towards it but stopped short. I suppose my secret weapon was my unattractive conceit in a belief that I could not be wrong. I could not believe what the map was trying to tell me. Would a race of mountain people as hardy as the Basques really build a road halfway up a mountain one side and another half way up the other side with nothing to link the two together? Did they never visit family? Did they never smuggle?

I painstakingly followed every squiggle and every squirm of the network of unclassified roads. These roads were smaller than a *départementale*; they were narrower than a *communale*; they were certainly far less important than a *vicinale*. Their white tracery was laced about the peaks like intestines at a ritual disembowling. They turned back upon themselves, they sometimes disppeared back into their own beginnings but I felt sure that they held the secret. I was convinced that there was a way through.

If my secret weapon was my conceit then it was certainly promoted by my cynicism. I was cynical enough to know that cartographers only showed what they were paid to show. This was a French map. If the French did not want you to know that a road leading into Spain existed then they would not permit the cartographers to show it.

This particular cartographic corruption is not unique to the French, it is transnational, it crosses all frontiers, even if they pretend that the roads do not. Our own Ordnance Survey started out on a falsity. The first edition maps which were ordered by the Ordnance Department of the British Army and which began to appear in the early nineteenth century, were forbidden from showing any installation which had a military importance. And so, a traveller arriving on the packet boat at Dover and gazing up at the imposing towers of the Norman keep and curtain walls of Dover Castle perched high on top of the White Cliffs, might search for enlightenment on his map in vain, for it would show that there was no such construction there at all. I suppose that the intelligent spy could then deduce that by its very absence from the map, the castle proved that it was of military significance.

Even quite recently I was using a Michelin map to navigate along the Franco-Belgian border and I discovered that they had omitted an entire village. I had some feeling in the matter for it happened to be the village I was looking for. My suspicion of the failure in the Michelin map was corroborated by the larger scale IGN map which detailed the village clearly; and the hideously concrete proof of the settlement's existence when I did find it. Upon returning home, I wrote and complained to Michelin. I received from them a duplicated reply to the effect that this (unspecified) omission/mistake had already been signalled to them but they thanked me all the same.

It was only much later that I realised that I had unwittingly discovered one of their safety checks. All mapmakers of any repute know that some unscrupulous publishers will copy their maps and not pay royalties – it is a lot cheaper than doing the survey yourself – and so they introduce certain deliberate mistakes into their maps. When the dishonest and ignorant competitors reproduce the very same faults in their own maps then they are taken to court. In the meantime we cannot find on the maps villages that do exist or imaginary farms (a favourite) on the ground that exist on the maps.

But I was convinced that I had found a route through the Pyrenees which did not exist on the map. I just believed that it had to be there. I was taking a terrific gamble for I would not know whether or not I was right until I had passed the point of no return. My route would take me up an ordinary minor mountain pass which, although it started out towards Spain, once it arrived at its summit, swerved back towards France. I had noticed, however, that at the top of this pass there was a track which forked off to the left as if intending to return to my hotel but which, if you were able to stick with its intricate insinuations, turned through three quarters of a circle to arrive at an even more remote pass nearer Spain. From this one I would have to descend and then climb to a third mountain pass which reached to within one kilometre of the frontier.

It was at this isolated point that the deceitful French cartographers wanted me to believe that the three roads all returned dutifully to France. I thought they were lying.

If I was right, then it would be downhill into Spain all the way. If I was wrong, then I would have to cross another two mountain passes to get back anywhere near civilization. This would be too much for me. I knew that I could not do it. Three mountain passes in one day was my absolute limit. It was imperative that I be right.

The receptionist handed me the bill. I paid it and carried my bags outside to my dripping bicycle. As I bent to my rear carrier I was pulled up short by the sight of my rear tyre. The sidewall was cracked. I had put the tyre on new at the beginning of the trip. I usually expected to get about three thousand miles out of this make of tyre before they needed replacement but this one had done less than a thousand. I squatted down and inspected it more closely. It was worse than I had thought. The crack ran around both sides of the tyre just above the rim of the wheel and in one place, a small strand of the textile casing was already pushing through. What could I do? There was no shop within a day's ride that could provide a replacement tyre and in any case, such a proposal would be academic since nothing would persuade me to pedal back out of the foothills of the Pyrenees now that I had come this far. I decided to go on. That decision was to cost me dear.

I pushed off from the hotel. Nobody waved or cheered. It all seemed so ordinary and humdrum. Here I was, starting out on the most adventurous exploit of my cycling career to date and there was nobody with whom I could share my misgivings. This is one of the disadvantages with being an obnoxious and unlovely person. When you want to do anything stupid or idiotic you have to do it on your own.

For the first few miles I cycled up the valley of the Saison river on a quiet *départementale* road no. D 918. Running parallel to my road but on the other side of the river ran another road, also numbered D 918. I could not fathom out why there should be twin roads going in the same direction.

It was perhaps an anomaly caused by the renumbering of the roads which was undertaken in the 1970s. What I could surmise was that the road had been formerly a *route nationale* for when the Ministry demoted the *nationales* to *départementales* they often just prefixed the original number with a nine. It was a fairly safe stratagem; even the largest *départements* would be unlikely to have as many as nine hundred minor numbered roads. But interesting though this is, it did not solve the riddle of why there existed two D 918s going in the same direction.

When I got home I looked out a 1949 edition of the Michelin map of the region which showed the same road numbered as N 618 and Mauléon-Licharre as Mauléon-Soule. And it was the same road on both sides of the valley because in order to travel from east to west in the Pyrenees, one often had to go northwards up a valley to a bridging point and then southwards back down the other side.

All this became academic a few minutes later when I left the D 918 and began to climb up towards my first pass. Soon I was gasping up a series of hairpin bends which took me violently from five hundred feet to nineteen hundred feet in less than four kilometres. I had forgotten what mountains were like. This was a rude awakening and a bad omen. If I was out of breath and struggling before breasting the first pass, what would I be like after the third?

I could hear the pop-popping of a small tractor which was labouring up the road behind me. It did not seem to be travelling much quicker than me. Eventually, under a long canopy of mist-dripping trees, it crawled past me. It was towing a small stock trailer in which half a dozen calves were rocking and bouncing gently. They gazed placidly at me, like a choir of giant nodding dogs on the back window of a white-line straddling saloon car. They were travelling only marginally faster than I was.

Hmm. Nobody looking? And I shan't tell anybody. Time for a bit of Plan B. I dropped into an even lower gear and began to thrash the pedals around. The tailgate of the trailer started to get nearer. I pushed harder.

One of my prize possessions at school had been a Will's cigarette card which colourfully portrayed the perils awaiting cyclists who hung onto the rear of slow moving vehicles. The card was my favourite not for its message – I did not possess a bicycle at the time – but because it was a good 'flicker' and by skilfully exploiting its stable and predictable aerodynamics I succeeded in amassing a considerable collection of cards won from my schoolfriends in the playground.

The image of this now long-lost card flashed across my mind as my guilty hand grasped a rusty bracket on the rear of the trailer. Getting a tow from a tractor is quite a skill. It is not a case of simply grabbing a handful of passing Massey Ferguson and then sitting back and enjoying the ride. The first and important factor to consider is what to grab. From the point of view of maintaining the cosy relationship that your joints may have established with your skeleton over the years, the side of the trailer appears quite attractive. You just lift an arm and there it is. Except that the trailer is often wider than the tractor and thus runs with its wheel against the verge. So where do you think you are going to cycle if you hang on to the side? If you choose the nearside you'll get dumped in the ditch with the first lurch and if you hang onto the offside you will be brushed off by any vehicle passing in the opposite direction. You can also easily end up under the wheels. So I always choose the back. You need long arms for this because you have to lean forwards over your handlebars and grab the bit you can reach but which does not draw you so close that your front wheel fouls the back of the trailer. It is also wise to work out beforehand the function of the various levers which sprout from these vehicles. The intended purpose of one of them will be to lower the tailgate, and unloading seven tons of sugar beet onto the highway not only creates an unnecessary and unwelcome hazard for the following traffic, but it can lead to a souring of relations with the driver whose aspirations for the load might have been directed otherwise.

Once you have grabbed the correct bit, then the work begins. What mechanical device is employed to transmit the movement from the tractor wheels to those of your bicycle? It is not magic. It is you. Your entire body becomes a tow bar. The tractor tries to pull your arm out of its socket so you have to strain against it to prevent it from dislocating your shoulder. So the motion has reached your shoulder and continues on through your body to try to bend you over the handlebars. You resist this by tautening your stomach muscles and stiffening your back. With your torso now rigid, the movement naturally moves down to your legs. If you try to pedal, your bicycle will stand still and you will disappear over the handlebars. What you do is you straighten one leg hard onto the pedal and hold it there and at that point the transmission train is complete. The bicycle now acquires the same velocity as the tractor.

Another factor which cannot be ignored is that the movement of the towing vehicle is never regular and all surges, retardations and swerves are magnified by the trailer so your arm has to serve not only as the first link in your power transmission but as a shock absorber, bending and stretching, twisting and yawing in order to keep your bicycle at the optimum distance. In fact, when all things are considered, it is probably less tiring to pedal the bicycle and ignore the tractor altogether.

But I didn't. With my fingers hooked around a rusty bracket, I lurched along in the wake of the trailer. Six pairs of docile eyes regarded me noddingly. One of the calves began to lick the salt from my hand. Bovine saliva trickled down my forearm to my elbow. Oh thank you.

Just when I thought I had got the hang of it, the tractor motor barked and the trailer lurched. This usually precurses a change into a higher gear and a launching into the supersonic speeds approaching ten or eleven miles per hour. At that velocity, every lurch and check threatens to drag you under the back or throw you off the side. I braced myself to counteract the G forces to be produced by the imminent tar-scorching acceleration. I need not have bothered. The tractor had arrived. It slewed into a gateway and I bade the calves goodbye.

I tucked my head down and stared at the small patch of tarmac in front of me. I did not need to see how it climbed or where it went. I could feel how steeply it climbed and I was not travelling fast enough to need to look ahead. If an obstacle appeared in front of me I had only to ease pedalling and I would stop dead.

I had left the trees behind with the salivating calves. The terrain was now sparse scrub and tufty grass with knuckles of rock poking through like arthritic hands gripping a counterpain. A road joined from the left so I grasped the opportunity to make a map stop. I always consult my map when I pause on a hill just in case somebody sees me and thinks that I have stopped for a rest. According to the map I was still two kilometres from the top. I cycled another five hundred metres and stopped to check the junction with the next track. Then another eight hundred to the next. I stopped here and ate a croissant from my foodpack. It was obvious to me that this behaviour betrayed that I was getting tired; and I was not even up the first pass yet.

At eleven o'clock I reached the summit at three thousand one hundred feet. This was where I was to take my first diversion. Before me and to my left I could see multiple pimples of mountain. According to my map there should be a road which forked left here. There was. It dropped quickly through four hundred feet. I shrugged mentally. When you cycle in the mountains, every foot of altitude you gain, goes into the bank. The trick is to try to spend your savings as slowly as possible. There was very little point in my worrying about that procedure now.

I would be earning and spending in a boom and bust economy all day until I crossed the frontier, then I would cash in an inflation-proofed pension which I hoped would take me to a hotel.

I was brought back to reality with a shock and it was a physical shock. A stone trench had been cut diagonally across my road to take off the surface water. I braked hard and crashed across it, wincing as I worried about my rear tyre. This gulley was a throwback to the previous century. It would have been dug long before the surface had been asphalted. Having checked my tyres, I gingerly eased off the brakes and began to roll down the hill. Around the corner lurked another drain. I crossed five in all before I reached the crossroads at the bottom of the dip. There I made another map stop. An enticingly smooth track wound off down to my left, down towards the trees. Not that road. The road to my right, I knew, once around the corner would begin a tortuous ascent back up the pass that I had just left. My road lay straight ahead.

It was unsurfaced. That is to say, it was loose shale. I could see its brown ribbon winding away along the edge of the mountainside, sticking closely, I hoped, to the nine hundred metre contour line. My progress was slow but the pedalling was not too arduous. The sun was now high above me and at every turn I was given a new perspective of the peaks of the Pyrenees. At one point, the track as such, disappeared. It faltered before a flat slab of rock which abutted a bluff. I dismounted and wheeled my bicycle onto the step. I did it carefully for there was only about ten feet of space between the wall and the drop. Ten feet sounds a lot until you divide it into the one thousand feet of the drop.

I was mightily relieved to find that the shale track continued around the corner. I paused and ate some bread and cheese to fortify me for the climbing ahead. A series of laces and hairpin bends took me around the end of a valley, through dark, damp, deciduous trees, up to three thousand four hundred feet. Here, the trees dropped off but the track continued to climb. My front wheel slithered and slid off slices of shale. Quite a portion of the effort I was applying in order to push me forwards was being diverted by the loose surface of the track. I do not know what surface I had expected, but I suppose bare rock and loose stones seemed appropriate.

I had met no-one for nearly an hour. The only proof of human existence that I had seen had been an occasional isolated farm, usually situated at the head of a valley, way, way below me. Then around the corner ambled a solitary brown cow. It stopped and looked at me. I returned the compliment. It lowered its head and began to browse the grass. I figured that I could wait for lunch. Just when I had accepted that it was quite natural to meet a cow up a mountain and that it had more right to be up here than I had, it was joined by half a dozen more. They, too, stared at me. Then the final two arrived and things began to happen. They formed up abreast and started to come down the track towards me.

Me? Frightened of cows up a mountain? You bet! I was off my bike in a flash and pressed up against the rock wall. This was survival technique that I had learned in the foothills of the Annapurnas in Nepal. When you meet a mule train, keep it between you and the drop because the animals will brush you off the mountain like they brush flies away with their tails.

The cows looked disappointed. They grumbled and filed past in a single, ordered line, averting their gazes. Just their luck to encounter a seasoned explorer!

I remounted and ground on upwards. My hope that my route had established an unshakeable affinity for the nine hundred metre contour line was rudely dashed when I reached twelve hundred metres – that is four thousand feet. On and on I ploughed. A lone cyclist amongst bare rock and buzzards. Why was I doing this?

Just to help me keep my muscles toned, my route now decided to alternately drop three hundred feet and then climb three hundred feet in a series of uneven swtichbacks. I was three kilometres from the mountain refuge at the top of the next pass. Just as I had slipped off the side of the previous pass, so would I arrive up the side of the next, meeting the motor road at right angles. It sounds unlikely, but it was right there on the map.

Up to four thousand one hundred feet and I rounded a corner of my mountain track to see an enormous Swiss style chalet, a strip of tarmac and a road sign. I had returned to the land of the tourist. Two men stood with their backs to me, gossipping on the corner of the road. Seeing me appear from out of their trouser pockets, they spun around to stare down my track as if it had just invented itself.

At the top of this pass was a restaurant, holiday homes and a tennis court. I really did not want to linger. After the ruggedness that I had encountered, I was afraid that too much contact with such debauchery as comfortable seats and hot coffee would soften me. However, I sat on a bench for a short time, just to gaze at the mountain tops.

The first mountain pass I had ever tackled had been in the Pyrenees and in climbing and descending it, I had discovered a weird effect. I had had to pedal up a one in eight incline for six miles and at my speed, that took me an hour and a half. During this period of time, my brain decided to take the easy way out and having started off by telling me that the road went upwards at the rate of one foot in every eight, it obviously decided that l did not need reminding of this fact as there were other stimuli to reinforce this information. Not the least of these was the resistance against the pedals when I tried to push them around. So after about half an hour, although I knew that I was going upwards, I saw the road as flat despite my knowing that it was not. Thus, when I reached a stretch of road where the incline moderated from one in eight to one in twelve, I quite naturally saw it as a short downhill stretch and took a welcome rest from pedalling. I promptly fell off.

As I picked myself up, thankful that I was alone, I looked behind me where I could see as plain as a pikestaff that the road descended quite steeply. I was confused. I eventually learned to look behind me whenever I thought that the road before me was beginning a descent. If the road behind me was still going down, then the road in front of me was still going up. Having mastered that principle, I thought that I was king and until I reached the top, I was.

Some of these passes are quite abrupt in transition. The Tourmalet, for example, has a stretch of only a few metres at the top before you begin the descent down the other side. This first pass was one such. My brain did not have sufficient time to get back into the office before I had started on my downward ride. Having convinced me that a one in eight was flat on the way up, it now scared the living daylights out of me by presenting the same incline in a downward direction as a one in four. It terrified me. I leaned right back into my saddle and pushed myself up from the handlebars, so convinced was I that I was about to plummet head over heels. Of course, I laugh about all this now. And I stop at the top of passes to allow my brain to get itself sorted out.

I tore my gaze from the sight of the mountain refuge and slowly climbed back on my bicycle. My knees were stinging and my hips aching and I had one more pass to climb. It was close by but before I reached it I would have to take some altitude out of the bank and spend it on loose women. With my brakes clamped hard on, I crawled down the hairpins, cursing, for I knew that shortly I would have to re-earn this altitude. Oh, what the hell! I had said 'loose women' not Sunday school teachers. I let go the brakes and the bike surged forwards. Singing happily at the top of my voice I rattled down the hill and screeched around the tight hairpins at the bottom. I might just as well enjoy it if I have to squander it.

I turned off to climb the third pass. I was now edging discreetly towards the Spanish border. This was the road which claimed that it went nowhere near Spain but was merely taking a stroll around the French side of the mountains. It was deserted. The incline was merciless and I was dog tired but I knew that I had to go on because going back would be too difficult. Up and up I went. Above habitation, above the trees. A thousand feet higher than the previous pass. At least the road was still asphalt. Eventually I reached a summit of five thousand one hundred and forty three feet. I looked back at the mountains. I was at the bottom of France, at the bottom of the map. All of the country was above me. I was coming up to the crossroads. This was where I could not make a mistake. According to the map there would be three roads, all of which returned to France. I believed that there would be a fourth road, going to Spain.

It was an elongated crossing of routes which stretched along the bleak spine of a raw hill. The roads ran towards each other, then veered away then merged and crossed at impossibly fine angles. Too fine to distinguish on the map. I was slowing down mentally now as well as physically. I could feel it. I held the map this way. I held it that way. If *that* was the road I had just come up then surely *this* was the road which would run westwards and then turn north back into France? Thus the road to my left should start off southwards and then perform a *volte face* and wind down a valley eastwards into France. Unless, of course, it is *that* road. In which case.... I sighed. I did not know what to do. I was stuck on top of a mountain, undecided upon which road to take and not knowing whether I had the strength to get back to civilisation.

As I stood there, I thought I could hear the groaning of a motor car engine. I could not be sure. Then it came again, unmistakably sounding and fading as the vehicle turned on the hairpins. I waited. I would swallow my pride and ask the driver. Anybody travelling this road would know where he was going.

Eventually a blue van crept into view. Something about that shade of blue seemed familiar. It was a van load of gendarmes. What a stroke of luck! There was no way that they could be lost. My jaw dropped open as the van drove straight past me and disappeared around the corner. It had just climbed five thousand feet to one of the most remote crossroads in France; there it had found what was obviously a foreign cyclist poring over a map and it had driven straight past. Was somebody trying to tell me something?

Right then, Martin, you're on your own. You got yourself into this mess, now get yourself out. First, find out exactly where you are. I study the shapes of the mountain peaks around me and then attempt to match them to the outline of the contours on the map. It is not easy to visualise in three dimensions what is described in two. After ten tortured minutes I arrive at the horrible conclusion that I am, indeed, where I think I am and that there are, indeed, only three roads and they do, indeed, all go to France.

Bum!

So much for my secret weapon. It has just misfired.

I decide that I might as well take the scenic route back and so I push off in the direction that the van had taken. I try not to think of the failure. Of the lung-breaking climbing that I have been doing since ten o'clock this morning. Of the ignominy of my smug assertion that I knew that I was right. My fatigue is showing through in my decision making. Surely it would be more sensible to go back the way I had come, along a route that I know, to the mountain refuge? It would only involve one climb. I stop at a fork in the road to think this over. If I turn around now and.... A fork in the road? My mind bumbles on. I don't remember seeing a fork on the map. I drag out the tattered accordeon. It falls open at the correct section. On the map, there is no fork.

The road back into France curves off to my right. The left fork points directly at Spain. I take it. It falls quite steeply into the end of a valley. The hill sides are green, the road surface, gritty. According to my estimation, I should come across a mountain stream which flows into Spain, for I had crossed the watershed.

The road veers sharply across the narrow valley. I can see the gulley with the sparkling water. When I come to the bridge it looks almost neolithic. It is a stack of stones in the middle of the river bed, supporting two enormous slabs of undressed rock. I bump carefully across it but I know that I shall have to recross this stream because, lower down, it forms the frontier between France and Spain.

I continue to descend. This is my pension. It should keep me in a small weekly allowance until I am well inside Spain. The green walls tower above me as the valley becomes narrower and then, unnacountably, my road swings through ninety degrees and begins to climb back towards France. I don't like the look of that. I need to keep the stream in sight.

Imprinted in the grass to my left, I can see the trace of a set of tyre tracks. I follow them. They take me to the stream and then run along its bank. I am still going down towards Spain. I must be nearly there. Suddenly the bank opens out to a flat grassy area and there sits the blue van. Five gendarmes, dressed in short dark blouson uniforms, are standing looking into the water. Two are smoking, their cigarettes hidden in their cupped hands. I smile inwardly at the thought that their boss must be one hell of a tyrant if they have to come to the furthest part of France to get a quiet smoke. Perhaps they hoped that if they got caught they could nip over the border and claim political asylum.

One of them spots me and says something. They all turn to my approach.

'Can I get across the river into Spain along here?' I ask them.

They look at the officer sporting a coloured ribbon on his jacket. 'There is no road,' he says,

'He could get across with his bike,' another says.

'Why have you come this way?' the chief asks.

I realise that by my innocent inquiry I have excited a professional curiosity. Rather silly of me.

'I was looking for a quiet road. I did not want to go through the tunnels. They are not good for cyclists.'

'But there is no road,' he insists.

'But your colleague says that I can get across.'

'You are not French are you?'

'No, I'm English.'

I become vividly aware of the ludicrous irony of fate. I, a foreigner, have vanquished all manner of delays and diversions to get myself via a devious route, nine hundred miles across France to a secret and remote border crossing point and I have managed to pitch my arrival so that it coincides exactly with that of five representatives of law and order. What were the odds against that? And why does it happen to me?

One of the officers who had remained by the stream calls to the others. They turn their attention to the water. I realise then what they are doing. They are looking for a good place to fish. I turn to the officer who had said that I could get across the river.

'So the border is just down there is it?'

He answers distractedly, wanting to go and look at the fish.

'Yes, just down there, by those trees.' He flaps a hand vaguely in the direction of the brook.

'And I can get across there with my bike?'

'Yes. Not with a car but you could with a bike.'

'I'll do that then.'

It is my challenge to them. I am proposing to cross the border into Spain without showing my passport or declaring any contraband.

'O.K.' he says.

Taking that remark as official permission, I push off and wobble along the edge of the tinkling water towards the trees. When I reach them I discover to my dismay that my passage is blocked by a barbed wire fence. It is sagging a little but the message it shouts is clear even if some of the vowels are missing. I cannot carry my bicycle over the fence. He had said that I could get across with a bike but not with a car. This fence is not even trying to differentiate between the two.

I look wistfully across to the other bank. That is probably Spain over there. I really do not want to accept that I have been beaten by a fence. Not after what I have been through. I stare at the twisted spikes and knotted strands but I can find no 'Open Sesame!'. Like a child inconsolable in disappointment I repeat to myself, 'but he said that I could cross the river, he said I could,' as if that would part the torrent like the biblical Red Sea.

Another minute passes in frustrated melancholy before I notice the stepping stones. He had said that I could cross the river. He had not said that it would be on a bridge.

It was not surprising that I had not seen the stones before because they were awash with foaming water. I stepped onto the first one and dragged my bike into the brook on the downstream side. This was a mistake. The tinkling little rill that I had admired was, in fact, a swift flowing torrent. It grabbed a hold on my wheel and started to push the bike down to Spain. With a certain amount of shoulder breaking exertion I managed to pull it back and retreat to the bank. There I changed sides and pushed the bicycle into the water on the upstream side of the stones. It was touch and go as to whether I would be knocked from my perch. I had to stretch across to the next stone and then bump the bicycle along the rocky bed so that it came past me and half way to the next stone. Then I had to transfer my weight to the same stone. It seemed that I was in a state of inequilibrium for ninety per cent of the time.

As I progressed towards the middle, I watched with alarm the level that the river was reaching up my bicycle. The lower half of the chainwheel was submerged. If the water reached the hubs of the wheels I thought that the resistance would be too much for me to cope with – already I was expending more and more energy in dragging the wheels through the water. I vowed that when I got home I would paint a Plimsoll line on the frame.

Two of the stone steps in the middle were completely submerged, the water slipping over them with a menacing power. There was nothing that I could do but carry on. My shoes and socks would dry out. I stepped out into the water. The river was now tugging at my ankle as well as dragging on the bicycle. I hauled on the handlebars and stepped onto the next stone. It was loose. It rocked and tried to shrug me off. I clung onto the handlebars. Thankfully, the machine was wedged and held me. The water roared around me, scouring over my feet and frothing through the spokes. It occurred to me that I must have looked a little evangelical for I appeared to be standing on the water. Having overcome that little pimple of excitement the remainder of the crossing was an anticlimax.

I sat on a stone and unpacked a dry pair of socks. I waved my toes in the sun until they dried. It was half past two in the afternoon and my secret weapon had worked.

I was in Spain.

chapter five

I sat there for half an hour, drying and resting. I felt a quiet exaltation. I had been right after all. I knew there had to be a way into Spain. I just knew it. Ha! So much for the disbelievers and the pooh-poohers. Yes, it had been risky, and yes, I was almost at the limit of my stamina but by studying the small overlap into Spain that was printed on the last of my French maps I could see that the nearest settlement was only ten miles away. There I would find somewhere to stay and the road to it would be downhill all the way, just as I had planned.

The distant sound of the gendarmerie van starting up brought me back to my task. It was three o'clock. The gendarmes had chosen their decent place to fish for the weekend. Time for me to go. I pushed my bicycle up the stony ramp to the track that I could see winding off into the heavy darkness of a deciduous forest in full summer leaf.

One of the most important things I would have to ensure was that I stayed on the correct side of the stream for at some, as yet, unestablished point in the future the track would tempt me to fork left and cycle off into the wilds of the forest. Rather as I had found Spain by turning right at Calais and keeping the sea on the same side all the way down France, so now I needed to keep the stream on my left to be certain that I got out of the forest before nightfall.

This was easier said than done. Two rather disagreeable qualities of the Spanish track swiftly made themselves apparent. One was that it immediately climbed towards a bluff which hid the stream from view and the other was its surface. I can best describe it as a cobbled street where every cobble was a rock. All shapes and sizes, many with projecting angles, they had been rammed and wedged into a semblance of disorder. I dropped to my lowest gear, which was very low, and dawdled up the slope at slightly less than walking pace.

I bit my lip nervously as I bumped over the hard ridges. I was reminded of the state of my rear tyre and the need to nurse it up to the top. Why did I not dismount and walk, I hear you ask? I will not distract you with complicated explanations. Please just accept that I can ride a bicycle where I cannot walk.

The track levelled out at the bluff. On one side of me was a steep drop, closely stacked with trees. Somewhere below I could hear the stream. Or was it the breeze in the leaves? No matter, now I can change up a gear. My hand wavered over my gear lever. I stopped and put my foot to the ground. Another fifty yards of the track was now visible, clinging to the uneven side of the narrow valley in a series of anguished curves. It was rock cobbles as far as I could see. Well it could not be like this for ten miles, I reassured myself. Grinding my teeth with tension I edged my bicycle along, trying to choose the smoothest route, crossing from one side to the other. This was not like the shale in France.

That had slowed me down by moving out from under my wheels as I had tried to get a purchase on it. This rock stayed put. It was absolutely unyielding. It was rugged, it was jagged, it jolted and jarred me and it would slash through a worn cycle tyre with no compunction whatsoever. With a decent tyre, I could have pedalled faster.

Perhaps the surface would improve after the next corner. It was unchanged. Forty yards after the bend there was another corner, and thirty yards later another. The track turned in serpent-like wriggles but they were the writhings of a snake in its final death throes. The clouds closed over the sky, the trees closed over the track. Every bump, every thud I expected to be followed by the sound of a rapidly deflating tyre. Nowhere did the road run straight. And everywhere it was rock, rugged rock. The blood was being pumped from the palms of my hands by the shocks on the handlebars. I tried to rest each hand in turn but was frustrated in the attempt by having to suddenly grab the brakes to steady the machine each time it tried to run away down a slope.

I thought that I would welcome the beginning of the descent. Had I been able to freewheel down it, probably I would have done. I clamped my sore and numbing hands to the brake levers and allowed gravity to provide the motive force, but I dared not run at more than four or five miles per hour. Even at that speed, a careless encounter with a razor edged rock would spell disaster. Bump, bump, lurch, thud, turn to the right, another turn to the right, now one to the left, a short steep descent, squeeze the brakes hard, knuckles going white, elbows aching, now a short climb, pedal, pedal hard enough to get over the rocks and up the slope but not too fast to damage the tyres. Haul on the handlebars, twist the wheel onto that soft bit.

Where am I? Am I on the right track? Am I going the right way? Where is the stream? I have seen no house, no hut, no fences, no drains, no tarmac, no signposts. Nobody.

I am alone in a silent forest on an ancient track as old as the Romans. Indeed, had a cohort marched around the next corner I would not have batted an eyelid. Here, in this forest, the only trace of man was the carpet of disordered rocks. It had surely been made for animals not vehicles. Pack mules and horses would need the unevenness of the stones to give them a grip in the climbs and descents. Who had been the last people to pass this way? Invaders? Pilgrims? Smugglers?

I crawled on. The ligaments in my wrists and elbows were beginning to burn with the strain. Paradoxically, going uphill was slightly less demanding than going down, but the track was going down. At one point I stopped and took out my compass to try to reassure myself of my general direction but I had made so many twists and turns that I had no way of knowing whether I was pointing at Gibraltar or Rockall. I did not know what the true orientation of my track was. Every fifty yards it pointed in a different direction and at no time could I see further than fifty yards. Often I saw less. I was utterly enclosed. I had lost the stream. I could see no sky. The gentle green light that I had started with had now become a sullen sombreness of neutral grey.

I kept going. I had to. I had to get out of this forest. I needed food, I needed a bed. I pedalled achingly onwards.

It was a discarded audio cassette lying in the grass. Garishly pink. I had never thought that I would be so pleased to see rubbish in the countryside but it announced that I must be getting close to humans. Two hundred yards later the track turned to tarmac and the forest suddenly ended in a deserted picnic site. I leaned my bicycle up against a table and took a drink from my bottle.

It was six o'clock in the evening.

I sat astride my machine and let it roll gently down the road from the picnic site. I had no strength or desire to pedal and it should not, in any case, be necessary. I reached the proper road and turned down the slope. I did not need the map. I knew that it could not be uphill. Uphill led back to France. With my head hanging loosely from hunched shoulders, I allowed the bicycle to slowly build up speed and I descended to a crossroads which lay at an altitude of a mere two thousand eight hundred feet. There I stopped. This could not be right. But it was. The three roads all climbed away from the junction. The southerly road, my road, climbed at a gradient of one in eight.

They could not do this to me. Since starting at nine o' clock this morning, I had already pedalled on rough tracks up from sea level to the summit of Snowdon. Twice.

I rechecked the map. I double rechecked it, but the damage had already been caused by my earlier, slovenly navigation. I had assumed that a road going down a valley would descend all the way. I had not examined every curve. This curve went over the top of the hill not around it.

No use crying over spilt milk. At least the surface is smooth tarmac. That will make it easier. I am still in bottom gear so off I go. I grind upwards, watching individual tarred chippings on the road surface as they slowly crawl towards me and then disappear under the bike. I distract myself by conjuring up an image of the steak that I am going to eat for supper. Everything is aching, my shoulders, my neck, elbows, wrists, hips, knees and ankles. I add mushrooms to the steak. Onward I go, up to three thousand four hundred feet – higher than the very first pass that I had climbed today. At what time had that been? Eleven o'clock? It now seemed like a lifetime ago. I add a grilled tomato.

I did not stop at the top to look at the view – I could not be bothered. I did not look at the map – I did not need to. I knew that there were settlements spaced at roughly five mile intervals all down this valley. I would sleep at the first hotel I came to.

As if that incline had been the final test, the road now occupied itself with the serious business of quickly losing altitude. I was now spoiled with smooth tarmac and flattered with crash barriers on the bends; what luxury!

The roof of a building hove into view. It was tucked down below the road, hunched against the valley wall by the torrent. As I whistled past I heard it humming. It was a hydro-electric generating station. That first settlement must be somewhere around here. Twenty minutes later when I came to the second power station I realised that these were the settlements. Self contained blocks of generating hall, workshop and maintenance shed, sitting smugly humming to themselves. They cared not one jot for the requirements of a weary and hungry cyclist. I continued to descend. I lost count of the number of hydro-electric stations I saw. I was unable to even begin the count of the number of hotels.

It is amazing how quickly one can descend a mountain. It can take all morning to climb a pass and just thirty minutes to travel the same distance down the other side. The breeze of my passing tugs at my shirt sleeve, the tyres swish over the tarmac, my head lolls wearily from side to side as I assess the hospitality of the various hamlets that present themselves. An hour after emerging from the forest I see a larger hamlet below me, sitting in a meander of the river. The valley here has begun to widen. I had taken as pure braggadocio the efforts of my tinkling little brook to sweep me from the stepping stones. I had underestimated it. It was now a serious river.

I turned onto the side road and crossed the water to the hamlet via a humped back stone bridge. At the end of the bridge a girl in a red cotton dress was playing with a dog. She was throwing a stick and the mongrel was chasing it across the square, its paws pounding up dust as it skidded on the impoverished grass. Having captured and subjugated the baton it then trotted back to the girl in that peculiar sliding sideways gait that uncouth canines like to affect. I needed some local intelligence and so, with a view to obtaining it, I approached the said dog's mistress.

She watched me with no great emotion. The dog ignored me completely.

'Is there a hotel here?' I asked.

At that moment the sun made a brief reappearance and the stone houses were bathed in a yellow glow. The river sparkled self consciously as if it had been trying to smuggle as much water down the valley as it could before anybody noticed and now found itself pinpointed in the customs officer's searchlight. The girl shielded her eyes with her hand. She looked up at me and said nothing.

It was then that I remembered that I could not speak Spanish.

Bit of an oversight, that.

But then, I had had my mind on other things. What the devil was the Spanish for 'hotel'?

'*Otel? Akee?*' I pointed at the village.

She shook her head.

Did that mean there was no hotel or that my Spanish was insufficient? I placed my cheek on the backs of my hands and made a mime of sleeping.

'*Iglesia?*' she asked and pointed at the church.

It was now my turn to shake my head. Her brown eyes watched me, solemn and unblinking. The dog tugged at the stick in her hand.

'*Dormir?*' I tried in French.

She smiled.

The dog wandered off.

The sun went in.

Perhaps I should have thought of learning a bit of the lingo before leaving jolly old Blighty, but you know, it had never occurred to me. We stood looking at each other.

A boy in a dirty white tee shirt and lime green shorts rattled up on a bicycle with no mudguards. He aimed a kick at the dog as he went past but the dog obviously knew his predilections and was already a yard out of reach before his knee had straightened.

'Ello Mister,' he said to me in English.

The girl switched her brown eyes from me to the boy and her expression, from solemnity to admiration. Immediately I felt jealous. No girl had ever looked at me in that manner at that age. Or at any other age, come to think of it.

'Hello. Is there a hotel here?' I asked.

'Yes mister.' He grinned at the girl. She gazed at him. If she had been ten years older she would have been already unlacing the ribbons on her nightdress.

'Where is the hotel?'

'Yes mister.' He grinned at the girl again.

I realised that I was merely a pawn in his successful game of seduction. My resentment was surpassed by my reluctant esteem for his prowess. Suddenly the girl said to me,

'Albergo?'

It sounded remarkably similar to the French word for inn – *auberge*.

'*Si, albergo*,' I confirmed recklessly.

She pointed down the valley.

'*Aoiz*'

I pulled out my map and cautiously fingered a point eight miles further down the road. She peered closely at it.

'*Si, Aoiz*,' she said. '*Albergo.*'

'*Gracias.*'

'*De nada señor.*'

The boy stood open mouthed. The girl laced up her nightdress and strode past him, whistling to the dog.

I decided to believe the assertion of an eight year old Spanish siren. There would be an inn at Aoiz and it would have a room for me. Be positive. But Spain had not yet finished with me. At ten past eight, when I was but half a mile from the village, the road suddenly lurched back up the hillside, climbing two hundred feet just to present me with the tourist view before sweeping down into the town. Two hundred feet does not sound much does it? It nearly broke me.

I had showered and changed and was sitting under the sparkling chandeliers in the hotel restaurant. Around me a dozen tables were occupied. On the plate before me sizzled my dreamed-of steak, but it was unattainable. I could not cut it. I tried again but I had no grip in either hand. The knife slipped from my fingers and clattered to the floor. I lowered my face as a hot tear of frustration and embarrassment trickled down my cheek. I knew that the waiter had been watching me. He fielded my knife for me and asked me something in Spanish. I shook my head and turned my wrist over to hide my raging red tendons.

'*Momento,*' he whispered and took my plate. He returned a few minutes later. He had cut my meat into small portions for me. I ate it with a spoon. Nobody noticed.

As I dragged myself up onto the bed that night, I vowed to decommission my secret weapon for all time. I was going to be boring and sensible from now onwards.

My absolute fatigue defeated the discomfort and I slept heavily. Half past seven on the following morning and I was refreshed and ready for breakfast. My first morning in Spain and my first Spanish breakfast. In truth, I did not expect it to be much different from my last breakfast in France. The frontier on which I had expended so much energy in crossing had been political, not gastronomic.

I was heartily comforted by my ability to understand and make myself understood. Although I spoke no Spanish, much of what they said to me seemed to have a direct and similar equivalent in French. The menus in the restaurant were written in French although that was no particular advantage to me since I have never understood a French menu. I can instantly give you the French for, 'a five-bearing crankshaft' or, 'a raked hull' but have never been able to work out what '*papillottes*' or '*goujons*' are. Mind you, I am no better in English. I was sixteen before I realised that fish had fingers and the Scotch laid eggs.

I had understood, 'a las siete y media' to indicate that breakfast was available from half past seven. That suited me. I would breakfast at eight and be on the road by half past. Breakfast is a very important meal for a cyclist. You need a good breakfast to set you up well for the rest of the day.

The overlap on my French map would take me only as far as Pamplona – probably less than a half day's ride. I needed to buy a Spanish map today. If I could not find one in Aoiz then I would certainly succeed in Pamplona.

I looked around my room. My bags were packed ready. It was five to eight. I went down to breakfast. Heavy wooden shutters had been swung across the windows. The further I spiralled down the staircase, the gloomier it became. So gloomy was it that I bumped head first into the wrought iron grille before I saw it. It barred the entry into the bar, indeed, it denied egress from the stairs. I must have come down the wrong staircase.

I climbed back up towards the light and wound around creaking corridors. At last I found the other staircase. It led me down from the second floor to the first and then stopped. I walked along the corridor. The only way down was by the spiral staircase with the wrought iron grille locked across the bottom of it. I was baffled. I returned to my room for a think. Was Spain on a different time to France? Had I come down an hour too early? Was it perhaps ten to seven not ten to eight?

I switched on the television. It confirmed that Spain and France used the same minutes. A lady with red lips and dangly ear-rings began to talk at me so I switched it off. I waited half an hour and went downstairs again. The grille was still locked. I shook it to make sure and to make a noise. The noise produced no human reaction whatsoever. I called, 'allo?' a few times. Still nothing. I returned to my room. I waited another half hour. At nine o'clock, now that must be breakfast time in anybody's language, I went down but the wrought iron grille contradicted me.

This was getting silly. I wanted my breakfast. I was hungry and I needed to be out on the road, not cooped up in this Pyrenean prison. I rattled the grille again and stamped my feet noisily on the step. Beyond my metal gaol bars I could see grey light squeezing its way around the street door. It did not look like sunlight but then I decided that the sun always rises late in the mountains because of the mist. I wondered what the hotel and catering staff used for their excuse. By craning my neck around and running the risk of jamming my head in the gate, I managed to reassure myself that my bicycle was still safely residing in the bar. Then I returned to my room. I lay on the bed and switched on the television. A purple dinosaur was saying something to a wasp. It seemed to sum up the situation.

At a quarter to ten, in a hiss of air brakes, a large coach pulled up in the otherwise empty street underneath my window. My shutters were apparently welded closed but by screwing myself up to the sill and peering down through the crack I could make out the scene below. The coach door opened. The driver alighted and opened the luggage locker in its flank. Three passengers presented themselves from somewhere below me. He took their bags and threw them into the hole. Then he leaned in and dragged out a wire crate which he lugged to the hotel door. He returned empty handed, slammed the boot, jumped in the coach and roared off. I made for my door. The wire crate had been crammed full of bread rolls. That was why no breakfast was being served – the bread had not arrived. I was certain that downstairs now I would find a hive of activity.

I could not have been more wrong. The wire crate full of bread rolls mocked me from the other side of the locked gate. Obviously the street door was left unlocked so that the driver could deposit and collect things and the gate was employed to ensure the security of the hotel proper.

But that deduction still did not get me my breakfast. I felt like a caged animal in a zoo, waiting for the keeper to feed me. I wondered if a hotel employee would turn up and start throwing bread rolls at me through the bars.

What should I do? Shouild I sit on the step and wait for Armageddon or return to the wasp and the purple dinosaur? The dinosaur won. I sat on my bed and wound up my indignation like a clockspring. Was it because I was English that two and a quarter hours after the time I had been told I could enjoy breakfast, no morsel of food had yet passed my lips? Why had I not succeeded in doing something about it? I could not imagine the Latin-blooded natives putting up with such scandalous treatment. Fine! Right! I'll go down there and I'll... I'll.... Well they had better jolly well look out for themselves, that's all.

I thought I could hear a movement as I came down the stairs. I was right. In the bar a black woman was scrubbing the floor. I rattled my key on the gate until she turned around. She gave me one questioning jerk of her head. I pointed to the bar.

'I've come for breakfast,' I said. I could see no point in trying to embroider my statement with Spanish. It must have been obvious what I wanted.

She made a clicking noise with her tongue and returned to her bucket. I watched her for a few seconds then rattled my key in an absolute frenzy of percussion. She turned around again. I grabbed the gate and rattled it. I felt even more like an animal caged in a zoo. She dropped her cloth into the bucket stood up and waddled towards me but instead of opening the grille, she unbolted a door on my side of it which gave me access to the bar.

'*Gracias,*' I said with feeling.

I walked over and dropped my bags by my bicycle. With a great flourish I pulled up a rattan topped stool to the counter, sat on it and clonked my key noisily onto the margin of the metal counter top which was not covered by the security blind. I was ready for breakfast. I just needed somebody to roll up the blind.

The minute hand on the clock clicked onto half past ten.

Then it clicked to ten thirty one.

Then ten thirty two.

Then ten thirty three.

The woman was still scrubbing. Whilst I would be the first to recognise that cleanliness in a place of food consumption is of paramount importance, on this occasion I was prepared to put up with a modicum of squalor in exchange for a little sustenance. I was not quite certain how to explain this bargaining to the lady concerned so I said merely, 'Coffee.'

She turned, shrugged and continued scrubbing.

The clock clicked to ten thirty four.

Ten thirty five.

This was ridiculous. I tapped her on the shoulder and by mime and language of a sort, explained that I wanted my breakfast. By mime and language of another sort she made it clear that she was only the cleaner.

At ten forty I set my jaw. I strapped my bags on my bicycle and pushed it out through the second open street door. I was fuming with rage. Breakfast at half past seven? Down here in the bar? Huh!

As I passed along the facade of the hotel a natty idea suggested itself to me. I opened the door which the coach driver had used. Before me sat the crate of bread rolls, behind it grinned my iron grille, still locked. I winkled four bread rolls out through the mesh of the wire cage and stuffed them into my pannier bags. Then I set off.

The town was eerily deserted. I think I saw only half a dozen people before I reached the main road south. There I found a bench overlooking the river. I broke open a couple of the bread rolls and stuffed them with some black chocolate from my emergency supplies. It was a good job that I had not considered anything that had happened yesterday to have been an emergency or I would have had nothing to eat for my breakfast this morning. That was excellent contingency planning.

But I was fulminating with indignation. It was not the money that mattered – I had paid for the room, dinner and all on the previous evening when they had asked me. I wondered now if that was why they had asked for payment first. What time would they get out of bed? I thought of the gate at the bottom of the stairs. What would have happened in the event of a fire? Staircase sealed, windows obstructed by jammed shutters. It really did not bear thinking about.

And then I realised that with both the street doors unlocked, anybody in the village could have purloined my bicycle and the iron bars would have prevented me from stopping them. Ironically the only person in the world who had no access to the bicycle was me, the rightful owner.

I was still choking over that dainty morsel when it started to rain.

chapter six

It rained all the way to Pamplona. An insistent drizzle whose stubborn determination left me in no doubt that it intended to reach the ground no matter what or who got in the way. It dripped from the peak of my sodden cap and splashed onto my nose. It trickled down my face, into the corner of my mouth and down my chin. It crept around my collar, it infused my clothes, it seeped into my shoes.

Although the road was a secondary route it was very broad and surely carried a considerable traffic at some part of the day but for the moment, the vehicles were sparsely strewn. The road preferred to avoid the settlements; snaking around them. I stuck with it. I could not be bothered to divert from the agreeably smooth surface to visit the odd forlorn hamlet. I was certain that other opportunities for rustication would arise before I reached Bilbao. As I circumnavigated one such village I felt, rather than heard, a rhythmic thudding. Was it a printing press?

A drop forge? No. It was church bells. They possessed the timbre of a cardboard box being kicked and rang with the resonance of a damp sock. But why were they sounding at all? Was there a plague or had the country just been liberated from an evil oppressor? Or was it to welcome me? The answer, when it came to me, was rather more mundane and insultingly simple. It was Sunday. I had lost count of the days but when I checked in my notebook it confirmed that today was the eighteenth of my journey, my first full day in Spain and a Sunday.

Arriving at the outskirts of Pamplona I ignored the signs which I was certain were trying to divert me around the centre and I made a bee-line for the middle. The wide avenue suddenly constricted into a narrow cobbled street with dark fronted shops and houses. I hauled my bicycle up on to the pavement. Or rather, I tried to. The kerb was as high as the bottom step on the Pyramids and when I tugged at my cross bar my bruised hands simply opened with the effort. I still had no grip. I hooked my forearms under the bar and hoisted my machine onto the sidewalk by swinging it up in the crooks of my elbows. That hurt me as well.

In the small general food store a lady in a white and blue apron provided me with the necessaries for a picnic lunch, a new pack of plastic razors and a small bar of soap. All I needed now was a map and I would be back to my full working specification. Further down the street I satisfied this lacuna with a road map of the Firestone Tyre Company. It was all I could find. It showed the country as far as my destination, Bilbao, but not much in between. Great tracts of land in this part of Spain were apparently white with green stipple. They were not complicated with a variety of altitudes, nor sullied by roads or speckled with settlements.

I navigated through Pamplona until I found a park. The rain had stopped and the sky was lightening. I ate my picnic and studied the map. The first thing that I learned was that

89

Pamplona was actually called 'Iruñea Pamplona' which seemed to explain the road signs that I had been following all morning. Another useful but unwelcome piece of information was that Spain had dual carriageways and motorways where France made do with cart tracks. With my finger I traced a cross country route to Bilbao, using as many of the yellow roads as I could. As there were no relief contours marked on the map I had to assume that when the road wriggled, it was going uphill. I later discovered that it also went uphill when it was not wriggling.

I pinpointed a town called Irurtzun. It was roughly thirteen miles further on and I thought that I had a good chance of getting there at about four in the afternoon. This would give me time to find a hotel, have a shower and be sitting down to a welcome hot dinner by seven o'clock. After the exertion of the twelve hour mountain crossing of the previous day, I felt that I had earned an early stop.

The road leading out of the city was broad and smooth and lined on both sides by factories and depots which were bizarrely interspersed with private houses. Ahead I could see the sky blackening by the minute. How could this be right? I was in Sunny Spain and it was the month of June. But the clouds were racing enthusiastically to meet me, running up the garden path to throw their arms around me and kiss me on both cheeks.

It was probably my anxiety about this reunion that caused me to overlook the diminutive policeman dressed in a rain cape. He was standing in the middle of the crossroads, looking like a lone pawn on a giant chess board. He blew his whistle furiously at me. I skidded to a stop and smiled sweetly at him whilst he went puce in the face in an effort to explain to the entire region of Navarre the full extent of my crime. I suppose I should have noticed that all the cars had been queueing.

He eventually calmed down and turned his back. I blew him a kiss. We waited. Me on my bicycle and the others in their cars. A solitary van crawled slowly across the junction and then nothing. Must be our turn now. No. We waited. A blob of rain plopped onto my thigh. I could see a bus shelter on the other side of the crossroads. If only I could just get across. I began to edge my bicycle forwards. The policeman turned, pointed at me and shouted. I edged backwards. I did not blow him a kiss this time.

The rain, having presented its visiting card and made its introduction, now enthusiastically slapped me on the back, remarked upon my rude health, enquired about an obscure mutual acquaintance whom I had never liked and guffawed at several of its own jokes.

Across the other side of the crossroads, the inside of the bus shelter was dry. Behind me, twenty motor car engines fanned and whined and twenty pairs of windscreen wipers went, *thud THUD, thud THUD, thud THUD.*

It occurred to me then that we must be waiting for somebody important to pass by on the other road. Royalty? Did Spain have a royal family? I supposed it must have. Wasn't it related to the family of pretenders to the throne of France? I could not remember. History at school had stopped at 1914 and had never gone further south than the Edict of Nantes. Oh well, if I was waiting for a regal cortège to go by, then that was all right. Indeed, I was at the front with the best view. This did not stop me from getting wet though.

At last the shiny black pawn espied the cortège arriving from the road to his right and energetically waved it forward.

Cyclists.

About four hundred of them.

Dressed in skin-hugging costumes in psychedelic hues. They tore across our road like a gaudy tropical snake pursuing a particularly juicy rat. Cyclists! I have stood here in the pouring rain to let cyclists through? The car behind me hooted. The policeman was now waving me forwards.

Cyclists?

I pushed off.

Cyclists! I wouldn't let them on the road. They ought to be banned. I glanced at the arid bus shelter as I went past. I was wet through to the skin because of cyclists? It was enough to make anybody a Royalist.

Cyclists!

The policeman eyed me suspiciously as I wobbled past him muttering, 'Cyclists, bah, flogging's too good for 'em.'

They had been going the right way. I obviously was not. The wind was hard in my face, forcing the rain under my spectacles and tugging at my anorak to slow me down. Then a ninety eight wheel lorry whisked past, four centimetres from my left elbow. I grabbed grimly at my handlebars in anticipation and two seconds later a vortex of draught pushed me a yard towards the kerb and then sucked me out towards the middle of the road. I leaned and threw my weight into the argument. Another lorry hurtled past and blew me into the concrete gulley. I skittered up against the crash barrelling. I said a very rude word. Then I said it again.

I would have to get off this road. I could not keep waltzing about the asphalt with impunity. Someone who could not dance would come along and tread on my foot. I dragged out the road map which had been cowering in the dry, lying under the top flap of my pannier bag. I began to unfold the concertina but need not have bothered. The wind immediately blew it full out and ripped it into two pieces. I stood there like some demon Royal Navy signaller, waving my hands about trying to get my two flags to roll up without daring to let them go. I had probably just dispersed the entire Home Fleet to the four corners of the North Atlantic. Now that I had dusted off that very rude word it seemed a pity not to use it. I did so. Five times in quick succession.

I screwed up the bits of map and pushed them into my bag. I bit on the toggles of my anorak hood to stop the pocket from filling like a drogue and then set off into the wind again. Thankfully, a few hundred yards further on, the heavy traffic, indeed, all the traffic, suddenly veered down a slip road onto the motorway, leaving me the main road to myself. About time too.

As predicted, I reached Irurtzun at about four o'clock and I was ready to stop. All my aches of yesterday had returned and my wrists were becoming inflamed again. Irurtzun was one main street of oddly shaped, multi storied buildings; flats above, shops below. The whole town was slyly sidling down the hill to a motorway junction. According to Firestone, the next ten miles of my road had been erased by this motorway but I did not believe them. And in any case, that would be tomorrow's problem.

I found a small hotel within a tyre's screech of the interchange and drank a coffee in the bar whilst I sized up its suitability. A bit of a pointless exercise really, since I was going to stay here anyway because it was the only hotel that I had found. I asked the man at the bar if he had a room for tonight.

'Five o'clock,' he said.

I really must learn Spanish.

I tried the question a different way, putting in French words like 'chambre' and trying to pronounce them as if they were Spanish.

'Five o'clock,' he repeated and to make it utterly clear, he tapped his watch.

The clock behind the bar clearly disputed this, showing the time as half past four. I decided that he was saying that the hotel opened at five o'clock. I ordered another coffee. The water dripped from my clothes into a pool on the tiled floor. At half past five a lady with orange hair bustled in. He pointed me out to her. She took a key from a drawer and showed me out into the street. Thankfully the rain had stopped, the wind had dropped, the sky was an innocent blue and had it not been for the road steaming like a damp commuter one would have believed a wide-eyed assertion that not a spot of rain had dropped this month. After all, was this not Sunny Spain?

The room was on the fourth floor of a block of flats, two doors up the street. It was what I would have called, 'a bedsit.' I was worried at first that she thought that I was looking for long-term accommodation but eventually I accepted that the hotel was a bar which had rented some rooms in the block of flats. That being said, it was clean, modern and well appointed. I would be able to squeeze my bicycle into the space at the bottom of the stairs in the entrance hall and so I took it.

Back at the bar I returned to the subject in which I always have a huge personal interest.

'When is dinner?' I asked in my one-day-old Spanish.

'Half past seven.' She shook a strand of orange hair from her face. I noticed that her eye shadow was green.

'Here?' I pointed to the bar. I was getting quite good at this.

'Yes. No.' She waggled her hand and her bangles jangled. She pointed to a flight of stairs which curved upwards from the corner of the bar and disappeared into the sombre shade of an upper storey. 'Upstairs.'

'Upstairs, at half past seven?' I confirmed.

'Seven, half past.'

I felt that I had made real progress.

By seven o'clock I had showered and changed into my dry clothes. My wet clothes I had already washed and they were drying from my washing line which I had strung across the shower cubicle. As I tripped gaily down the eight flights of stairs to dinner, I felt like a new man. Well perhaps not exactly a new man, but at the very least, a recently refurbished one.

The bar was abuzz with conversation and aclink with glasses. I sat at a table in the corner and pretended to study my map. I was actually inspecting the clientele – a predominance of brown in the clothes, black in the hair and broad in the belly. They were all men. The pitch of the conversation was the lower registers of baritone and the hue, that of a mud filled estuary. Where were all the ladies? Where was the colour? The vivacity? The tinkling laughter? The glamour?

At half past seven I folded my map, tucked it under my arm, and sauntered up the curved staircase, trying not to look like a ravenously hungry cyclist who wanted to get his dinner before everybody else.

The dining room ran the full length above the bar. It was set with neat circular tables and plush chairs. Miniature alcoves had been created with low screens of dark wood and these would have been lit by the wall lights shaped like candles to match the giant versions hanging from the ceiling in the middle. I say, 'would have been lit' because they were not. No lamps were lit. The room was in darkness. There was nobody there. I turned and ambled down the staircase with a contented grin welded to my face. Just checking out the restaurant for er... for later.

By eight o'clock I had worked out on the map my route for the following day. A quick reconnaissance up the stairs confirmed for me that the room was still as quiet as the grave and just as welcoming. Downstairs, the barman was a jovial, red faced fellow, roaring at customer's jokes and then drawing on a fag which he lay on a plate of nuts. I wanted my dinner.

'To eat?' I asked, making a mime of succulent food entering my mouth.

'Yes. Upstairs.' He pointed to the corner staircase and then shouted a retort down the bar at a sixty year old man.

'Upstairs?' I insisted.

He turned and began to pull a beer from the tap.

'What?'

'To eat. Upstairs?'

'Yes, yes.' He waved his hand at the corner again.

'At what time?'

'A moment! A moment!' he called to a pair of swarthy men with red neckerchiefs. He turned to me and jerked his head up. 'What?'

'At what time, to eat?'

He was certainly giving me the recommended dose of repetition in my language training in order to reinforce learning. I wondered if he had read the manual.

'Half past seven.' He picked up his cigarette and flicked the ash into the nuts.

'Half past seven?'

I looked pointedly at the clock which showed five past eight.

'Half past seven,' he repeated. He screwed up his eyes and drew on his cigarette. Was I going to challenge him on this blatantly false assertion of his? He exhaled grey smoke and stared brazenly at me.

'Thank you,' I said and returned to my corner.

This thing about the time was obviously a cultural factor that I had not quite come to grips with yet. 'Half past seven' for breakfast this morning had meant, 'ten minutes to eleven if you are prepared to go without a hot drink and forage what you can from the doorstep delivery.' I hoped that, 'half past seven' this evening did not mean, 'ten minutes to eleven.' My last cooked meal had been twenty four hours ago.

I popped back up the stairs again at half past eight. Nothing had changed but when I redescended, three ladies had now arrived in the bar. They were shorter than the men but just as broad. They were monumentally coiffed, extravagantly painted and expensively dressed. They stood at the bar drinking glasses of wine. Perhaps this is what we are waiting for – the other halves of the couples. Maybe now we will see some action. But the only action was a change in the pitch of the conversation and the occasional sharp retort of a slap on a backside.

At nine o'clock I went up to the bar, selected a peanut from the dish and returned to my table to chew it. The irony was not recognised. I should have asked for a knife and fork but although my knowledge of Spanish had proceeded apace within the last twenty four hours, it did not yet extend to cutlery. It was pretty good on telling the time. There was not much more that I could do. Unlike the hotel of this morning, there was not a crate full of food lounging at the bottom of the stairs which I could pillage.

At twenty past nine three more ladies arrived. These were younger and slimmer and were apparently known to everybody in the bar except me. I discovered why when they disappeared up the stairs and switched on the lights. Don't rush. It might be a trap. I waited to see if anybody else had noticed. If they had, it was not apparent. They continued to spit nutshells, drink wine and slap bottoms.

There comes a time in a man's life when he has to be a leader. Assuming the heavy mantle of responsibility with a debonair attitude, I rose from my table and went upstairs. The restaurant looked charming. A young lady met me with a menu and a smile and conducted me to a table. I ordered my food and the first morsel reached my palate at ten minutes to ten.

When I left at eleven o'clock the restaurant was in full swing. As I made for the street door I asked the barman where I could eat breakfast.

'Here,' he said, nodding at the bar.

'And at what time?'

'Half past seven,' came the reply.

chapter seven

You know what I am going to say, don't you?

At eight o'clock I am standing at the bar with a cup of coffee and nothing else. The same brown masculine mass is expectorating on the tiles and the barman is jovialising indiscriminately.

This is obviously what the Spanish call, 'breakfast'.

Before leaving Irurtzun I wander back up the street to the supermarket and sit outside on the wall, basking in the morning sun until the shop opens. Sun! I had forgotten what it was like. Having made my purchases, I am rolling down the main street when I see two cyclists on the opposite side of the road, poring over a map. A man and a woman in their early sixties perhaps. Their bicycles are dusty and loaded with camping gear. They call me over.

'Hi,' says the woman. 'I am Mariet and this is Pieter.'

'My name's Martin.' We shake hands. I look at their bicycles which are laden down with all sorts of bundles and bags. 'Where are you going now?'

'Home. Back to Holland. You?'

'Home, back to UK.'

'You're going the wrong way.' They laugh.

'I'm cheating. I'm taking a ferry from Bilbao.'

'Ah so.' They look at each other.

'Did you pedal all the way here from Holland?'

'Yah.'

'And you are pedalling all the way back?'

'Yah. We've been right round Spain. Right down to Algeciras.'

I said, 'wow' because it seemed appropriate. When I later looked at a full map of Spain I realised that 'wow' was a little understated. Their total mileage would easily be five times mine.

'You could go back to Holland by ship,' I suggested. 'Go to the UK by ferry, cycle from Portsmouth to Dover and then ferry across the Channel. The ship leaves Bilbao on Thursday, you could be in Dover by Sunday.'

'Let's go and have a coffee,' Mariet indicates that we are outside a bar.

They wait whilst I lock my bicycle and we go in.

'Coffee?' she says.

'Yes please, thank you.'

I gaze around the bar in amazement. The surface of the counter is covered from end to end with food. Mariet picks up a sandwich and starts to rip it apart with her teeth. My mouth waters but I stoically stand fast and decline her offer of food. Actually, it was not stoicism, it was crass stupidity and I knew it but could do nothing about it. If my hotel could not provide me with breakfast why should I be expected to get it elsewhere?

'So, this scheep from Bilbao,' Pieter asked through a mouthful of sausage, 'How much does it cost?' .

'Just a minute.' I burrowed in my pouch and pulled out my ticket. I showed it to him.

'It's a lot of money.' He raised his eyebrows.

'Well, you have to take a cabin. I have to pay extra for a single cabin. You would go cheaper in a twin berth.'

He showed the ticket to Mariet who also pulled a face, then handed it back to me.

'It is still a lot of money. It will not cost us that to go back by bicycle.'

'You are camping?'

'Yah. It is very cheap in Spain. And we are in no hurry. I am an artist in Harlem. If I want to take a couple of months holiday in summer there is nobody to tell me not to.'

That sounded like just the kind of life that I could cope with. I made a mental note to investigate the entrance requirements when I got home. Then I stopped dreaming and turned to more practical matters.

'Where have you come from this morning?'

'Just up the road.' He took out a map. It was a Michelin. What was it with tyre companies that they were obsessed with making maps?

'Ah,' I said, 'my map shows only the motorway between here and Lekumberri but I want to go on the old main road. There must be one still there. What does your map show?'

'The same, but the old road is still there.'

'And it is open?'

'Yah, yah. For cyclists. No problem. We came down it this morning. Yah, no problem for cyclists.'

His assertion reassured me. We both understood the fine qualification, 'for cyclists.' Very few 'closed' roads were really closed for cyclists. This had been proved to me on several occasions. One of the most heart warming proofs was given to me on an early visit to the Pyrenees, years ago. I had set off with the intention of grinding up the pass to arrive at the summit at about two in the afternoon. I had been a little disturbed to discover that the foothills of the Pyrenees were violent little hillocks with one in six gradients everywhere. This had upset my timetable. It was two o'clock before I had arrived at the bottom of the pass, let alone the summit. I was just a mite off schedule. Up I had pedalled, sweating in the afternoon heat. I should have been in the morning shade. Round and round, back and forth, zig and zag, higher and higher. At one point I had waited at a place where the road widened to allow a tourist coach which had been grumbling up the pass behind me to catch me up and go past. The pensioners had gazed placidly through the smoked glass, comfortable and insulated in air conditioned splendour.

About a quarter of an hour later, as I still struggled on heavenwards, I had met the coach coming down. The driver had stopped and informed me that the road was closed ahead. 'Even for bicycles,' he had insisted. But then he would, he was a driver. Sour grapes. I had plodded on and sure enough I came to a sign which informed me that the road was closed two hundred metres ahead. Would I like to follow the twenty three mile diversion which would take me back down the mountain and up another, further from my destination? I found it difficult to believe that workmen closing a mountain pass would put the warning sign at the top and not at the bottom. It did not make sense. Why allow travellers to climb the hill to discover that they could not get over it? This would be particularly unpleasant for those of us whose motive power came from our own muscles and not from controlled combustion of distilled carboniferous detritus. I pressed on.

When I came to the road works they were inescapably demonstrative. It was not so much that the road was blocked. It was more a case that it was missing. Workmen were installing a huge concrete drainage pipe to take the winter rainfall under the road and in order to do so, had simply dug the road away. A ravine faced me. I walked up and down the edge, trying to see if there was any possible way that I could climb down and up the other side, carrying a bicycle. On the opposite bank, the man on the digger watched me. I came to the awful conclusion that the road was impassable. I had arrived too early, for the pipe was in place but the road had not been tucked back over it.

I pulled a face at the digger driver. He waved at me to wait. In a raspberry roar he started his excavator. Even as an adult I loved to watch these machines working. They made the moving of mundane moraine look like ballet dancing. In a sequence of beautifully choreographed movements, the long arm scooped up bucketsfull of sand which it gracefully deposited in a makeshift causeway across the highest part of the pipe. With an effortless precision, he tamped the top with the bottom of the bucket. He swung the arm away, sat back and with a flourish of his hand, invited me to cross.

What a star! He was probably a cyclist himself.

And several years later I had weaved around some *'road closed'* signs in the Massif Central and come across a team of workmen mending the bridge. The decking had been ripped up and they were welding the girders. With not so much as a grumble they had stopped sparking and pulled their equipment aside. I had walked along one girder whilst running my bicycle parallel on another with the mountain stream visible below me as it thundered over the rocks.

So I knew what another cyclist meant when he said that the road was not closed to cyclists.

The road to Lekumberri was climbing gently up a prettily wooded valley which was patched with occasional pasture lands. Sometimes it was cows, sometimes pigs, sometimes goats and because the road was closed, it was beautifully quiet. I occasionally caught the odd rumble of the motorway on the other side of the hills and from time to time a local resident would rattle past but apart from that, I was alone. This tranquility was useful. It allowed me to recall my conversation with Pieter and Mariet which thus reminded me that there was an actual deadline to my journey. At eleven o'clock on Thursday I needed to be in the ferry queue in Bilbao.

It was raining steadily by the time that I reached the top of the hill. I call it a hill since the summit was at a mere eighteen hundred feet. As I edged my bicycle down the greasy, unused incline on the other side, I realised that by chance I had chosen the best direction in which to travel. Parts of the descending gradient were one in five, they would be lungbursters on the way up. I stopped in a fortuitous bus shelter and ate my picnic. There were no seats so I had to eat standing up. The day had taken on the tone of an old black and white photograph. Colours which for a short time had been vivid in the sun, were now muted and neutralised under the rain.

Before reaching the next big town, Tolosa, I was to have a new and nerve-racking experience. The road passed through a tunnel. It was on a corner where there had not been sufficient space to make a detour around an outcrop. It was hewn out of solid rock and I entered it in a state of innocent unpreparedness. I had switched on my dynamo, of course but I was not ready for the absolute blackness which I plunged into. The pupils of my eyes would not dilate to allow me to see where I was going because every time that I looked up, I saw the bright white spot of the light at the end of the tunnel. The edge of the carriageway was not marked with a white line and when I lowered my head to try to see where the road was, jagged points of rock would lurch out at me from the rough-hewn walls. My dynamo light was as much use as a wooden compass; I never saw one sparkle of its meagre light reflected on the ground in front of me.

As I was veering from right to left in the blackness I suddenly jumped to an explosion of noise as a vehicle entered the tunnel. The din echoed off the walls and rolled around the soundbox of the tunnel. But where was the car? Which way was it going? Could it see me? I was utterly disorientated. In a rising crescendo of noise, a dark saloon raced up behind me and hurtled past. I say, 'a dark saloon' but it was only a guess. It did not have any lights on. Oh my God there's another one coming towards me. Am I on the correct side of the road? Where is the wall? I can't see a bloody thing. I came out of that tunnel ten years older.

I found another tunnel just around the corner.

My determination to get to Bilbao now took a hold of me. I sailed straight through Tolosa and on towards Azpeitia. It would be another fifteen miles but I would be nearer Bilbao and what else can you do when it is raining? It was not as if I wanted to check in to a hotel, run upstairs and get changed and then come down and slosh around the streets of Tolosa.

The road was steep and unforgiving. No sooner had I breasted one rise than I hurtled down and began all over again. My wrists were paining me again and once a bump in the road knocked the handlebars from my deficient grip and for one frantic moment, I grabbed in a mad frenzy at anything and everything to avoid disaster.

I was very tired when I arrived at Azpeitia. I found a poor looking pension which was surrounded by waste ground upon which rusty bits of lorry had been dumped. Rotting trailers and crippled earth-moving machinery peered forlornly at the walls of the inn through fronds of scragggy foliage. My room was so mansarded that I could not stand up straight and the toilet was down the corridor but the room did have one asset which no other had provided thus far – a working, two-bar electric fire set into the wall. I stripped off and hung my clothes out to dry in front of it. They immediately began to steam.

I was so weary that I just went straight down to dinner and it was not until I was half way through it that I realised that I had not asked at what time I could eat and we had started at half past seven. Perhaps that was where I was going wrong. I should not ask, just assume. Or was it that somewhere in today's journey I had crossed an invisible date line and we were back to normal hours again? I would probably never know.

On the wall of the pension hallway – I could not in any sense call it a hotel reception – hung a map of Spain. It was thanks to this that I understood the magnitude of Mariet and Pieter's wanderings and also discovered that although I had thought that the Pyrenees stopped at the Atlantic Ocean it was only the name that stopped. A range of peaks descending from three thousand feet to fifteen hundred would accompany me all the way to Bilbao.

I handed my bank card to the proprietor of the pension. He looked at it with interest, turned it over and then gave it back.

'No,' he said.

'No?'

'No. Pesetas.'

I frowned as I quarried into my money bag. I was trying to pay for dinner, bed and breakfast and all that I had was fifteen pounds in small pesetas. I decided to plead poverty and emptied all my money onto the counter. Completely unruffled, the man counted out what he needed and pushed back about three pounds worth of pesetas. I scooped it back into the bag before he changed his mind. Spain was definitely much cheaper than France.

As I set off under a leaden grey sky I could sense that my mind was now set on Bilbao and the ferry. No diversions, no amusements, this was serious. I would try to reach Gernika Lumo tonight and Bilbao, Wednesday night, ready for the ferry in the morning.

I plodded up the interminable hills and tried to avoid the candid admission that this trip had been a bit of a failure. The project of coming to Spain had been born from a desire to see my friend who was moving to Bilbao and a wish to escape the damp drabness of a French summer and yet, the warmest, driest weather that I had experienced so far had all been north of the Pyrenees. It had rained from the first moment that I had set foot in Spain. As for visiting my friend... well, more of that later.

The electromagnetic radiation from my brain must have been transmitted high into the ionosphere because suddenly, the sun broke through the clouds. I stopped and symbolically removed the anorak that had become my Spanish uniform. Two minutes later I removed my top shirt. A minute after that I was looking for some shade to stop under. There was none. The skin on the back of my neck was burning. The temperature had suddenly risen to over eighty degrees. I felt that there was no need for such exaggeration. I had only expressed a little moan about the rain, honest.

By lunchtime, I had had enough of the Spanish sun. It was like being a burger under the grill. I expected at any moment that a giant spatula would descend from the sky to scoop me up and throw me onto a plate with some floppy salad and cardboard chips.

I found some heavily foliaged trees surrounding a square in the town of Markina and so I sat on a bench to prepare my picnic. The schoolchildren were shrieking and trilling in the playground opposite and mothers of younger children were congregated under the shade, whilst their darlings rushed around in the sun. The children were all wearing trousers, not shorts. They probably thought that the weather was cold today.

An elderly gentleman dressed in grey trousers, a blue jumper and black beret was slowly picking his way around the sandy square with the aid of a bowed walking stick. Along the far length he hobbled; then up the side, always carefully avoiding the shade of the trees; now a right angle turn to bring him along the side of the square where I was sitting. He stopped before me.

I looked up. He turned his body and inspected me. I nodded at him. He turned back and continued his circuit.

When I had first purchased bread in Spain I had wondered what it would be like. Everybody knows what French bread is, but do you know what Spanish bread is like? It's the same as French bread. Silly me. I cut open a portion of baguette along its length and inserted some slices of sausage. I did not fall into the trap of trying to slice the tomato. I would eat that in my hand. The old man was just finishing the other short side and turning onto my stretch.

I crunched into my sandwich and met the watery gaze of his greeny brown eyes. He looked at me. I nodded at him again. There is not much more you can do with a foot of baguette clamped between your teeth. Once more he inspected me and then continued his journey. On his third circuit he stopped and inspected me again. Was it so strange to see somebody eating in Spain? Given the difficulty that I had encountered so far in trying to get food I had to suppose that it was.

His behaviour reminded me of Frank's Goldfish Syndrome.

'I heard an interesting statistic about goldfish the other day,' Frank said.

'Is there one?'

He was not to be deflected.

'The memory span of the average goldfish is only eleven seconds.'

'What is?' I blew imaginary air bubbles through pouting piscatorial lips.

'The memory–' He looked at me with narrowed eyes. 'You're not taking this seriously are you?'

'Goldfish,' I prompted.

'They have a memory span of eleven seconds.'

'You said that before.'

'So anything that happened to them more than eleven seconds ago, has gone.'

'This is why you can't train goldfish to be guard dogs,' I told him. 'They can never remember where they live.' I thought this was quite an intelligent observation but Frank ignored it.

'I was imagining the standard set-up. A fish bowl with one of those little plastic castles sitting in the middle. So there are two goldfish swimming around the bowl but the time needed to complete a full circuit is more than eleven seconds, right?'

'A big bowl, then?'

'Right.'

'Or slow swimmers.'

He sighed heavily.

'So as they pass the castle one goldfish turns to the other and says, "I've never noticed that there before." Then they swim around again and by the time that they reach the castle more than eleven seconds have elapsed, so the fish says to his companion, "I've never noticed that there before." They swim around again and as they go past the castle–'

'Ye-es,' I said. 'But you're wrong aren't you?'

'Well no. Neither fish would be able to remember the beginning of the journey because a complete circuit would last longer than their memory.'

'So,' I said, 'the fish could not say, "I've never noticed that there before", because he would not be able to remember what he had seen before, when he had been at that point. He would say something like, "Oh look, a castle." Then he would go round again and say, "Oh look, a castle."'

'I suppose so,' he said grudgingly.

'But we're both wrong.'

'Why?'

'Well, you said "a fish bowl." A fish bowl, by its nature, is circular. So the castle situated in the middle of the bowl would always be at the same distance from them. It would not suddenly surge into view. Either they would be able to see it all the while or not at all.'

'It could be at one end of the bowl.'

'You cannot have an end to a circle. You should know that.'

'It could be oval.'

'Fish bowls are not oval, they are circular.'

'But they could be swimming on an oval course within a circular bowl.'

'So we have two eleven-second memory fishes who are describing an intricate elliptical course within a circular bowl, they interrupt their complex geometrical swimming pattern to make the observation that–'

Frank said, 'I don't want to talk about this anymore.'

I finished my picnic and left my Spanish goldfish swimming slowly around the square. I cycled to Gernika Lumo.

What is the Spanish for 'Early Closing Day'? The English phrase sprang to my lips when I arrived in Gernika Lumo. The streets were empty. They ran as ghostly canyons in dark shadow between vast blocks of modern buildings. Shutters were down, balconies deserted, shops closed. The only movement came from the desultory shunting of a banging locomotive in the station yard; the only chatter, from the squawking caged birds hanging from windows.

I found a hotel where the customers were still being served lunch at three o'clock. The lady told me to come back at five for the hotel. All the indicators regarding eating hours that I had received since entering Spain had been shouting out one word very loudly to me but I had been utterly deaf to their bellowings.

Siesta.

In Spain, it is early closing day, every day.

It's called, 'siesta'.

When I returned at five, shutters were up, cars were hooting, pedestrians ambling and balconies bulging. On the square before the hotel stood a group of English cyclists. A tandem and three singles. Eddie and Sarah on the tandem, Rob, Margo and Ian on bicycles. Eddie was a fit forty year old with steely blue eyes which had an unsettling penetration about them. His hair was silvering at the temples which served to make him look distinguished. Eddie was the departmental head in the multinational company in which they worked and the others were his underlings. Every year they took the ferry to Bilbao on a five day excursion ticket and enjoyed a ride around this part of Spain. It was a sort of comradeship bonding thing. They just got on well as a group. They were so lucky.

Sarah, on the back of the tandem was about twenty eight. She had long hair which the sun had begun to bleach and long slender legs which the sun had successfully tanned. Her cycling shorts and top indicated that the rest of her was probably equally well proportioned. Rob and Margo, on the bicycles, were a married couple in their late twenties. Rob was a trifle dumpy and apparently liked tee shirts which broadcast a message. I had no idea who 'Frankie' was and why I or, indeed, the Spanish, should need to be informed that he, or she, 'goes to Hollywood'. Was this regular commuting we were being told about or a ritual such as, 'Martin goes to Woolworth's'? Margo, his wife, had short cropped brown hair and a frank, open face; freckles, brown eyes and a Northern accent. Ian looked like a trawlerman. He had a full beard. It also showed silver but did not add distinction to his face. Like Eddie, his eyes were blue but they had a faraway gaze in them – usually when he was looking at Sarah. His manner was that of someone not at ease with people, a little self effacing.

We stood chatting about journeys whilst we waited for the man to open the trap into the cellar. This, I was informed by the others, was where they stored the bicycles.

'What's it like on a tandem?' I said to Eddie.

'Great! That right Sarah?'

She nodded warmly.

'I could never go on a tandem,' I admitted. 'If I was at the back I would not trust myself to the skills of the person steering and if I were steering I would forever be suspecting the one at the back of not pedalling.'

'Sarah's a good stoker and I'm a good steerer so it's the perfect match.'

Those blue eyes bored into me as if challenging me to dispute this corporation of fortune.

'I should think the others have trouble keeping up with you don't they? I mean a tandem can really move.'

'Not uphill,' brown-eyed Margo said gleefully. 'We always go past them uphill. Every time.'

'Not every time.'

She clearly mouthed, 'every time' to me behind Eddie's back.

'The thing is,' Eddie explained, 'a tandem is slower up a winding hill because of its long wheelbase. We take a longer line around the hairpins. But on the downhills and the flats there's no catching us, is there Sarah?'

'Too right,' she affirmed.

At that moment the twin traps of the cellar were flung open and a black haired berry of a man waved us to hand our bicycles down to him.

'Hold hard, gang,' Eddie said. He took a pace to the edge and peered down the steep steps. 'Bit of organisation required. Form a chain. Ian, you're the shortest, you go onto the third step.'

Ian shuffled up.

'I'll hold your bike,' I said to him. He smiled gratefully, his lips red in his beard.

Ian said something to the cellarman who nodded and stood down. He clambered onto the broad-stepped ladder and stood with his torso projecting. We removed our cycle bags and abandoned them in untidy heaps on the flags, then we passed our machines down the line to be swallowed up by the dank darkness of the *bodega*. I think that is the correct word.

In the restaurant that evening, the waitress showed me to their table, assuming that I was of the party. Before I could correct her, they had insisted that I join them. I sat in the empty place opposite Ian.

'How far did you get to in your trip?' I asked.

'San Sebastian.'

I pulled out the tattered remains of my Firestone. The paper had dissolved into a pulp of tissue wherever the rain had soaked it. 'Where is San Sebastian?' I asked.

He looked at the map and gently carressed his beard. Then he put his finger on a town back along the coast towards France.

'There, Donostia.'

I was puzzled. 'San Sebastian?'

'San Sebastian, Donostia – it's the same town. One name is Spanish, the other, Basque. Like Gernika.'

'Gernika Lumo,' I corrected.

'But that is both names. Gernika is the Basque name and Lumo is the Spanish name. Or the other way around, I don't know which. They print both names on the maps.'

'Oh, so that is why Pamplona is 'Pamplona-Iruñea'? It's called one or the other depending on which language you are using.' He nodded. 'Where are you off to tomorrow?'

'Well...' he glanced across at Eddie. 'We'll probably–'

'We're going up to the coast aren't we gang?' Eddie's steely eyes swept around the table. He got nods of assent. 'We're going to take a dip in the sea now that the sun has arrived.'

'Yes, that's where we are going,' Ian confirmed. 'There's not much to see now in Gernika, not since the Germans bombed it.'

'They did what?'

I am perpetually refreshed by the serendipitical rediscovery of my own ignorance. I suppose you all knew about Gernika and the Spanish Civil War but, as I have already explained, my school history stopped at 1919 and went no further south than Nantes. The Spanish Civil War was thus excluded on two counts.

In 1937 a squadron of German bombers attacked the town of Gernika on market day. Gernika was not a military or defended town so the military rationale seems a little obscure. The town was utterly destroyed, over two thousand civilians were killed and Gernika became synonymous with the horror of the newfound aerial weapon – bombing. Recalling the appearance of the town as I ate, I realised that it should have been obvious to me that something monumental had happened here.

We chatted on through the meal. Ian was the only one of the group who had any useful knowledge of Spanish. It was he who was able to translate the word for 'veal' so that Sarah could be upset by the idea of the poor little calves; it was he who was able to get the wine sorted out into what they wanted and it was he whom Eddie interrupted or talked over as soon as he tried to make inroads into the communal conversation. As an outsider, knowing nothing of their lives and little of their relationships, I would have said that Ian was blindly in love with Sarah and that Eddie felt threatened by this.

However, not my problem. They were agreeably impressed by my journey down through France. For the sake of veracity I toned down my account of the Pyrenean crossing – I left out the pack of wolves baying at my heels and the meeting of the grizzly bear face to face on the glacier. We parted on the morrow. They, to spend their final night at the coast and me, to go direct to Bilbao to be in place for the ferry. I admired the confidence they possessed in their cycling prowess which allowed them to sleep quite serenely thirty kilometres from their ferry whose departure would occur at half past twelve on the following day, whether they were present or not.

Actually, the ferry does not depart from Bilbao itself. The city of Bilbao is about eight miles inland, up the River Nervion. The ferry leaves from the port at the estuary – Santurtzi. For my last night in Spain I was obliged to stay in a rather expensive hotel but it did have a view of the harbour. I sat watching the boats and mused on my great adventure. Twenty two days earlier, I had ridden ashore at Calais, turned right and kept going. From the top of France, right down to the bottom; I had crossed the Pyrenees in a manner which would be a permanent memory and a useful yardstick of what I was capable of. I had been fried in France and splashed in Spain and I had done it all because my friend who was engaged to a Spanish girl in Bilbao had invited me to stay with them.

I lifted the receiver and dialled his number.
In London.
London?
Yes. You see, I knew when I started the journey that he would not be in Bilbao when I got there. He had not moved yet. He had given me the address and telephone number of his fiancée and told me to ring her, she would be very willing to accommodate me. But I did not ring her, of course. After all, we had not been introduced.

Do you mean to say, that you have just cycled fifty miles a day for three weeks, in pouring rain and blazing sun, up mountain and down pothole to arrive at your destination at a time when you knew your friend would be in London?

Yes, well when you put it like that, it makes it all look rather silly.

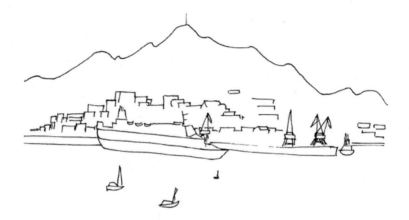

chapter eight

As required, at eleven o'clock I was in the queue for the ferry. The vessel itself towered high above the terminal. Nothing less like a ferry could I imagine. This was a cruise liner with a vehicle deck.

I had been directed to the front of an empty lane at one side of the park. It was the lane reserved for bicycles and motor bikes and for a time I occupied this corridor in regal isolation until a retired couple wobbled up on bicycles loaded down with tents and sleeping bags. Despite the brilliant sun, they wore trousers and windcheaters – there was probably no space in their bags to store them. The lady smiled at me from under her white fuzzy hair but the man stood his bicycle on its stand and stomped off towards the terminal building, his red nose pointing before him like the warhead on a ballistic missile.

The marshals began to load the cars. We were still just three bicycles in an otherwise empty lane. Where was Eddie and his 'gang' I wondered? I was sure that they had said that they were taking this ferry. The man came back and stood by his bicycle, an angry vein pulsing in his temple as he glared at each individual car embarking. Suddenly he exploded at the sight of a large saloon towing a speedboat on a trailer.

'Just look at that!' he spluttered. His wife hardly glanced at him. 'Look at him! Why did he have to bring that with him? A bloody speedboat. Bloody showoff! That's all he is, a bloody showoff! Why does he need a speedboat on holiday? Can't he live without it for a couple of weeks of the year? Eh? Can't he?'

Then he began to worry about getting the best place on the car deck for their bikes so that they would be first off at Portsmouth. As if that mattered after a thirty hour voyage. But it did to him. He would have dearly liked to have been at the head of our little queue which still consisted of only three bikes. I think that it riled him that they were numbers two and three in the queue and not one and two. He bustled around his wife muttering, 'Soon be us, soon be us. Get ready.' Then he cajoled her into a place right behind me and edged himself up to a position behind my left shoulder.

At last it was our turn. The moment we got the wave he stood up and stamped on his pedals and with a pointed exhortation of, 'come on dear,' thrown loudly over his shoulder for the benefit of his wife, he tried frantically to out-accelerate me on his heavily laden bicycle in a race to the ship.

'Isn't it lovely weather for the time of year?' I observed pleasantly as I paced effortlessly alongside him.

'Humph!' he grunted, his eyes bulging with strain. Then he noticed the passport kiosks for the first time and he realised that all his effort to get up to a good speed had been wasted. 'Get the passports out dear,' he shouted over his shoulder. He would have needed to have shouted because his wife was still fifty yards behind, struggling to get her bike going.

Whilst he fumed and chomped I languidly pulled out my

little red booklet and handed it over for inspection. At last his wife trundled up.

'Passports,' he snapped at her.

'Yes, I know dear.' She handed her passport to the official.

'Well what about mine?' he said. 'Give him mine as well or we'll be here all day.' What he really meant was, 'or that other chap will get on the boat in front of us.'

'You've got your passport dear,' she said calmly.

'What? No, you've got them in your bag.'

'No dear, you asked for yours so that we could go through quickly, don't you remember?'

'I did not.'

'You put it in your jacket pocket, dear. The left one.'

'Doh, silly thing,' he muttered and pulled out his passport. 'Never had this trouble with the old blue ones. You could always tell when you had one of those in your pocket.'

About half a second after I had left the kiosks, he steamed past me again, his eyes fixed fanatically on the bottom of the ramp. I stopped pedalling and pulled over to let his wife go by.

'You had better go first love, I'm in no hurry.'

She shook her head sadly as she cycled past me.

'Nor am I,' she sighed.

When I finally entered the dark bowels of the ship and reached the end of the car deck, the chargehand waved me forwards, past the elderly couple tying up their bicycles, and gave me a rope and a small space by the exit ramp. I thought the husband was going to fight me for it. He nearly burst a blood vessel.

After twelve hours on board ship I knew for certain that I could never take a cruise. I would go round the twist. Well, further round the twist than I already am. The seats were all designed to look inviting and they supported you lovingly for about thirty five minutes after which they would shrug you off. They were either too hard, too upright, too shallow, too low, too deep or too cramped. What the company wanted was that you should spend your time and money in the restaurants and shop. There was a perpetual movement of evicted sitters wandering about the ship, ready to claim that elusive treasure – a comfortable seat.

Several years later, after my third or fourth crossing, I discovered that there were only four comfortable seats on the entire ship, two on the port side, two on the starboard. They patently did not belong on board because they were the wrong colour and they were the correct shape. You could sit in them for hours at a stretch and not require a crane to winch you out or physiotherapy to get you mobile again. I wondered if the seats had been smuggled on board by some enigmatic society for the comfort of subscription paying members. I kept the seats' location a secret from all but my closest friends. And it's no earthly good you writing to the publishers, I'm not telling you. I don't want to find you sitting in my seat even if you are reading one of my books.

As I wandered around the floating shopping mall that was my transport, I walked through a narrow lounge down one side of which the early risers had installed themselves in upholstered chairs and erected defences of bags, bottles and newspapers to repel all carpetbaggers. Each community was deep in conversation and, the passing from one to the other, as I did, was akin to tuning a radio across the frequencies and catching a phrase from each station.

'...started going wrong when they split the atom. Up until then, everything was all right.'

'...do a doughnut with like, custard, in it instead of jam. They're famous for it.'

'...down to her navel.'

'...more lire to the pound than pesetas, John says.'

'...and we didn't see any dolphins last time.'
'...no, no, no, not that one. I was talking about the road through Bodmin.'

I admit that I am an incorrigible eavesdropper and despite the adage, I have never heard ill of myself. In fact, rather more humiliating is the hurtful admission that I have never overheard anybody ever make even the slightest of allusions to me.

And me a famous author.

But listen to this one.

I was in a secondhand bookshop. You know the kind of place – Victorian rooms lined with dusty, bare-wood shelves from floor to ceiling, strip lights that cast shadows onto the spines of only the books you are interested in, a cat curled up on a radiator and classical music playing on a cheap radio lodged somewhere near the desk. I had been browsing there some time and had worked my way along most of the shelves and was on the home run back towards the front door when I heard a conversation that was struck up between the proprietor and a customer, neither of whom I could see.

'Can I leave those here then and collect them later when I go by.'

'Yes sir, I'll put them down here. I'd better write your name on them.'

'Chatterton.'

'Chatt...er...ton. Hmm. We've got a Chatterton up at the corner. The florist.'

'Yeah. My sister.'

'Oh, your sister. I haven't see you in here before. You don't live in the area then?'

'No, just visiting. Thinking of moving down though.'

'Oh.'

Silence.

'So... she's your sister then?'

'Yeah.'

'Older than you is she?'

'No, younger.'

Given that these two were apparently utter strangers on a first meeting, the next question seemed so utterly incongruous, both in content and tone, that it made me pause in mid-browse.

'How do you er... how do you get on with her then, your sister?'

And if that paused me, the reply froze me to the spot.

'Hate her! Hate her! Wish she was dead!'

The venom in the voice brought a chill to the sunny shop. I stared at the spines of the books shelved before me. I was nearly at the front door. I had finished browsing really but I stepped back and reviewed a shelf or two whilst I strained my ears.

'You don't get on with her then?'

'Younger sister you see. Before she came along it was lovely. Just me and my Mum. All day long. Life was just perfect. Then she came along and it all changed...'

I was at the front door again. I really had finished. I could not see what other course of action was open to me other than to go out onto the street but I wanted to listen to this poisonous diatribe.

'Then it all changed. I hated her for that.'

I opened the door and the street noise rumbled in. I strained my ears as I stepped over the sill.

'–never forgave her for that.'

I released the door. It began to close on its spring.

'–that's why I murdered my father.'

Click.

The door shut.

'That's why I murdered my father?' Had I heard correctly? There was no doubt about it. I stared at the dumb door. What do you do in a case like this? Rush back in and pretend that you have just recalled some urgent quiet browsing that needs to be undertaken within earshot?

'That's why I murdered my father.' How often, if ever, have you heard somebody say that? Then I concocted the fanciful proposition that they might have been reading the parts from a published play. How else could it be explained? People don't just say to strangers, 'that's why I murdered my father.' I edged to the shop window and tried to peer over the display. I could see the shopkeeper still nodding as he listened to the revelations of a man in his early sixties. The latter had his back to me and was wearing a vaguely nautical blue shirt and a panama hat. And neither man was reading from a book.

I was so disturbed by my gleanings that I forgot to walk up to the corner to see what his hated sister looked like.

I did not hear anybody on the ship admitting that they had murdered a parent but, if cornered, I could have done grevious bodily harm to the chair designers.

Continuing my search, I discovered Eddie and his gang uncomfortably distributed along an L shaped bench in the piano bar. They looked like a mouthful of bad teeth.

'So you made it alright then?' I said as I sat down. 'I was beginning to wonder, when you did not show up at the loading time.'

'Yes we made it,' Eddie said briskly then he jumped up. 'Come on,' he said to Sarah. She flicked her hair, grinned a silly excuse and hurried after him. Ian watched them go.

'Well, I hope it wasn't something I said,' I laughed.

'No, it wasn't you,' Margo grinned. 'He's feeling a bit sensitive. On the way to the ferry he decided to lead us along a stony track.'

'And I got a puncture,' Ian said gloomily.

'We only just caught the ferry,' Rob finished.

'Oh well, cheer up. You're here now. Who wants my duty free voucher? I'm teetotal.' I waved the card in the air.

'We haven't got any more room on the bikes.' Rob

sounded disappointed.

I offered it to Ian. He looked a little startled.

'Oh well, if you are not going to use it...'

'I'm not.'

'Well thanks. Thanks a lot. I think I'll pop along there now whilst there is still a choice.'

He got up. We watched him weave his way through the staggered seats.

'Poor old Ian,' Margo muttered.

'He's a bit shy is he?'

Rob and Margo looked at each other.

'Well, sort of,' Margo said. 'He's not had much of a good time lately. Sarah used to be his girl but then she ditched him for Eddie and Eddie ditched his wife for Sarah. They've just gone back to the cabin for their daily bonk.'

'Margo!' Rob said.

'Well they have. It stuck out a mile.' She gave a rich gurgle. 'If you see what I mean.'

By lunchtime I was verging on insanity. The food was disgusting and the bookshop, full of fluffy penguins. In order to stave off the mind-numbing boredom I bought a paperback about the international terrorist, Carlos 'The Jackal', who had rampaged bloodily about Europe in the early nineteen seventies. I found a quiet corner of the bar in which to read but five minutes after I sat down some pimply youth with a microphone began to show off how numerate he was by calling out integers. He did not fool me. I could see he was reading them from a bingo machine.

I retreated to the small self service coffee bar. I bought a cup of coffee and a croissant and tried to immerse myself in the terrorist scene of a couple of decades ago. To my astonishment I learned that Carlos and I had lived in the same street in Paris. It was a narrow quiet street in the seventh arrondissement. I was not surprised that he had chosen it for a hideout. I flicked back through the pages to fix the event in time. Blimey! Carlos and I had lived opposite each other for about a year. Whilst half a dozen police forces around the world were searching for him we were probably sitting side by side in the launderette watching our socks going round and round. Wow! I must have passed him in the street loads of times. I read further. I then discovered that I had worked alongside one of the agents of the Japanese Red Army. Perhaps I shall write a book about it one day.*

I looked up and gazed with unfocused eyes at the mural screen before me. It ran around one and a quarter sides of the coffee bar and represented a Nordic landscape of calm water and cliffs and small islands. Not quite the Bay of Biscay but then I remembered that I had seen the shipbuilder's plate somewhere. This ship had been built in Scandinavia with the original intention of using it for cruising around the fjords – thus the decor. It had faded now. What had probably been brightly coloured cliffs and caverns, rooftops and harbour walls was now an almost abstract scattering of warped geometrical shapes with their images mirrored below a horizontal line representing the water. There was a small island with its reflection like a pyramid; a timber jutting from the water at an angle; a lone dwelling of some sort perched on a hill top. It was greys, and browns and greens and blues.

I sipped from my cup and my eyes settled gently on the landscape directly opposite me. A line of odd shaped hills cut off straight at the water line. My eyes lazily travelled over the woman's naked buttocks, up her back to where her long hair trailed off over her shoulder. I blinked. It was supposed to be a fjord. I looked again. The only two hills on the entire frieze which were not angular were juxtaposed like a pair of enormous buttocks. They were buttocks. A woman's buttocks. There was even a cave at the water line between

*Carlos lived at 11 rue Amélie. My thriller, *Rue Amélie*, was published by Queen Anne's Fan in 2009.

the... Oh my God! I sat up in my chair and looked around. Nobody else seemed to have noticed. This was not the ink blob test of psychiatrists, this was for real. An enormous naked woman was sprawled across the Nordic countryside in a quite immodest pose.

I did not have a camera with me. I took my writing pad and a ball point pen and sketched it, just as it was. I would bring a camera on my next trip so that everybody could see.

On my next crossing I discovered that the café had been refurbished. The screens had disappeared.

But I've still got the drawing.

chapter nine

I went back to Bilbao, of course, many times. I learned, however, to tell English friends that I was going to 'Spain'. If I mentioned Bilbao it always provoked the response, 'Where? What on earth for?' Indeed, why should anybody go to Bilbao? It is a decayed industrial city set in the wettest part of Spain. It is Sheffield-near-the-Sea, complete with rusting blast furnaces and derelict iron ore mines, washed by endless days of Mancunian quality rain. Garnish this with the possibility of being blown up by Basque terrorists and the probability that you won't get breakfast and it does not present a very appetising dish.

Alan, Raquel and Mama live in a district known as *'Las Carreras.'* This rang warning bells for me because from my knowledge of French I deduced, quite cleverly, that in Spanish this meant, 'The Quarries.' Not an unreasonable deduction given that the local topography consisted of enormous holes in the ground but I was wrong. It means, 'The Races'. I have no idea why the area is called that and nobody could enlighten me.

The railway station snuggles up to the bottom of the garden and the petrol refinery lounges about in the valley across the road. For days on end we live under a muggy blanket of hydrocarbons which mixes with the low cloud to obscure the sun that is happily scorching the remainder of Spain. So why do I keep going there?

One fairly mercenary reason is that I get fed and lodged for free. Well, almost for free. Occasionally I am requested to take an English class at the private school that Alan and Raquel run – the Academia Seneca. It seems that the schooling system in Spain is such that the children attend in the morning and then play sport in the afternoon. Those parents who wish their children to actually learn something enrol them in a private school for the afternoons where they learn what they should have done in the morning.

My English classes are a substantial learning shock to the native students. I am absolutely untrained in teaching and I do not speak Spanish. Students always know that the teacher really speaks their language and so they rarely force themselves to make a worthy effort. As soon as they reach a hiccough, they revert to their native language and the teacher obliges with an explanation. Not so me. I respond to their Spanish cross-questioning with, 'I'm awfully sorry, but I don't speak Spanish. I'm jolly good at English though. Why don't you try me?'

Eventually they come to learn that the language they had been studying as a disembodied academic discipline is now the only tool that they can use in order to communicate with this idiot in front of them. I love to be there when they suddenly realise that this is what learning a foreign language is all about. It is not about ticking boxes in an American text book or putting words into the speech balloons of a strip cartoon; it is about being able to talk to and understand foreigners. The look of achievement which I see course across their faces is worth the deceit, for in truth I can usually understand the gist of what they are asking me in Spanish despite my denials.

I suppose another reason why I visit Alan and Raquel is because I quite like them.

Very cleverly, Alan introduced me to Las Carreras by a route which was guaranteed to appeal to me: a cycle track. Bilbao has been known for its iron for at least five centuries. A 'bilbo' was an ancient word for a type of sword – 'bilbo' being the older customary spelling of Bilbao. Had I delved into the works of Scott I would no doubt draw your attention to the phrase, 'at drawn Bilbo,' but I haven't so I shan't. And were I a Shakespearean scholar I would quote that part in *Hamlet* v ii 6 which says; 'Me thought I lay worse than the Mutines in the Bilboes,' but I am not, so I won't. I wonder if this is what theatre critics call, 'dramatic irony'?

The point that I am coming to is that Bilbao has been producing iron for centuries and the fortunes of the town have risen and fallen with the demand for its product.

The middle of the nineteenth century brought British entrepreneurs and railways to Bilbao and thence began the heyday of Bilbao's iron industry. British ships delivered tons of Welsh coal to the blast furnaces which were built along the banks of the River Nervion and for the return cargo they loaded up with the pig iron for reworking in the steel mills of South Wales. The hillsides of Vizcaya were blasted and scoured for the rich iron ore that they contained. A dense network of railways, in fact, the densest network that Spain has ever known was scarred across the countryside to bring the ore to the furnaces. The lines ran around and through the hills, they leapfrogged each other with metal bridges and hurtled down through dynamited cuttings and roughly hewn tunnels. Workers flocked from everywhere to this industrial Mecca. The population of Bilbao in 1870 was seventeen thousand; thirty years later it was eighty three thousand and it continued to grow by one thousand souls every year for the following two decades.

Raquel's father was one of those who migrated from the Extremadura – a poor area in the south of Spain whose name translates as 'very hard' – to seek for work in the Basque country. He ended up working in Portugalete at the factory of the British boilermakers Babcock and Wilcox.

And then suddenly, there was no more high quality ore and the railways were not needed. Many of the lines had been financed and in some cases, managed, by British companies. After all, three quarters of Bilbao's iron was exported to Britain. The railways were closed. Some of them lingered on, pretending that they served a social purpose but the motor omnibus soon put paid to them. The rails were ripped up and the trackbeds, abandoned.

And now they are being reborn as cycle and walking tracks. I have cycled from the top of Santurtzi to the back of Las Carreras on a beautifully smooth ribbon of red tarmac complete with white lane markings and reflective warning signs. Evidence of the railway heritage is everywhere. In one place I pedalled under a stone and iron bridge which had carried another branch of the line over and about. I could see where the loaded wagons would have doubled around the curve on screeching wheels like a fairground ride to thunder down and join my track. At the bottom of the valley to my right, derelict industrial buildings were being bulldozed into terraces ready for blocks of flats.

The great advantage to a cyclist in using a former railway track is that, when they constructed the line, the engineers knew that their maximum gradient would be dictated by how well a smooth steel wheel could grip a smooth steel rail. The result is that railway lines do not go straight up the side of a hill and down the other; they take the much more gentlemanly option of wandering around the edges on the same contour line and occasionally boring through a big bit with a tunnel. Nobody would spend that amount of money and time in making a level track for cyclists, but converting an existing track for the use of bicycles is very cost effective.

However, on my first return to Bilbao I had no bicycle. I flew in for the wedding. It was winter so I wore a raincoat. It was twenty two degrees centigrade when we landed. The Spanish customs officer wanted to know what was in the heavy brown paper parcel whose string was cutting through my fingers. Well, what do you think? What would you take to Spain for a wedding present for a couple who ran a private college? Sixty two secondhand Ladybird books of course, what else?

With no bicycle I discovered that there was a distinct advantage in having a railway station lurking at the bottom of your garden. Even more so when your station is the penultimate stop on the branch. You can sit in the kitchen and drink coffee until you see the train go up, then you know that it will be back down in twenty minutes to take you into town.

The old town of Bilbao stands on the right, or northern bank of the river. It is a knot of tightly wound stone-laid streets hemmed in by dark-balconied buildings. It was right here that the first prosperity of the city was established. Here were all the shops, the businesses and the banks. In 1300 the town was given a sort of charter of self government by the lord of the Basque country and this helped to reinforce its supremacy over the town of Portugalete which was the port at the mouth of the river.

The Basques were known as fearless seamen which was quite fortunate because the entrance to the river was fairly hazardous on account of the harbour bar. Once the ships had negotiated this obstacle, however, there was little impediment to their sailing eight miles further up the river, especially if the town they found there was furnished with the merchant banks, the agents and the customs houses necessary for their masters to conduct business. The deleterious effect of the harbour bar was not neutralised until the great sea mole was built at Portugalete in the latter part of the nineteenth century but by then, Bilbao was well established as one of the largest settlements in Spain.

In the early twentieth century, the space needed by the ever-expanding Bilbao took it across the river to the parish of Abando which it annexed and then laid out with majestic avenues on a modern grid pattern. Today, the roles are reversed with Abando being the thriving commercial area and the old town, a quiet backwater.

Wandering around the narrow streets of the old city and looking at the eighteenth century town mansions, I wondered what had assured the prosperity of Bilbao before the industrial development of its iron ore. The answer humbled me in my ignorance: the Spanish colonies. How could I forget that Spain had colonised most of South America? Bilbao was one of the ports which had grown rich on the cross Atlantic trade. Already in the sixteenth century it had been granted the right to establish its own commercial laws and the definitive version of these formed the basis of the commercial code of all Spain and of many South American countries. So really, Bilbao is probably quite an important place.

As I climbed the steps to the Abando station for the train to take me back to Las Carreras I was suddenly struck by the observation that everything in Spain is upstairs. The trains are on the second floor, hotels are above shops, people live in flats. Alan's house is a bizarre mixture, almost as if putting an Englishman into the equation threw out the calculation. They live on the first floor and another family occupies a maisonette which consists of the ground floor and second floor. Alan and Raquel are the filling in a sandwich. Neighbours can be heard at all hours of night and day, stomping up and down staircases at the end of the building; Alan's bathroom window opens out onto his neighbour's balcony.

What is this fixation with living on top of one another?

In European terms, Spain is a big country. At half a million square kilometres it is larger than Germany, larger than Italy although smaller than France or Turkey. The population density of the UK is two hundred and forty souls per square kilometre; in Spain it is sixty eight and the way that the Spanish build means that there is one person at the bottom and sixty seven living above them. Everywhere I looked, multi-storied blocks of flats were creeping into the Spanish countryside; a countryside which is an enormous expanse of unpeopled land. Why build upwards when the horizontal is so empty? Is it a subconscious desire to see further? Are the Spanish really that worried about being the shortest people in Europe?

The train twisted sinuously around the shiny brand new Guggenheim museum which sat like a gigantic foil-wrapped cream cake at the water's edge. Behind it, across the river, the ancient jetties were rotting into the murky slime and warehouse facades crumbling into the street.

The noise inside the train was deafening. It was not mechanical – the air conditioned carriage swished us along with an occasional sibilant, *'Hurrengo geltokia'* from the loudspeakers, this being the Basque for, 'the next stop'. No, the noise in the train was one which you would never hear in England. It was that of conversation. Strangers, friends, mothers, workmen, everybody talking to each other. Whenever the Spanish get together they talk. They sit on benches in the park and reminisce. They stand on street corners and argue. They gossip, three abreast, across busy doorways. They expound theories behind reversing lorries. They throw enquiries from the ascending escalator to a recipient on the descending one. And they even say hello to foreigners.

When I turned up at Bilbao airport for my flight home, I found a pink and yellow spotted cow standing on the pavement outside the terminal building. Knowing that I am teetotal, are you not just a little curious about that statement? Of course, my being a seasoned traveller meant that I had to ignore the cow as everybody else was doing. But I bet you are having difficulty ignoring it.

When I got to the check-in queue I found a vibrant corroboration of an assertion that Alan had made to me that the Guggenheim Museum was opening up Bilbao to the tourists. Here before me were eight Americans who would never have even heard of Bilbao five years earlier. Their voices were as loud as the colours of their clothes. As I shuffled along behind them, I could see that they were the indisputable proof of that much stated adage that travel broadens the hips. Or did I just make that one up?

And much later that day, as I wearily dragged my feet up my garden path, I wondered where had I put my front door key. I tried the door handle. It opened. I had not taken my key with me. For the two weeks that I had been in Spain, I had left the doors of my house unlocked.

I suppose I could be thankful that there was nobody standing talking in the doorways. At least I could get in.

But, safely in England, I found that Spain was not an easy country to dismiss from my mind. Thoughts of Raquel and Alan and Mama kept intruding. I remembered once an incident which had arisen at the Academia where Alan and Raquel teach and I occasionally assist. It was a question put to me by a pupil which had sparked it all off. The situation was made more surreal by the gaps in their vocabulary and in my comprehension which coincided to make it necessary for Raquel to be called in to the classroom in order to interpret the request.

'They want to see your bottom.'

I looked at her as only an Englishman could in such circumstances. It was obvious that she had mistaken the word and was not aware of what she had just said. It reminded me of the French wife of an acquaintance who, wishing to play Scrabble in French, had written off and asked the manufacturers to send her a bag of French letters. I gave Raquel an inane smile and hoped it would serve to cover the embarrassment that she must have been feeling. I was a little perturbed that I was unable to detect the evidence that any such sentiment was fomenting in her conscience. I was further perplexed when she continued.

'Can you stand up, turn around and lift up your jacket?'

Not much equivocation about that then.

It is astonishing how unprepared one's upbringing can leave one for the rigours of real life. I can honestly and categorically state, maybe with a little chagrin, that this was the first time that anybody had asked to see my bottom for other than medical reasons. I was not certain what Etiquette decreed should be the correct form to decline a request to display one's fundament. It had not been covered in the short course of commercial correspondence that we had done in the sixth form, so I tried prevarication.

'My bottom?' I said.

'Yes, your bottom. They want to see your bottom.'

'My bare bottom?'

'No, not your bare bottom. Unless you want to.'

'I don't understand why they should be entitled to see something that I have never seen. Why do they want to see my bottom? Is this something that thirteen year olds usually ask? Is it part of the curriculum?'

'They want to see if your bottom is like Alan's.'

'Well, apart from its nationality it must, perforce, have some similarity with Alan's due to the communality of its functions with his. Have they seen Alan's? But why?'

I was utterly lost.

'Spanish girls like men with big bottoms.'

'Bully for them.'

'But they think that Englishmen all have little bottoms.'

'Well, surely that should be a matter of concern only to

English men, not Spanish girls.'

'Yes but I have married an Englishman.'

'A splendid choice.'

'But they want to know why.'

'Well tell them then.'

'OK. So you will show them your bottom then?'

Was she misunderstanding me on purpose? I sighed in resignation, turned around and lifted up my jacket.

'Finished?' I asked.

'Yes thank you.'

'So what was their conclusion?'

'You've got a little bottom.'

'And?'

'They like big bottoms.'

'Well that suits me. I suspect that it is merely a case of their liking Spanish men and that they cannot find a Spanish man with a little bottom so they make big bottoms a desideratum. Rather like Welshmen preferring women with thick legs because all Welsh women have thick legs.

'It's true? Do Welsh women really have thick legs?'

'I don't know, I've never asked.'

'But you don't need to ask, you can just look.'

'Do you mind? I'm English. I don't go around looking at ladies' legs.'

'Why not? It's quite normal. Spanish girls go around looking at men's bottoms.'

'Apparently so. Look... is it lunchtime yet?'

And on another day I had announced,

'I thought I would go for a ride on the *bidegorria* this afternoon.'

'Well Raquel and I shall be teaching but dinner is at the usual time,' Alan said.

'Half past ten?'

'No, eight o'clock.'

I was scandalised by the bare-faced lie.

'But... but, we have never eaten at eight o'clock,' I stuttered. 'Last night Mama didn't even light the stove until half past nine.'

Alan let my protest lie unaddressed. His charity made me feel mean. Who was I to expect food to be served to the timetable of an English digestion? It seemed that my motto was, 'when in Rome do like the Goths and Vandals.'

He glanced up at the ceramic plate clock on the kitchen wall. I've always treated with circumspection those who feel that a plate tacked to the wall by a nail is prettier than one pinned to the table by food.

'Watch out for the old men on the *bidegorria*.' he warned me. 'In the morning it's the women who walk but in the afternoon it's the men.'

The *bidegorria* was the track shared between cyclists and walkers – *'bidegorria'* being the Basque word for 'green way'. This I found confusing since the tarmac was red. However, upon this tarmac was painted a white line to allocate the relevant sides of the track to the appropriate users. In practice, the edges of the separation tended to get blurred.

'Well, I've met the women already. They are not much problem. I just say *'hola'* as I approach and they tidy up the ranks.'

'Well watch out for the men and their sticks. They wave them about a bit. Get one of those in your front wheel and you'll know about it.'

I was intrigued by these old men and their sticks. I should have been frightened. They were absolutely lethal. The walking sticks were used for everything except walking. A man would swing his stick to casually swipe the top from a trackside shrub as he strolled towards you. Apart from the discomfort of dodging a four foot floret of fragrant fennel as it winged its way straight at your head, meeting a group of such men was like jousting with a combine harvester. You would be picking maize pods and pampas fronds from your lycra for the rest of the day.

Then you got the declaimers. For some reason you always approached these from the rear. Short stumpy men arguing about something. The one losing the argument was always the chap nearest you and as you passed, *wheeesh thwack,* he would emphasise his point by suddenly throwing his stick arm up sideways, knocking your sunglasses into the ditch and taking a slice from your scalp.

And then there were the fitness freaks. I have nothing but admiration for the amount of walking that the average middle-aged Spaniard does. Not only on easy paths but alongside main roads, miles from anywhere you will come across a couple of Spaniards walking to... somewhere. But the stick-wielding fitness freaks carry their canes in both hands horizontally across their body as if they are engaged in that cinematic stave fighting that was the favourite resort of Little John and Robin Hood when, having no swords, they had to fight their way out of the Blue Boar Tavern. Then, as you get nearer, they hoist the stick upwards, one, two, puff, blow; downwards, three, four, puff, blow; twist it vertical, push away from chest, straight arms, five, six, puff, blow. You half expect them to spin it around one finger and then launch it heavenwards as would a majorette.

An explanation for this behaviour did not come to me until several days later when Alan asked me if I would pop down and get some bread from the shop. This was the shop above which a Basque terrorist cell was cosily installed, as Alan and Raquel discovered some months later when one day the village was surrounded by two hundred machine gun toting Guardia. I bet that livened up the fiesta.

So I went to the shop. This simple expedition would have been fruitless and frustrated had I attempted it during my first visits to Spain because shops in Spanish villages have an interesting attitude to trade. In the money grabbing, consumerist Western World, shops, even in small villages, sport at least one brightly lit window, a couple of illuminated signs swinging on creaking chains and perhaps an A-board leaning drunkenly on the footway to obstruct passage to those who thought they would pass by without making a purchase.

But when I cycled through apparently thriving Spanish villages looking for somewhere to buy bread and other necessaries I was regularly disappointed and mystified by the absence of shops. I did not know that the shops were there but they were hiding. A Spanish village shop is a crafty beast. For a start, it is probably an ordinary house, perhaps with a slightly larger window but with a complete absence of any signs announcing a commercial bent. If you do manage to discover it, it will be closed. Or rather, it will pretend to be closed. The shopkeeper will be sitting inside looking at you but you cannot see him or her because everything is in pitch darkness. When you summon up courage and push open the door, probably stumbling down three uneven steps as you do so, the shopkeeper will reluctantly switch on the single fluorescent tube and then stand directly underneath it so that his face is distorted in ghoulish form and his produce is washed in a hue of sickly pale green.

I am not scared of addressing foreign shopkeepers and making known my desires. I've been about, you know. I can remember when Sainsbury's was all blue and white tiles and you had to queue at each counter in turn.

But here I am in Alan's village, falling down the stone steps into the shop in order to buy a loaf of bread. The fluorescent tube is already lit. The shoplady is standing beneath it, grinning like Vincent Price, her arms folded. Four other ladies are giggling and in the middle of the shop a stocky life-and-soul-of-the-party man in a black beret and wielding a stick, is holding forth. No actual commerce or trade is being enacted. Before his adoring audience this sparkle-eyed man is strutting, throwing to each woman in turn a remark or riposte to keep them bubbling and shrieking. When he sees me he draws me into the show, but entirely on his terms; advancing upon me, waving his stick and then turning to make a ribald aside to the ladies.

I have the excuse of being a non-Spanish speaking foreigner to keep me on the margins and I hug myself to it cosily as I watch the cabaret before me. The man talks about his sausage and their melons and I know that it is not the sales stock of the shop which is being referred to. As I watch, I cannot help but notice the similarity to the hen house. This man is the cock and the ladies are the hens, clucking at his jokes and coarse references and I, of course, am the rival which is why he keeps strutting up to my end of the shop and waving his stick at me before turning to launch another side-splitting joke at the ladies. He needs to keep me from the hens. He is crowding me up against the potato sack.

Well, I eventually managed to purchase a loaf of bread and I took my discovery back to Alan.

'Those walking sticks the men carry.'

'Oh yes?'

'They are swords. The men are *caballeros* and the sticks are their swords. You watch them next time. They never use them to walk with, they carry them as you would a drawn sword; they swing and swipe with them, they wave and brandish them, they poke people in the chest. They are swords, that's all.

'Ye-es,' Alan said. 'Did you get the bread?'

I gave it to him in a rapier thrust.

The more I thought about Spain the more I had to admit that I could not boast of possessing overwhelming evidence that the country welcomed me back on my visits but then, why should it? All I seemed to do in Spain was grumble. But by the resigned looks I received on each return to England, I could surmise that a proportion of the UK population, viz: that which had met me, was very hopeful of the export potential of my persona and heartily disappointed to see the sample returned unpurchased, year after year.

Except for Keith.

Keith was very annoyed when I went to Bilbao. It had taken me a shovelful of persuasion to get him to come in on this little soirée that we were preparing at the request of the local Women's Institute group.

'Just a few songs and a bit of laughter for Christmas,' said our Drama Club Secretary. 'Could you arrange that for them Martin? About forty minutes they want.'

Well, I knew that I could concoct a programme that would have them rolling in the aisles if they dared. Several other thespians were willing but I felt that we needed Keith in with us; for his expressive face, his vast knowledge of theatrical technique and his faultless sense of timing. So I polished up my musical parodies and dusted off my old revue scripts.

'This is the sketch I want you to do with me, Keith. It's a Christmas story,' I explained.

'Yes, well it is their Christmas party.' Keith had always been quick to grasp the essentials.

'It's about this shepherd at night sitting on a hillside overlooking Bethlehem.'

So he took it away to read and evaluate and it produced the desired effect – he joined us.

Our little group, like many others, had its ups and downs but we were chugging along nicely, dredging up songs and poems and shuffling them into some kind of order when it happened. There is always somebody who, in order to inject some spirit of urgency into the proceedings, will insist on getting out their diary and calculating how many rehearsals we have remaining.

'We have only got three weeks left,' she wailed in as desperate a voice as she could muster. Don't forget that this was a drama club.

I did not quake one micron as I devastated her with the correct calculation.

'Actually we've only got two weeks.'

'Two weeks? Oh my God!' The forearm went to her brow.

'Don't let him panic you,' Keith reassured her, 'it's three weeks on Thursday.'

'No, Keith, it's two weeks on Thursday.' I took out my diary. 'It's the ninth. Look, it's written in my diary. It cannot be the sixteenth because I'm leaving for Bilbao on the fourteenth. I've already got the ticket.'

One by one, they silently showed me their diaries.

As I said, Keith has an impeccable sense of timing and a very expressive face. But his command of English has to be heard to be believed.

Yes, Keith was very annoyed when I went to Bilbao.

The Women's Institute never even missed me.

chapter ten

Two disparate factors eventually conjoined to render it desirable that I undertake a focused expedition to Spain. The first was that I purchased a guidebook in Spanish. This was not the most approachable source for somebody who still could not order breakfast in the language but I felt I had to buy it. It was a definitive account of the *Vias Verdes* – the system of old railway lines which had been converted into cycle tracks. This was something that I just had to try.

It pains me somewhat to divulge the second factor: I needed to return to my secret road over the Pyrenees in order to take photographs to convince the cheek-sucking cynics of my acquaintance that I had really done what I had said that I had done.

But how was I to get to Spain? My tenuous love affair with the maritime link to Bilbao had tarnished decidedly over the years. I no longer found it amusing to trip over trays full of dirty crockery dumped outside my cabin door by those too lazy to return them. Surviving for two days on Mama's cold omelette which I had smuggled aboard as the only palatable food became monotonous. And the shop did not stock my books.

The crunch came the day when I made a mistake in booking my ticket and reserved myself a single berth instead of a single cabin. There is no such thing as a single cabin. It is a double cabin in which one pays a premium to enjoy single occupancy. So, half an hour before sailing, I am sitting in my cabin with my effects spread liberally around me when I hear a key fumbling at the door. Knowing this to be a confused passenger trying the wrong cabin, I do nothing. I know his key cannot open the door. But it does. Into my matchbox struggles a hairy giant with a rucsack the size of a fridge freezer strapped to his back.

'Hoy!' he greets me in some unknown language and swings his pack violently down onto the opposite bunk, catapulting my bits and pieces a foot into the air.

I was speechless. I ran out and gibbered at the cabin steward who checked my ticket and confirmed for me that this monster was to be my companion for the next thirty six hours.

In a daze I wandered back to my hole. I tried to put a brave face on it and be positive. He did not speak English. I tried him in French with no response. My smattering of German and Spanish had no effect whatsoever. He climbed into his bunk and, as far as I could discover, he never left it until we reached Spain. At whatever time I returned to the cabin in the search for a bit of privacy, peace and quiet I would find his hateful lump heaving and belching on the shelf. The atmosphere in the cabin was rank. He flatulated and eructated across the Bay of Biscay whilst I wandered around the ship with the desperation of the entertainments officer on the Marie Celeste as I tried unsuccessfully to find somewhere to snooze which did not leave me shaped like a banana or was not positioned three feet from an amplified loudspeaker.

So, for this new expedition I found an alternative route to Spain – a double deck coach which towed a specially designed bicycle-carrying trailer and which would transport me between the UK and pre-arranged points in France. When I prised myself from the seat after the fourteen hour journey, I was not convinced that this was the best solution. I could not fault the company, they had delivered what they had promised. Perhaps I was just not of the best shape and condition for such an enterprise.

But it was eight o'clock in the morning, the sun was shining and the Spanish border was a short ride away. I was gambling on reaching San Sebastian in time to catch the half past five train to Bilbao.

I took the old main road through St Jean de Luz and Hendaye. The effects of the early sun were soon dissipated by a film of thin cloud which made the day heavy. Just out of Hendaye I chose the scenic route up the winding road to Hondarribia and regretted it very quickly. It was steep, the weather was humid and when I reached the top the view was smeared by a vaseline of heat haze.

As I ran down the hairpins, trying to encourage the sticky breeze to blow through my shirt, I reflected that I might already be lengthening the odds against my catching the train. According to the map, the village I was making for was on the east side of an inlet of the sea. Opposite was its twin village. Nothing on my map showed that there existed any means of crossing the bay other than by swimming. I had made up my mind that there would be a ferry of some sort. If I was proved wrong, then I would have added twelve kilometres to my journey, five of which would be on a very busy dual carriageway.

I settled upon the psychological approach. Rather than grant to the locals the possiblity of contradicting my unfounded belief that a boat existed, I would couch my enquiries in terms that showed that I knew the truth. So as I rattled down through the narrow cobbled streets towards the water, instead of asking of passers by, 'is there a boat?' I simply shouted, 'where is the boat?'. Without hesitation they directed me onwards.

The boat was small. It was so small that my bicycle was longer than its beam. With the good humoured help of the three matrons who were already installed on the bench, I personhandled my machine into a position fore and aft and then sat opposite them, holding the bicycle upright in the well of the diminutive boat.

The old man pushed off and we rocked and swayed across the choppy water, the motor spluttering like a retired colonel in a Tunbridge Wells teashop. Was I following the route of St.Jacques of Compostello, the ladies wanted to know? Was I a pilgrim? When I explained that I was only visiting friends in Bilbao, their interest in me died and they started talking to each other about hospitals.

I reached San Sebastian with a good hour to spare. I concocted a picnic of what I could muster from the food shop and then selected a bench on one of San Sebastian's stately avenues and watched the world gyrate as I ate.

The train from San Sebastian to Bilbao is a *Euskotren* – a sort of Basque narrow gauge railway. Compared to the rolling stock of the broad gauge national RENFE, the blue rakes looked like toy trains. The man in the booth who sold me a ticket told me to come back fifteen minutes before the train started. When I returned as instructed, he walked me down the platform and showed me in the little carriage where I could install my bicycle in the special space which was designed to take a wheelchair. It was even equipped with a seat belt with which I readily secured my machine.

'What happens if somebody disabled gets on?' I thought that this was a sensible enquiry.

'There is nobody disabled in San Sebastian.'

Some answers just take your breath away, don't they?

A toy train it might be, but it took itself seriously. All along the journey to Bilbao we passed wagons loaded with rolls of steel for the finishing mills of the region. Many of the stations had a busy goods yard and there were various junctions and sidings leading off into noisy factories. The old fashioned, thriving agitation of the railway implied that time in Spain had been preserved at 1950. With my cynical eye I suspected EC subsidies to be the aspic.

I was travelling the entire length of the line unlike the many schoolchildren, workers and housewives who were hopping on and off. I am sure they appreciated the light music drifting from the ceiling loudspeakers. By the end of the journey I had heard the tape several times.

It was dark when we arrived. I became anxious lest the train not allow me the time to alight with my bicycle, for I had seen the difficulties that passengers had experienced with the door locks. The moment my travelling companions began to gather their belongings I started to unlash my bicycle. Stooping to peer through the navel-height windows I caught a glimpse of the station sign. Bilbao something. As I stepped from the train with my bicycle under my arm, it occurred to me that I was being a little silly since there surely would be ample time to get off, for Bilbao was the terminus and the train would stay here for the night.

That much was true. And had I left the train at the terminus it would have applied, but I had not. Open mouthed, I watched the train disappear into the blackness of a tunnel on its way to Bilbao Atchouri. I was somewhere in a part of the suburbs which I had never visited in daylight so to add a little excitement to my consternation, I balanced my bicycle on the escalator and hung on as it lurched me precariously up to street level. There I questioned some elderly men as to the route for the town centre. I reckoned that if I could get to the centre I would know where to go.

'You go down here,' the man with the beret waved his arm at some traffic lights.

'No, go that way,' said another through his cheroot.

The third man brought them to silence by forcibly

lowering their gesticulating arms.

'Go straight up here,' he said, pointing at the seething dual carriageway. 'At the top is a square. Straight ahead is a big road. Do not go on that road, it is not good for bicycles. Go on the next road and it will take you down to the river.'

Well that was what I understood him to have said. I really ought to learn Spanish.

He was right about the road straight ahead being not good for bicycles. It was a six lane motorway strutting across the valley on concrete legs. I found his road down to the river and stuck my tongue out at the Atchouri terminus station as I went past. Silly name for a station. Sounds like a sneeze. Across the bridge by the theatre I went and up those bloody steps to the Abando railway station. The train was waiting for me at the platform. I walked straight on with my bicycle and half an hour later I was at Alan and Raquel's.

You may remember that the first time I came here, I had known before starting out that Alan would not be in the town when I reached it and because I did not tell you this until the end of the journey it made me look a bit stupid, so let me inform you straight away that it was no surprise to me when Alan went into hospital on the day after my arrival for a multiple heart bypass operation. These things are planned. We had known well in advance and he had generously decreed that there was no need for me to cancel my proposed holiday and I had selfishly agreed with him.

The night before, I tried to interest him in the pictures in my guide books. They showed smiling cyclists zinging along billiard table smooth Via Verde tracks in a rustic tableau of tranquil countryside lighted by a brilliant sun shining from a cloudless sky but, well I don't know, he seemed to be distracted and have other things on his mind.

So after breakfast, Alan nipped down to the hospital with his pyjamas and a good book and I started my first train journey. It was to be another of the narrow gauge lines that wind along the northern coast of Cantabria. This one ran from Bilbao to Santander, the port further to the west. I would be getting off before the terminus again, but this time it would be intentional. I could see from my guide book that my first Via Verde departed from a station called El Astillero.

All these Vias Verdes have a history. In this part of Spain it is almost certain to be linked with extracting coal or iron ore and shipping it down to the coast for export or smelting. The first metre-gauge locomotives would have been manufactured in Germany or Great Britain with the rolling stock built locally. As the Spanish iron and steel industry found its feet so did Spanish-built locomotives begin to appear, puffing along at the head of a rake of hopper wagons. The railway company would have bowed to local pressure and run the occasional passenger train to serve the needs of the community but the inescapable *raison d'etre* of the line would have been to serve the needs of extractive industry.

But the line from El Astillero had had higher aspirations. It was none other than the beginning of the projected Santander-Mediterranean railway. A railway which would carry all kinds of goods from one of the busiest Atlantic coast ports, across the isthmus to the Mediterranean in a matter of hours and thus save the time, bother and expense of running around seven eights of the coastline of the country in a ship. It was to climb through the Cantabrican mountain range to link up with existing lines at Burgos and thence via Calatayud to the Mediterranean.

The first thirty miles from El Astillero to Ontaneda were opened in 1898. Forty years later, the missing link to Burgos was still an unrealised project. The iron industry was in decline, the motor bus in the ascendant. The line was never completed.

I duly alighted at El Astillero in the late afternoon. A few miles to the north, the clouds lay ominously heavy over the sea but that should not worry me for the track ran twenty miles southwards to the town of San Vicente de Toranzo. There, I knew from the book, there was a hotel and I was certain that at this time of the year it would have room for me. For a while I wandered unproductively around a sort of maritime industrial estate until I found somebody who directed me to the other side of the town. It was reassuring that he had heard of the Via Verde.

Unfortunately, so had the gas company. They had dug it up to bury a pipe which they had then covered with a six inch layer of granite chippings. I found this surface utterly impossible to cycle on. I dismounted and, cursing the tide of progress as it spread into the backwaters, I pushed my bicycle. Even that was difficult. You don't see many people pushing bicycles along a pebble beach and now I knew why. And it was not a matter of a few yards; it was for the first kilometre.

My arms and legs were aching when at last I rolled onto smooth tarmac. Along this particular stretch were, evenly distributed, benches and little Spanish ladies in tee shirts and knee length shorts. The benches were no problem, maintaining a reassuringly characteristic inertia, but the ladies were a trifle frustrating since I now needed to make up some time and having to slalom around mobile barrages of chattering matrons every one hundred yards was an annoying obstacle to my smooth progress.

By the time the next village hove into view, a fine mist was falling on me, or rather, with the reputed Iberian attitude to haste, it was hanging in the air and letting me collect it up as I rode along. I could not see where the track went in the village. Did it become this road or that road? One went up, the other down and neither at a recognisable railway gradient. I found an old man working high up the bank in his garden and called out to him. His dog thought this was great fun and answered me promptly and with several diphthongs but his master, whose back was turned to me, ignored me completely. I shouted again. Still no response. By this time the hound was becoming a little impudent in his language. The man was the only living soul that I had seen in the hamlet, I needed to ask him. So I... (persons of a nervous disposition can now skip to the beginning of the next paragraph if they wish) So I threw a stone at him. It hit him squarely on the back of his leather coat. Well what would you have done?

He slowly turned, saw me, and hobbled down the bank. I explained as best I could that I was looking for the continuation of the old railway track. He smiled happily at me and waggled his fingers at his ears. He was deaf. How the devil was I going to make him understand me? He could not lip read me because I was not speaking a Spanish that any native would recognise. I became a one man mime show, one minute a steam engine, the next a bicycle, then a weary traveller sleeping in a bed. I could see that he was very grateful for this strange itinerant foreigner who had travelled all the way to his village just to entertain him. I thought he was going to give me a round of applause and a repeat booking. Instead, he came down from his vegetables and walked me through the village. By the dried up stream at the bottom, a girl was flicking pieces of cake to a blackish bird. She glanced at us with passing interest and then flicked another crumb almost into the beak of the bird.

We wound up the other side of the dip towards the sound of a fast road. That worried me. Then the man stopped at a *'No Entry'* sign and explained to me that the track had become houses between here and the next village but after that, it picked up again.

And the next village was...?

I had an awful presentiment.

He pointed up the road which said *'No Entry.'* Even without my Spanish he could see that I was demurring but he insisted enthusiastically that this led me to the big road to the next village. He was probably right and there was not much else I could do so I thanked him and pedalled past the signs up towards the sound of traffic.

It turned out that this road was the exit slip from the main road. That surprised me but not half as much as my contra-directional progress surprised the dozy drivers when they hurtled around the corner. Thankfully, the main road sported no central barrier so I was able, as he had no doubt explained to me, to cross quite safely and cycle on to the next village. There the track took off with a vengeance. The mist had not reached this far and the dry tarmac even had miniature street lights alongside it. I cycled through a child's hopscotch pitch and my tyres printed random white bands of chalk for a number of revolutions like a giant stretched bar code.

The rain caught me up after the village, as I crossed a field on the flinty remains of the trackbed. The latter ran flush to some ancient farmbuildings. The occupants must have lived with the trains rattling past their very front doors. The main road that I had used earlier was still alongside me on an embankment, but it did not stay there. With the rain trickling from the tops of my thighs I gazed in dismay at the solid earthen wall across my track. I pulled out my guidebook and studied the plan. On it, the green line representing the Via Verde simply sailed through the red of the road. I wonder how it did that? By dint of searching left and right, I found a footworn track which led to a concrete drainage pipe under the embankment. With my head squashed below the handlebars, and the traffic drumming above me, I managed to squeeze through to the other side. There I was presented with a field of six foot high maize but I could see, crossing the middle of it, the unmistakeable low embankment of the railway.

I looked at my timepiece. It was six o'clock and raining steadily and I still had about ten miles to travel to find the hotel. I set my jaw at a determined angle and slithered and slid along the edge of the field till I came to the track again.

I like blackberries. In the right place. This was not the right place. The track was an impenetrable tangle of ten foot high brambles. I did not bother to check in the guide book to see how the green line dealt with blackberries, I was pretty sure that I knew the answer.

My jaw unset itself from its determined angle and dropped loose in defeat. I retraced my route, slopped around the dripping maize and crawled back through the pipe. The rain had now set in for the evening and it was growing dark. I togged myself up in my waterproofs, dragged my bicycle up to the main road and pointed it in the direction of Santander. If I had stayed on the train this afternoon and had not bothered with this fanciful Santander-Mediterranean Railway track, I would have been in a dry hotel three hours ago.

With the rain now coursing down in gourdsfull I pedalled fast along the broad hard shoulder. Most of the traffic gave me a very wide berth. Some slowed down to goggle. The Spanish do not cycle at night and so the drivers had never seen a bicycle with lights on. In the UK I had spent fifteen years commuting along busy main roads at all hours of the night and early morning in rain, fog, gales, snow and ice. I was now wearing a reflective Sam Browne belt. My bicycle sported two front lights; four white, two orange and two yellow front reflectors; three rear lights, three red rear reflectors plus two orange and two yellow. Like a soggy perambulating Christmas tree, I flapped and swayed down into Santander accompanied by a gawping escort of wide-eyed Spaniards.

chapter eleven

After breakfast in the hotel restaurant, I phoned Raquel for news of Alan who was due to be operated on later that day. They said he was 'comfortable.' That probably meant that he was bored out of his mind.

The hotel was an intriguing amalgam of locations. It meandered from one side to the other across the various storeys of a complete block of buildings, changing style and character as it did so. On the noisy, fast avenue it was a lively restaurant with dark wooden tables and lots of cigar smoke. If you went onto the mezzanine towards the interior the decor slowly mellowed into wallpaper and formica until you passed through an unused beige room provided with floor to ceiling mirrors. From there you negotiated two sets of doors like an air lock and entered a world of corridors and carpets until you descended the staircase to the hotel entrance whose glass and marble facade stared with cold disdain on a completely different street. Here I had been instructed to leave my dripping bicycle in the small lobby. When I had asked for some old paper to put under it to catch the oily mud which would drop from it, the lady had dismissed the idea with the assertion that they cleaned the floors every morning and that nothing could mark good Spanish marble. I drew two conclusions from this. One, that she had never done that experiment in the chemistry lab at school when you poured sulphuric acid on marble to produce volumes of some important gas or other and, two, that it was not her who did the cleaning.

Sure enough, when I rejoined my bicycle in the morning it was lovingly surrounded by irregularly overlapping grey concentric tide marks but the moment I moved it they were swabbed away with a professional ease by the cleaning lady.

I was in no hurry to leave the hotel because I had half a day in hand – the train for my next jump along the coast did not leave until half past three. The plan that I had been obliged to abort, would have seen me spending the night in the hotel at the end of the mythical Via Verde and cycling into Santander during this morning, but I was here already so now I had some time to waste.

The town is set on a wide, sweeping bay which shelters an excellent deep water port although they are now having to dredge this regularly to remove the sand bar which is trying to establish itself across the entrance. With a naturally protected and easily defendable position such as it has, Santander must have been an important port from the time of the first seagoing vessel and, rather like Bilbao, its prosperity came from its trade with America and the later development of mining in the hinterland. But it is a town which has been dogged with Armageddon-like bad luck.

One of the necessary imports for the flourishing zinc and iron ore mines was dynamite and on the afternoon of 3 November 1893, the steamer *Cabo Machichaco* was moored at the quay. Whether it was seventeen or twenty cases which initially caught fire, people still argue over. The distinction is irrelevant since the entire cargo and ship eventually blew up. It wrecked the quays and flattened the streets far into the town with a loss of life recorded as 'in the several hundreds.' Over the following ten years the port was rebuilt and the houses were replaced. This gave rise to the universal condemnation by visitors that Santander was, 'a newish looking town with no buildings of merit.'

On 15 February 1941, just when the newish looking town must have been weathering nicely into that historical cliché that the tourist so expects, it was struck by a tornado tearing in from the Bay of Biscay. The sea broke over the mole and thundered into the town. The damage led to the outbreak of numerous fires and, fanned by the afterdraught of the spiralling wind, they consumed forty streets, hundreds of houses and left about twenty thousand people homeless. In remarkable contrast to the earlier catastrophe, no lives were recorded as lost. The town was rebuilt with lower buildings and wider avenues – a guise which provoked the next generation of tourists to turn up their noses at its 'modern urbanity.' Poor old Santander, it just could not win.

My day quickly established itself in the hot and sunny category. This was a pity since I was destined to spend it not on my bicycle but mostly in another narrow gauge train. I was aiming for Gijon. 'Think of donkeys,' a useful polyglot friend had coached me. 'It's pronounced, *hee hon.*' he said. As indeed it was. Santander is served by two railway termini which are placed two hundred yards apart. Although at this stage of my journey I had no intention of returning via Santander, the knowledge of their mutual proximity was to serve me well later.

At a quarter past three I was installed in the hot train, impatient to be moving. At a quarter to four I was in the same position, nursing a more intense impatience. Some kind of hitch had occurred. The passengers wandering in and out of the carriage obviously had special knowledge that allowed them such liberty of movement without the fear of being left behind by this, the last of the two daily departures to Gijon. I had no such intelligence and even less faith so I stayed put. At about ten to four a couple of college students bounced in and then frightened the life out of me by grabbing the back of the seat in front and lunging it backwards at me. I flinched and raised both arms to protect myself from this unprovoked assault and wanton vandalism. Luckily, my aggressors did not notice and the seat clanged into its alternative position, now facing the direction of travel. That was my introduction to reversible tram seats. I must have led a very sheltered childhood for they had never figured in my life until that moment.

More students wandered in, clanging seats back and talking all at once and eventually, forty five minutes late, we stuttered out of the station. This tardy start to the journey was merely an inconvenience but when the conductor checked my ticket, it assumed a different hue.

'You're going to Gijon?' he asked.

Knowing that this was obvious from my ticket, I merely nodded. He looked at his watch, sucked on his teeth and shook his head discouragingly.

'What's wrong?' I asked. 'I change trains at El Berron, don't I?'

'That's what is wrong. We might arrive too late for the connection.'

'Is there another train after that?'

'No.'

I did not want to stay on this train as far as Oviedo unless it was unavoidable. I had scheduled that town for the day after. The point of going to Gijon was to enjoy two *vias* which would take me up through the hills to Oviedo. It would make it all a little contrived if I started from Oviedo.

The train dawdled and banged its sinuous route across the countryside. I followed our progress by watching the station names pop up on the electronic notice board at the end of the carriage and then finding them on the map printed above me. People got on. People got off. It became dark. Three enormous American students climbed aboard and talked noisily amongst themselves in open mouthed Spanish. I played British and sunk back into my seat. At one station we changed conductors, the departing official pointing me out to his replacement as a trouble maker.

Two stations before El Berron, the new conductor came to see me.

'You're going to Gijon?' he said, looking at my ticket whilst twisting his black moustache. I was convinced that they were doing this on purpose just for an excuse to make the donkey noise.

'Si. Hee Hon,' I replied.

'You change trains at El Berron.'

Two can play at this game, I thought.

'For Hee Hon?' I enquired innocently.

'Si, Hee Hon.'

'And the train for Hee Hon, where does it go to?' I knew damn well where it went but he didn't need to know that.

'Hee Hon.'

'And after Hee Hon?'

'It stops at Hee Hon.'

'So Hee Hon is the terminus?'

'Hee Hon is the terminus.'

I had to stop then because I was on the point of hysteria and foreigners can be touchy about their language.

We pulled into the junction station and I lugged my bicycle from the train, looking hopefully for my connection but knowing in my heart that it would have left thirty minutes earlier. Suddenly the conductor jumped from my train and accosted a young lady with shoulder length hair, tight jeans and a big bottom. I heard the word 'Hee Hon' again and she turned, smiled at me and nodded.

'Follow that señorita,' the conductor ordered me, 'she is too going to Hee Hon.'

'Following that señorita' was not quite as easy as it sounded. For a start, I had a bicycle and she did not. She could ripple through the crowds, well, not quite ripple but the width of her bottom was less, slightly less, than that of my bike. Also, the station appeared to be lit with Christmas cake candles and hurricane lamps which would register zero on the Beaufort scale. I am sure this was an erroneous impression that I acquired due to the paucity of ambient light but the fact remained that we were barging along through a very dark crowd. Not only that, but I had grasped merely a fleeting glimpse of the aforementioned señorita's visage in the light from the train before she had turned around. I stumbled on through the gloom, tripping over rails and sleepers and bouncing off shadowy figures whilst desperately praying that the denim-wrapped Spanish bum that I could just perceive wobbling in the gloom before me was the very one which was going to Hee Hon.

I never found out if it was or was not. Around a pitch black railway shed and up a ramp I fell across another train. It was sitting with its doors open and people were clambering on as if it were the last lifeboat on the Titanic.

'Hee Hon,' the guard was shouting. 'Hee Hon.'

How was I going to get my bicycle onto such a crowded train? The problem existed solely in my British imagination. The Spanish just squeezed aside in all good humour and stood patiently whilst I backed my bike up against the carriage side. It was not a problem as far as they were concerned. I warmed to them.

The guard then began to call out station names and to tick them on a slip of paper as if calling the register at school. If nobody responded to a station he called it out again. If there was no response at the third call, and the station did not present a sick note from its mum, then it was struck from his list. And with this form of democratic bingo, was our journey into Gijon decided. We rattled through the unclaimed stations without stopping. No good calling 'house' now, you had had your chance.

Right opposite the terminus in Gijon I could see a hotel sign so I hurried across the road towards it. Through the wrought iron and glass windows of the dark wood door, I could see the staircase leading up through a welcoming orange glow to the reception. There was no time to lose as it was already a quarter to ten. Leaving my bicycle at the bottom, I opened the door and went up.

You never know quite what you are going to get in a Spanish hotel. This one had gone for the open plan look. The stairs led up to a huge balustraded mezzanine, tiled in polished marble. Across this were scattered in haphazard fashion, half a dozen leather sofas, each the size of a small saloon car. In the dim light with the feeble lamps reflecting on humps of shiny leather, it looked like a pub car park on a rainy night. Rather incongruously, the top of the stairwell was closed by a small gate such as conscientious parents erect to prevent their progeniture from accessing the lower storeys at high speed in an inverted posture. I unlatched it, passed through, and carefully relatched it behind me.

I was then at a loss to know what to do next. Apart from the sofas and a scattering of reading lamps, I had the choice of an unlit corridor or a solid wooden door. I could see no installation which sugggested a reception desk, with its paraphernalia of key board and pigeon holes. I decided that, in deference to the lateness of the hour, it would be politic to make my presence known now, rather than plunge headlong into the labyrinth of sleeping corridors.

'Koee hay?' I called, realising a split second later that it was the Hindustani phrase for, 'Is there anybody there?' and not the Spanish. It's funny what tricks your memory plays when you are tired and confused with circles in your head. As it turned out, the Hindustani was sufficient. The wooden door opened and several things happened at once.

A voice said, 'Si?'

The old dame in the bed screeched and pulled the sheets up to her chin. My glance fell upon the young lady in the white housecoat, kneeling on the floor.

'Si?' she said again. She was holding the door open.

'Have you got a room?'

'A room?'

'A room for tonight.'

'A room for tonight?'

'For one person.'

'For one person?'

I was beginning to wonder whether I could slide that old faithful, 'Hee Hon', into our conversation.

'Yes, a room for tonight,' I insisted and then added, with just a touch of petulance, 'It's a hotel isn't it?'

Silly question. Her eyebrows puckered angrily.

'No, it is not a hotel.'

She slammed the door. I turned around, tripped over the stupid safety gate and just saved myself from a calamitous descent by hanging on to the banister rails.

Back at my bicycle, I looked up at the illuminated sign swinging above the door. It said *'Hotel'*. Rather than having ideas above its station, this one appeared to have ideas opposite its station.

I remembered the incident of Alan going down the road one day to buy some honey. It was at an old farmhouse languishing in a dip in a narrow lane not far from their house. He knocked at the door and the old fellow came out.

'Have you got any honey?' Alan asked.

'No, we haven't got any honey.'

'Have you run out of honey?'

'No.'

'Will you be getting any honey soon?'

'No. Why? Do you want some?'

'Yes. You sell honey don't you?'

'No, we don't sell honey.'

'But you've got a sign up there.' He pointed to the four foot high white letters painted on the farmhouse wall. *'We sell honey.'*

The man stepped out into the road and carefully read

the legend.

'Oh that! That was there when we bought the house ten years ago. WE don't sell honey.'

I did not find a hotel until half past ten. Nobody had told me that this weekend was some Spanish holiday or other. They had all decided to go to the seaside.

At Hee Hon.

I wonder if they have donkeys on the beach?

In the 1970s Gijon was second only to Barcelona in terms of tonnage handled and it was from its quays that the coal and iron ore of the Asturias region were exported. The coal traffic gained in importance with the increase in consumption which arose at the end of the Civil War. The road system of the region was primitive and utterly unable to cope with the demands made upon it and so the owners of the mine at La Camocha applied to build a railway down to the port. By the time that it was opened in 1946 it was a standard gauge line effectively owned and run by the Spanish national railway company, RENFE.

Gijon on the Sunday morning was the time to visit the excellent museum devoted to the railway history of the Asturias region. In this former station I was able to touch the machines that had puffed along the very tracks that I was now attempting to cycle. Soon my heart would be singing to the sound of tyres hissing on tarmac as I took the gentle climb up my next Via Verde to the Camocha mine. But before starting, I needed to buy some lunch as I only had left some scraps from my previous day's train picnic.

The route to the beginning of the Via Verde took me through a suburb of tenements. There I found a popular grocer's shop. Perhaps a couple of tomatoes, a slice of ham and a newer loaf than the rubbery truncheon in my cycle bag? Yes, that should do the trick. The vegetables, the fruit, the cereals, everything was stored in cardboard boxes tipped on their sides. That the shop was popular was evident from the number of customers waiting to be served but nobody was serving them. The two ladies at the front of the queue were quite unconcerned with this and chatted animatedly about everything and everybody. We waited patiently but still nobody appeared. After about four minutes, one of the ladies at the front got fed up, said goodbye to her chatterbox companion and turned to walk out. I could not understand her action. Just when she had reached the front of the queue, she had given up. I deduced that it was a matter of camel's backs and straws. But I was wrong. As she walked past me I could see that her shopping bag was full. At the same time I noticed that the chatterbox companion had refolded her arms and was now beginning a conversation with the next lady in the queue. They nodded and buzzed and squawked and shook in a most familiar fashion. After a couple of minutes of this, the chatterbox scooped up a handful of potatoes from a nearby box and dropped them into the other lady's bag. The theft was perpetrated so naturally that I wondered if anybody else had noticed. I looked around. The other customers did not appear worried. There was still nobody behind the counter to serve us. The two ladies yakked on then some red peppers went into the bag.

You almost certainly got there ages before I did. The chatterbox was the shopkeeper. I had been in the shop for nine minutes and she was serving her second customer. I counted down the shop. I was number twelve. I would stand here for an hour before being served. Well I wouldn't and I didn't and that is why I am now pedalling through a beautifully maintained and lighted railway tunnel towards the tourist viewpoint marked in my guidebook. There is nothing to surpass a pretty panorama for freshening tired bread and spicing up bland sausage.

I had made the right decision. I could see the track leaving the tunnel; it was a smooth grey asphalt ribbon stretching out before me. A shiny asphalt ribbon. A rather wet one. It was raining. Perhaps it was a passing shower. I stopped at the portal and peered out. The sky was the colour of dirty seagull in all directions. Some yards further on sat the bench, gazing out in solitary satisfaction at the tourist viewpoint, raindrops dropping from its slats. There was little attraction for me in sitting in the pouring rain no matter how fine the view so I ate a rubbery snack in the tunnel entrance and pulled on my waterproof jacket.

Having finished, I pushed out into the fine drizzle. I afforded the tourist panorama a soggy glance as I passed. The view would have been one down a pretty shallow valley of pastures and trees. I say, 'would have been' because two hundred yards from the bench the vista was blocked by a dripping grey concrete viaduct which carried a spanking new motorway over a quagmire of churned raw mud, rusty oil drums and broken timber. Who cares about pretty views when motor cars need to go somewhere quickly?

I climbed upwards to the end of the track where I was surprised to find a working coal mine. The enormous hopper lorries parked in the yard underlined the reasons for the demise of the railway.

I was pleased with myself. I had been very clever with my planning. This track took me into a range of shallow coastal hills of a mere two thousand feet altitude where, in about eight miles, another track would avoid the steepest part of the range and lead me along gentle railway gradients down towards Oviedo. I knew from my guide book that the track would be dead easy to find. It started at the old railway station.

'There's no railway station here.'

The men stood under the dark overhanging eaves of the cave-like roadside bar and picked their teeth and shook their heads. Raindrops dripped disconsolately from the roof onto my head and shoulders.

'It's an old railway station,' I insisted, but they still shook their heads.

'No there's no station.'

'And no railway. We've never had a railway here.'

Then a lad of about fourteen pushed to the front and, to the apparent surprise of all the veterans, affirmed that the old railway station was the house just down *there*. I nearly kissed him.

The station had lost all its ferrovial appurtenances but I nevertheless recognised it for what it was. I stood on the overgrown low platform and struggled inside my final waterproof layer. At this moment, the owners of the house arrived in their car. It squelched to a halt alongside the platform and they got out.

'Is this track good for Lieres?' I asked, pointing down the alley. It was luscious green weeds and small deciduous trees leaning across to form leafy archways.

He said yes. She said no. They conferred rapidly in some bubbling wet Spanish, then he turned to me.

'You should be able to get through the tunnel.'

'Tunnel? What tunnel?'

'In about eight hundred metres. They've blocked it with a bank of earth but you should be alright on a bike.'

'Blocked it?'

'Take a run at it, you'll be alright.'

'Take a run at it?' My voice went up an octave.

'Take a run at it.' He mimed jerking handlebars easily over a molehill. 'It's only about four metres high.' He rubbed his chin. 'Of course, there might be four metres of water behind it.'

I was unable to confirm or confound the accuracy of this speculation for I never discovered the tunnel. Long before I had run his eight hundred metres the track had disappeared into a flora-strewn topography that denied ever having seen a sleeper. In the pouring grey rain I slogged up the steep hairpins that my clever navigation was supposed to have avoided and sloshed down the other side, forty three kilometres to Oviedo.

As soon as I got to a hotel room I stripped off my sodden clothes and showered off the road grit. Then I phoned Raquel to ask about Alan. She said his operation had been successful and they claimed that he was still 'comfortable.' The former, I was mightily pleased to hear; the latter, I doubted very much.

That evening, sitting on the bed with my clothes gently steaming on the radiator, I looked anew at the guidebook which I had used as my bible for this expedition. Was there some factor that I had not taken into account? The book flaunted all the correct testimonials. It had been published by the organisation that claimed to have opened up these Vias Verdes so it should speak with authority. It was only one year old so it could hardly be called outdated. And yet, the line from El Astillero finished in a drainpipe, the viewpoint at Camocha had been built across by a motorway and the track which was supposed to take me through the hills was so overgrown that the ancient locals denied ever having seen a railway there. Where was I going wrong?

I went to bed that night with a disquieting feeling of unease. The performance of the book did not bode well for the morrow, or indeed, for the rest of the trip.

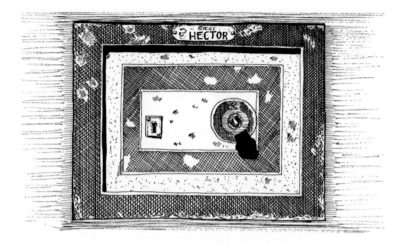

chapter twelve

Oviedo is the capital of the Asturias region of northern Spain. It stands as an inhabited molehill in a plain of maize and other cultivations. This is deceptive for although its buildings and streets proclaim opulence, the wealth was not generated by growing cereals. First came the arsenal – a sure fire winner as long as men contemplate with relish the annihilation of their fellows – and then in the nineteenth century, the coal mines. Well, what a surprise. I expect you are sick and tired of reading about coal and iron but, quite frankly, apart from luscious pastures, ancient monuments, stupendous mountains, interesting food and some really fascinating people, there is not much else here.

The coal mines of the Asturian basin were the most productive in Spain when they were at full stretch. Their importance even led to the establishment in Oviedo of a mining college. But going to school was not the only thing that miners did in Oviedo. In October 1934, they set up a revolutionary committee and took over the town, looting the banks, burning churches and shooting anybody with pretensions of an education. In ten days of bloody fighting, Oviedo was devastated; the destruction was of a terrible order; the miners exploiting their familiarity with dynamite to simply blow up the buildings they desired. Thus perished the Sacred Room and its 9th. century religious relicry, Oviedo University and even a portion of the cathedral.

The army finally wrested control from the rebels in a ferocious battle around the Northern Railway Station which was destroyed in the fighting. The station was rebuilt in 1946 and now, over fifty years later, it is being altered again. My cycle tyres leave tracks in the builders' sand as I weave my way around raw concrete pillars on my way to the platform. The train I board deposits me half an hour later at Trubia, a town on the eponymous river.

I have wanted to use that word 'eponymous' ever since it suddenly came into fashion and appeared in every Sunday book review for a year. The lengths the critics would go to, contorting their grammar and twisting the whole direction of their observation back upon itself merely so that they could write 'eponymous'! I am convinced that book reviewers have a distorted sense of mischief and I suspect that this, coupled with their well known propensity for ridiculing their readers, gave birth to an unwritten challenge wherein every critic in every paper had to use the word 'eponymous' as many times as they could within the space of one year. It's funny what people will do for words.

I was once invited to a garden party by the vague acquaintance of a man I think I had met somewhere. As I stood admiring the flower bed and shorn lawn whilst holding a glass of fizzy water in one hand and a paper plate of cardboard food in the other and trying to use my knife and fork with my third and fourth hands whilst pushing the hair out of my eyes with my fifth and warding off the host's Great Dane with my sixth, I was accosted by a man with blue eyes and a velvet accent.

'What do you do?' he said.

I was more interested in what he was eating.

'Where did you get the bread roll?' I replied. If I could get hold of one of those I could cram into it the contents of my plate and free up three of my six hands. And then, belatedly remembering my manners I responded correctly, 'How do you do?' I did not attempt to proffer my seventh hand. I was saving that for emergencies.

'No, not, "how do you do?" – What do you do?'

'When?'

'When what?'

'What do I do, when?'

'When...?' He seemed lost for words. I wondered whether I should make a lunge for his roll whilst he was still distracted. 'Well, what do you do? You know, when you work?'

'Oh, what work do I do?'

'Yes, what do you do? For work,' he added, in case I had lost the thread.

'I write.' My reply was short for I had just noticed a rather attractive young lady almost wearing a black dress.

'Oh really?'

I flicked my eyes back to Velvet Voice to check whether or not he was taking a rise.

'Yes, I write.' I began to shuffle sideways to open up an escape route.

'So do I,' he smiled, closing the gap and stringing a coil of barbed wire across. Then he dug a trench in front of it and planted his anti-personnel mine. 'I have just written a dictionary.'

The girl was looking at a classical statue and murmuring something to her companion; a lady some years her senior.

'A dictionary!' I exclaimed, taking a step backwards in mock amazement. 'Fascinating!' I assured him. She was leaning forwards to read the inscription on the stone. There was even less of her in the dress than before.

'Yes, an Italian-English dictionary.' He drifted vaguely to his right and blocked my panorama.

'Oh so you're a linguist then?' It was the kind of inane response that should have sent him packing.

'Not really, no.'

I studied him critically. I was still not utterly convinced that he was not making fun of me. The girl was walking away. Blast him!

'But you speak Italian?' I insisted.

'A bit. Enough.'

'Enough to write a dictionary.'

'Well, you don't have to know much.'

'Just the entire language.'

'No, that's not how it is done. I just bought the *Harraps*, the *Collins* and a couple of others and sort of paraphrased what they said. It gets a bit tricky sometimes because they all seem to say the same thing.'

'I suppose it is inescapable that the definition of a word in different dictionaries would tend to have some common points. You can't invent meanings for the word, just in order to be original can you?'

He appeared quite shocked.

'Oh Good Heavens no, you can't do that. It would be quite unethical.'

Although I considered that his approach to ethics rivalled the Dartford Tunnel's for its obscurity (read that bit aloud then think about it) I decided not to reflect upon it too intently. The girl was coming back. Nice bits were wobbling. She stopped, just near enough to overhear our conversation. I moved slickly into intellectual overdrive.

'So did you discover the secret keyword in any of the nuclear compilation systems of the dictionaries you copied? Er, you consulted?' I corrected quickly. He was baffled. The girl was interested.

'The nuclear key...?'

'Well surely you know how a dictionary is compiled?

'I've just written one.'

'Quite. But what would you have done if there had been no dictionaries to consult?'

He thought about that. The girl had edged nearer. His face brightened.

'A bit like the chicken and the egg?' he suggested.

I had no idea what poultry breeding had to do with dictionaries but I let it pass. I glanced at the girl. She had dark eyes and they were smiling. Ooh I felt good.

'The way they compile a dictionary,' I explained, 'when there is not one available to... er... adapt.' I tried to remain diplomatic. 'Is to choose a keyword which becomes the nuclear linguistic root of the entire work. All definitions stem from that one word.'

He was beginning to struggle, I could tell. His mouth was opening and closing silently. I was still tempted to make a grab for his bread roll.

'I see,' he said slowly.

As a bald confirmation that his ocular system was functioning correctly and that his brain was able to interpret the signals sent by his retinal nerves, I would not have argued with that pronouncement; but as a suggestion that it implied his comprehensive understanding of my explanation, I would have rudely laughed it out of court.

'Now take the *New Century English Dictionary*,' I said. 'I happened to be looking through it the other day and I discovered their keyword, quite by chance. I just knew it had to be that one.'

His jaw hung slack, his eyes were glazing and his head was nodding gently up and down. I jerked my head at the big house.

'If you pop off to their library and find a copy, I'll show you the key word.' I nodded encouragingly towards the pile of grey ragstone. But when he turned to go, the girl was not there so I resolved to track down the source of the bread rolls and get my food down to a two handed format.

I was standing at the tableclothed trestle, viewing the vol-au-vents and perusing the pickles when I felt a tug at my sleeve. I still had not found the bread rolls but old Velvet Voice had found the bloody dictionary.

'Here it is,' he said excitedly, 'this is the one isn't it?'

'Oh yes, that is the one.'

'So are you going to show us how to find the keyword?' the girl asked.

I had not noticed her behind him. I gulped.

'Yes. The keyword. You'll need somewhere to sit if you are going to read the entire dictionary.'

'I don't need to read the entire book,' he protested.

'You will have to if you find the keyword.'

'Really?'

'Really. You can't stop yourself.'

He settled himself on a stone bench on the terrace.

'Right. Are you ready?' I said.

'Yes.' He was bright eyed and eager. The girl, who had drifted along with us was less intrigued, more, amused.

'The word is...'

'Yes?'

'It's....'

Could I remember it?

'Well?' he said.

'Um. It's er... it's near the front.'

'A lot of the words are near the front.'

'Those that are not near the back,' said the girl.

Suddenly it came to me.

'Cincinnus,' I said.

'Sin what?' Velvet Voice started to leaf through the volume.

'C I N C I N N U S,' I spelled out.

'Cincinnus? What does that mean?'

'Well, look it up and find out. That is how it works.'

'Got it.'

'What does it say?'

'Well I don't understand any of it. "A uniparous cymose influorescence–"'

'That is exactly the point. Now how many words in the definition of 'cincinnus' do you not understand?'

'Six. No, seven.'

'So what are you going to have to do?'

'Look them up?' he suggested, unsure of himself.

'Exactly. Off you go then. I'll just–' I turned to the girl. She had gone.

I went and tracked down the bread rolls. I stuffed a roll and then stuffed myself. But the day did not finish there for fate had reserved for me a bitter-sweet dessert.

'He's up to fifty three and still searching,' she said, her eyes glinting with devilish amusement.

'Fifty three?'

'Yes. "Uniparous" gave him two more words he did not know. Then "cymose" gave him another three.'

'Well, that's the way it goes,' I said. 'He'll end up reading the entire dictionary.' I took her elbow gently. 'Why don't you and I–?'

She shook her head as she eased her arm from my guiding hand.

'I've got to drive him home. He's already drunk several glasses of wine.'

'Oh you're–' I suddenly realised the relationship. 'Do you live far away? I mean you could just drop your dad off and come back. The day is young.'

'Not my dad.' She waved her fingers under my nose. One of them had a gold ring on it. 'My husband. Sorry.' She shrugged.

And would you believe it? Next time I looked, they had taken 'cincinnus' out of the dictionary.

I did not mind the rain, not really. It was quite gentle. It dampened the dirty facade of the factory which formed one side of the street, giving a mother-of-pearl sheen to the black wall. The other side of the street was the river – the eponymous one if you remember. The factory had been here since it was, quite appropriately, founded, in the eighteenth century – for it is the National Cannon Foundry. What with rebellions, arsenals and cannon foundries, this region must have been quite a fashionable resort for the bellicose.

But thanks to their enthusiasm I was able to enjoy the Via Senda del Oso. Built in 1874 to carry the iron ore and coal down to Trubia, the line wound its twenty one kilometres into the foothills of the Cordillera Cantabrica. According to the guidebook, this track would be the most spectacular of my trip.

The surface was well metalled and I pedalled off happily under the dark green trees which were dripping with rain. I was alone, there were no walkers and no other cyclists. They would not appear until the afternoon when the weather would be more settled. In fact, now I come to consider, even the weather in Spain gets out of bed late.

As I approached the mountains, outside one village where the track had been forced to divert for a few hundred metres, I came across a set of metal steps and a platform. I had already noted that the fence which ran along the mountain side of the track was about ten feet high and serious. This suggested to me that there must be some military presence nearby. However, although the intended purpose of the platform to me was obscure, its possible use was obvious. I clambered to the top with my camera in my hand and, sure enough, I had a terrific view down the valley. As I was lining up a really artistic shot and trying to keep my index finger from in front of the lens, I felt that strange sensation that somebody was watching me. How could they be? I was alone, ten feet above the countryside, standing on a platform. The feeling persisted and increased to such an intensity that I involuntarily looked behind me. I found myself staring into the eyes of a large brown bear.

It was sitting on the rocky scree opposite me. Now I knew what the fence was for. Once the bear realised that I was not going to throw any cakes at it, it ambled off.

The track continued to climb. Soon I came to the first tunnel. All the tunnels on this line had been hewn out of solid rock. The inside was a jagged jumble of tortured teeth and warring wedges. It was these tunnels that, during the ninety year working span of the line, had claimed the lives of numerous brakesmen whose job it had been to swing from wagon to wagon and screw down the brakes to prevent the heavy trains from hurtling to destruction.

I stood looking at the pool of forbidding blackness. I had bad memories of tunnels. The biggest problem was the obvious one. Tunnels are dark and cycle lamps do not illuminate anything. I strapped an extra lamp to my head, in the fashion of a coal miner. I had already learned that a rider needs a light that shines where he is looking, as well as one which shows where the wheel is pointing. However, as I crossed the portal to this tunnel, it illuminated itself from one end to the other, thanks to the concealed lighting triggered by an infra red detector. I felt a little overdressed.

And then I came to the defile. It was breathtaking. Here the two peaks squeezed together to almost touch; only a few metres separated them. Through this crack roared the torrent. Hacked into the riverbank opposite, squirmed the road. The railway had blasted and chiselled a ledge thirty metres above the water. It dodged in and out of tunnels, some with great windows pierced in their sides through which the river could be heard raging below. The tension that these three routes caused by forcing themselves through the same gap made my scalp tingle.

I carried on up to the old station in the village at the top. There I drank a hot chocolate. Then I freewheeled back down to the bottom. It was glorious, despite the rain.

After another night in a hotel in Oviedo I was convinced that I had got the hang of this trip. It would be all right from now on. Spain had put me to the test and I had prevailed. The next track on my itinerary started in the middle of nowhere and ended even further in obscurity. I would have to take the train over the mountains to the town of León. There I would take a train south and get off at Palanquinos. From this hamlet an old track ran due southwards for thirty kilometres, dead flat, across the fields. At the other end I would have to pick up the road system and go cross country to Valladolid.

By eight o'clock I was rocking gently to the slowing rhythm of the train as it attacked the gradient. The tight curves made the wheels screech. Up and up we laboured, sometimes lost in the obscurity of tunnels, sometimes hanging magically to a valley side above the town cowering hundreds of feet below us. The weak sun passed from the left of the train to the right and then back again as we wriggled all ways to find the gentlest slope. Looking across the valley I could see a second railway line running northwards. It was ours. Ten minutes later we were on it, looking across at this one as we headed back towards the coast in order to go around a mountain. Huge trucks belched fumes as they kept pace with us on the road. We would hide in a tunnel and creep out the other end to surprise them. Sometimes they were below us, twisting up through hairpins, sometimes above, straining over a bridge.

By the time we breasted the summit of four thousand feet, the sky was overcast a uniform grey. We paused at the top station. In the yard were railway trucks loaded with coal. Right on top of this mountain there was industry. I could see where half of a peak had been quarried away, leaving an ugly raw gash. These mountains must be getting lower every year. Further on we passed an enormous power station belching smoke and steam up into what must once have been pure mountain air. This mountain was polluted. We came down the other side and reached La Robla. Of course, I should have remembered. La Robla was an enormous coal mine. The narrow gauge railway had once run from here all the way through the mountain range to the banks of the river Nervion in Bilbao to deliver coal to the blast furnaces. I had remembered the name. I had just never realised that you could have a coal mine on top of a mountain.

The Oviedo side of the mountain range was lush and green because it benefitted from the maritime climate and the rains. The León side of the range was termed 'arid'. This is a climatological nomenclature. I point out this distinction because despite its classification, the region was lying under widespread rain. The railway station at León was tall and gaunt and grey. I pushed my bicycle into the booking hall and looked up the time of the train to Valladolid which would take me to Palanquinos. There was one daily departure and it was not until two fifteen in the afternoon. If I waited that long, nightfall would find me at the southern end of my cycle track, stranded in the middle of nowhere so I pulled on my waterproof trousers and pedalled off to complete the ten miles to Palanquinos. I realised that this was probably the furthest that I had penetrated into darkest Spain. All my cycling to date had been within easy reach of the coast. I suppose it was the old Colonial spirit – always keep within range of a British gunboat. Another discovery which surprised me in in my appalling ignorance, was that although we had climbed to four thousand feet to get over the mountains we had not come down the same amount the other side. I was still three thousand feet above sea level but the topography was open rolling plains. I thought that it had to be mountains if you were that high.

Half way to Palanquinos the rain decided to give up so I stopped and removed my waterproof overtrousers. This operation I undertook quite openly in a village square. It had not occurred to me that the girls waiting in the bus queue would not realise that I was wearing cycling shorts underneath and I was only alerted to this possibility by the outbreak of shrieking and giggling punctuated by ear splitting whistles. Although I thought myself immune to this kind of ridicule, it had an unfortunate effect, which you shall learn about shortly.

At Palanquinos I made straight for the railway station. I knew from the guide book that the old railway line ran direct south across the fields at right angles to the existing line. I remembered the photograph of the smiling girl as she pedalled through a shady grove of trees. I found the track. It left the village in the guise of the stony hard shoulder to a busy road. I was confused because there was no road on the plan in the guide book. Ah yes, the guide book. It always seems to come back to that doesn't it?

I gritted my teeth and started off. The road was dead straight and dead level and the traffic was driving at such a speed that if I strayed onto their carriageway I would be dead dead. Perhaps the road would leave me shortly. I plugged on into the rising wind, the grey clouds massing before me, the maize heads bobbing one side and the murderous traffic whisking past my left elbow on the other.

I ignored the first spots of rain. Cyclists usually do. They are born optimists. They have to be. It is only a shower. I can see lighter sky on the other side of the cloud. After five miles it was obvious to me that the next fifteen would be the same. Slogging up the hard shoulder of a treacherous main road into wind-driven rain was not what I had come to Spain for. I decided on a quick *volte-face*. Taking my life in my hands I crossed the road to the shelter of some farm buildings in order to don my waterproofs. If I could get back to Palanquinos I should be able to catch the train to Valladolid that I had already ascertained would be leaving León at half past two and passing through Palanquinos. I was convincing myself of the sense of this course of action as I fished around in my pannier bag for my trousers. They were not there. They were not anywhere. The shrieking of the girls must have distracted me and I had cycled off with my trousers lying unattached on the top of my rear carrier. Somewhere across the wind-blown plateau of León, my waterproof trousers were striding boldly without me.

I put my head down and pedalled hard back to Palanquinos. The wind blew the rain along behind me but it was still wet. In the village I found a small café. I recall it as being brown. Brown walls, brown customers, brown hot chocolate that I drank. Around the picture rail hung illustrated tea-towels depicting various towns in Spain. The lady brought me a couple of metres of kitchen paper to dry myself. When she saw it immediately reduced to an uncooked doughnut she went away and came back with two tea towels. As I dabbed at my dripping body I glanced furtively around the room to discover which wall she had pulled them from but I could see no obvious gaps. Perhaps they had been awaiting pre-exhibition cataloguing.

I sat by the steamed up window and watched the vehicles splashing by. At half past two I got on my bicycle and rode the hundred yards to the station. The building was a rectangular two storeyed stone house with a pitched roof and bricked up doors. I cycled around it to the platform side. The doors were bricked up on this side also. And the windows. Somebody had taken everything away. There was no awning to shelter under and no bench to sit on. The station building with its bricked up windows could almost have been a solid block with the doors and windows printed on the outside. This set me to thinking and as I looked at these three platforms dropped as they were on a monotonous plain, they conjured up in my mind the idea that this was a gigantic train set on a carpet in somebody's front room. They had snapped the rails together, put some platforms down and plonked the station building on one of them but they could not be bothered to drag the bridge out from under the sofa, get the newspaper kiosk from behind the television or unwrap the set of three benches from its tissue paper. All they had found was the solitary figure of an inappropriately attired cyclist and with a malicious sense of humour they had dumped him down into their chosen weather. This figure now squeezed itself into the slight shelter of an architectural rebut and watched the rain sweeping across the four tracks and the barren platforms.

And then it occurred to me. I did not know which line the train would come in on. I knew from which direction it would arrive but not on which line. There were no staff of whom I could enquire. I could find no timetables nor could I see any signs to inform me. I was standing with my back to the station building. Before me ran two railway lines, then an island platform of low stone, then another two lines then a far platform. I had never really paid attention to railway practice in Spain. Did they drive on the right or the left?

In England, the trains drive on the left. I knew that France did the same because we had sold them their first locomotives and built their first lines and so they had been obliged to use our system. Ha! ha! I bet that annoys them. However, this knowledge did not tell me which side the Spanish trains ran on.

I calculated that I would double my chances of success by occupying the island platform which had access to two tracks. I looked right and left and then clambered down onto the permanent way, bumped my machine over the rails and heaved it up onto the middle platform. There was no overbridge of course, that was still under the sofa. I looked up and down in both directions but the colour light signals seemed to work both ways for all tracks so there was no clue there. I would have to wait and see. Here, on my stone island in a sea of shining wet steel, I had no protection from the rain and it soused down. I wondered how far my trousers had got. They were probably warming their gusset before a nice cosy fire in Valladolid by now. I leaned against my bicycle, my shoulders hunched.

Why, oh why, am I here?

At long last, through the grey mist of driving rain I saw a headlight approaching. I tried to convince myself that it would pull up at my platform. If it stopped at one of the others I would not be able to reach it, for the train itself would prevent me from crossing the track. I sighed in exasperation. How do I get myself into these situations? I waved a big fluorescent yellow waterproof arm backwards and forwards above my head and then, to my astonishment, the train doused and relit its headlight. He had seen me!

Well I do not know what all the panic was about. You really do make a fuss over nothing. The train stopped in front of me and I got on. Easy peasy.

When the conductor came along he sold me a ticket and grinned at my socks which were drying on the radiator. I realised what a lucky escape I had had and what a good decision I had made. The countryside we were crossing was a vast, treeless, rolling plain, devoid of any shelter and only sparsely populated. I would have perished from exposure. Well, perhaps it was not as extreme as that but I certainly would not have enjoyed it.

Valladolid was a town living to a northern European pulse not a meridional one. It was half past five and workers were hurrying about, boarding buses and trains. Perhaps the town was frantically trying to catch what it had lost, for in the past, Valladolid had twice been the capital city of Spain but had been finally ousted by Madrid.

I launched myself into the traffic in a search for a hotel. You would think that task would be simple in a town of this size but whichever way I turned, either I ended up standing in front of a modern hotel made of glass or pedalling around the statue of a chap called Cristobal Colon. I found one hotel where the manager admitted it was fully booked but suggested that I should return at eight o'clock in case they had had some cancellations. I was distrustful of any arrangement that a Spaniard might make with me which depended upon something happening at a stated time. I took another turn around old Cristobal and pitched up at the glass palace. This would cost me an arm and a leg. My prejudiced view of the hotel was somewhat moderated when I discovered that an industrial clothing shop was trading next door. I went in and purchased a pair of waterproof trousers. Just in case. You never could tell. It might rain tomorrow.

As you would expect, the hotel reception was a vast hall of mirrors and marble with glittering chandeliers and reception girls in tight skirts who insisted that they could speak English. I did not argue with them. They would not have understood me.

I ordered pork chops for dinner. The lady came to clear away my plate.

'Was it good?' she asked in Spanish.

'No,' I replied clearly and shook my head to make sure that everybody in the room understood my Spanish.

The meal had excelled in two respects. It had been easily the most expensive and definitely the worst meal that I had ever eaten in Spain.

chapter thirteen

I lay under my acres of duvet and listened to the town awakening. It was still dark outside. The floor to ceiling drapes glowed with a fiery fringe from the sodium lamps lining the avenue. This hotel room, with its built-in wardrobes, its lobby and its bathroom was probably greater in volumetric capacity than all my other hotel rooms put together. Indeed, the room was even greater than I could have imagined for unknown to me, the drapes were still concealing an enormous rectangular bay window. I had noticed this architectural whim in several towns. Do not ask me what it is called because I have no idea, but it manifests itself in a column of projecting windows fixed to the facade of the building rather as it is the modern fashion to put a glass lift shaft on the outside of a shopping mall.

But as I lay in bed, amusing myself by trying to interpret the rumbles and clinks coming from outside, I was unaware of this appendix to my room. I discovered it as I returned from the bathroom in that cleansed and relaxed state that coddles one's mind and body after a satisfying shower.

In a brutal explosion of sound and vigour, the curtains suddenly blasted apart as the vast double glazed panel of the bay window burst open and swung free. The writing paper, the menu, the television instructions and other various publications which had been dozing on the bureau immediately awoke and began a whirling dervish dance around the room at head height. One curtain tail swiped the telephone to the floor and slapped the television across the face whilst the other lunged menacingly towards the tall standard lamp. Bullets of wind-driven rain drilled onto the desktop. I started forwards and dived through the curtains. The window was about eight feet tall and the wind had got a better purchase than I had. Back and forth we staggered, me, forcing it into the frame and the tornado insolently puffing it open before I could discover how to work those complicated combined bolt and hinge gizmos that always adorn these installations.

At last brain triumphed over brawn and I managed to wrench the lever down, pulling the casement into the frame. Everything went quiet. Outside in the avenue, the seven or eight passers by who had happened to look up were gazing with interest at where, two storeys up the front facade of the hotel, in a presentation glass box tastefully illuminated by the convenient street lamp, an Englishman was standing, stark naked. I bowed stiffly, then stepped backwards through the curtains and pulled them across with a flourish. I expect the noise of the thunderous applause was cut out by the, now closed, double glazing.

When I checked out, I explained to the receptionist that the window bolt did not work properly. I did not mention my impromptu performance to the populace of Valladolid in case she sighed for my autograph.

I picked up the street plan and asked that she show me how to get to the Canal de Castille. I knew before she began to speak that it would involve a circuit around my old mate Cristobal Colon.

'Tell me, who is the statue I keep going around?'

'That is Cristobal Colon.'

'Yes, that's him. Who is he?'

'You have not heard of Cristobal Colon?' The girl was aghast at my ignorance. So am I, sometimes, but let us get matters into proportion. Many towns possess a local bigwig, a benefactor or a fine and flourishing family that has endowed the church or donated a park, but outside their manor, they are nobody. They are the big fish in the little pond. This, of course, does not reduce the adulation by the minnows and the more intense they make it, the more important the person appears in their eyes and thus, the more the standing of their pond is exalted. Such is very dangerous ground for the ignorant visitor amongst whose cohorts, I allow, I regularly plant my ensign. The populace is very sensitive to any suggestion that their Important Person should not enjoy equal gravitas in the greater scheme of things as God, the Queen or Marks and Spencer, so in response to the receptionist's scandalised reaction to my ignorance I merely replied,

'No, I'm afraid not. What did he do?'

'Cristobal Colon?'

'Yes. He must be famous for something.'

'He is very famous. Every school student knows Cristobal Colon.'

I can only tolerate the minnows' blind adulation up to a reasonable limit. I wondered if minnows had an eleven second memory as well as goldfish.

'In Spain, perhaps every student knows him, but not in England,' I assured her as equably as I felt capable.

I thought I had displayed considerable restraint by not declaring that I doubted if anybody outside the town walls knew anything about Cristobal Colon. I most probably could have stopped the first hundred people in the street and asked them, 'Who is that statue and what is he famous for?' and they all would have been unable to answer. I felt this girl was taking municipal pride a little too far.

But now she was bent on contradicting me even about my own country.

'Yes in England they know him. He is known all over the world,' she insisted.

The gauntlet was down. No time for sophistry.

'What for?' I demanded bluntly.

By this time, the hotel porter, the bell boy and a even a gaggle of girls behind the hardwood panelling in the back office were being fed snippets of commentary in Spanish so that they could be as aghast as my opponent.

'You don't know what Cristobal Colon did?' She was now pretending to believe that I was trying to tease her.

'I've no idea.'

She looked me straight in the eye and said,

'He discovered America.'

I had never heard such a preposterous lie.

'No, no, no. That was Christopher Colum...'

I stopped and ruminated.

Ah.

Well I didn't know that was his proper name. Did you? Anyway he was an Italian, not a Spaniard. He came from Genoa.

The hotel automaton decided to teach me a lesson for my impertinence and as I struggled my bicycle up the concrete ramp from the underground garage, with a short screech of triumph, it started to lower the door. I was immediately back in my primary school playground, circling around and chanting 'Oranges and Lemons.'

Here comes a candle to light you to bed,
And here comes a chopper to chop off your head.

I survived the attempted execution and steeled my resolve against the inevitable dismay provoked by the sight of the rain pouring down onto the pavement. This avenue was being pedestrianised. The far edge of the carriageway was still pockmarked sand but before and beyond me stretched a broad perspective of grey marble flags. They were shiny wet and reflected the stunted trees as distorted black skeletons. I knew today was going to be an all-rain day. I sheltered under the overhang of the bay windows and methodically climbed into my new waterproof overtrousers, zipped up my trusty anorak and pulled on my peaked cap. If I could start off dry, perhaps I would stay drier longer.

Wet marble can be treacherously slippery so I pootled along at walking pace from one shiny silver grey square to the next. By the time that I had noticed that the next square on the patchwork was different from the rest, it was too late. I had plunged into a nine inch deep hole, two feet square, which had been prepared to accept some unidentifiable piece of street furniture. The hole was filled up to the rim with grey water – a more effective disguise on a promenade of shiny wet grey marble slabs to be viewed in the half light of a stormy morning could not have been constructed. This grey water now poured into my shoes because I had been thrown forwards from the saddle as the bike had nosed in.

I paddled about in the lagoon whose water reached well up my calves. When I managed to lift my bicycle from its depths, I found that the impact had burst my inner tube.

I had travelled just fifty yards in my day and had acquired two shoes full of sandy water and one tyre empty of air. Perhaps I was being superstitious but I did not think that this was a very good start to the day.

Mending a puncture in the street in the pouring rain is an impossible task. No puncture patch will stick onto wet rubber. I squelched my bicycle into the nearby park where I found a shelter. It took me about three quarters of an hour to replace the inner tube with one of my spares. The burst tube I threw away. It was irreparable. I set off for the Canal de Castille.

Although the track alongside the canal was a tow-path and not an abandoned railway, the path had been classed as a Via Verde and was thus described in my guide book. The river which runs southwards through Valladolid is the Pisuergo and it rises high in the Cordillera Cantabrica – the mountain range which runs along the north coast. After Valladolid, the river turns westwards and flows into the Duero which the Portuguese call the *Douro* and which

185

reaches the Atlantic Ocean at Porto.

My plan was to cycle northwards up the Canal de Castille which also occupied the valley of the Pisuergo. It was a distance of ninety miles and knowing that the surface of the towpath would not permit me to travel fast, I had allocated three days in which to do it.

The canal was part of an original and ambitious plan hatched in the eighteenth century for the eventual construction of a cruciform network of four canals to serve all of the region. The excavation and subsequent exploitation of this system had been intended to drag Spain out of feudalism and into the Industrial Revolution. Big words. Only the Canal de Castille was built, the others never got off the drawing board. And, delayed by economic crises and war, the construction of even this canal took far too long. In the more developed countries of Europe the Industrial Revolution had passed onto the next stage and by the time that the canal was opened in 1835, Spain's first railways were only a couple of decades away. The traffic deserted the waterway, the canalside industry decamped to the railways and the locks were allowed to fall into ruin. The Canal de Castille reverted to its second designed function – that of irrigation.

I joined the canal at an ancient loading wharf and, on a whim, chose to cycle along the eastern towpath. I could not tell from the guide book which would be prettier but I had chosen well. A short distance north of the town, the canal running high on the hillside enjoyed a beautiful aspect eastwards across the serpentine meanders of the river down in the valley. The leaves on the deciduous trees were already turning to gold and yellow. Nearby stood an ancient distance marker and carved into the timeworn white stone I could just discern the softened letters of the original name of the canal – *'Canal del Roy'*. I was ashamed to admit that I had no idea which king had named it.

The rain had thinned out into squalls stooping from a harried sky of autumnal blue. I kept my waterproof trousers on although I had found that their rubberised coating was gripping and pulling the hairs from my legs and it would continue to do so until I learned to tuck them into my socks. The trousers, that is, not the hairs. The day was undoubtedly brightening and my enthusiasm rose in proportion. Finding a bench, I sat down and changed into dry socks taken from my bags. The wet ones I rolled into a spare plastic bag. They would have to wait until the evening hotel stop to be washed and dried.

Dry socks and a lightening sky bolstered up my spirits to the point where I started to take stock of my journey so far and realised that it was not the disaster that I had been claiming. The odd drain pipe to crawl through, the non existent breakfast – these were all things that could be coped with and with which I would certainly regale my friends and readers upon my return. Even the rain – well that was surely funny was it not? To come to sunny Spain and get drenched to the skin day after day after day? Yes, of course it was.

Whilst I had been constructing these arguments in my mind a rumbling noise drifting across from my left had grown to the point where it was beginning to interrupt my thoughts. A quarter of a mile distant, traffic was thundering along a motorway. A motorway which did not appear in the guide book. And it was getting closer. Suddenly it lunged across the fields and nestled cosily up against the west bank of the canal. To add to my pleasure, the rain began again. For the next hour and a half I endured a barrage of drumming and roaring as cars and lorries swished by at speeds completely unrelated to the road conditions. Thank goodness I had chosen the eastern towpath and at least had the width of the canal to isolate me. I should have kept my mouth shut. With a flick of its tail the motorway leapt the canal on a bridge whose buttress completely blocked the towpath on my side. My track veered away in fright. I plodded on through the puddles and loose gravel, hemmed in by a chain link fence. I was still with the motorway, but it was forcing me tangentially further and further from the canal. I could see the tops of the poplar trees which lined the canal and they were now three hundred yards away. My track had become a motorway towpath. Coaches and trucks hurtled alongside me, assaulting my ears and buffeting me with a cocktail of fine spray and road grit. I could find no way of crossing the motorway.

I realised eventually that I needed to go back to the last roadbridge over the canal and cross to the other bank, for I had noticed that the towpath on that side of the canal had managed to squeeze under the motorway.

I turned around and cycled back the two miles to the bridge behind me. I crossed to the other towpath and started out again towards my day's goal – the town of Palencia. I was now rubbing elbows with the motorway traffic but held my breath in anticipation of its hopefully crossing the canal and disappearing off to my right.

Here it comes, here it comes and... I stopped. Were my eyes deceiving me? I hoped fervently that they were for the towpath on my side seemed to disappear into the canal. I edged nearer. Opaque green water stretched from buttress to buttress. It slapped and slopped against the concrete where my towpath slipped discreetly under its wind-rippled surface. Above me the vehicles hooted and scooted in derisive triumph. I will cycle through a deep puddle but not straight into a canal. I turned around and cycled the two miles back to the bridge. I looked at my map. Since first passing this bridge an hour earlier, I had cycled eight miles and I was no further forward. I would have to take the main road into the town of Duenas and rejoin the canal there. I pushed off but was immediately arrested by a road sign preventing passage of me and my bicycle for this section of the road to Duenas was via the motorway so I returned to the bridge. The only solution left to me now was to take the road in the opposite direction and hope that it turned northwards. Either that or cycle back to Valladolid.

I gambled on the road and lost. It did not turn northwards. An hour and another seven miles later I was back at the bridge. When choosing the route for their new motorway, the authorities had annexed a stretch of the old main road. I had discovered a town inaccessible by bicycle – Duenas.

I was wet through to the skin. I was fed up and I had wasted the last two hours cycling fifteen miles to be back in the same place. At a damp hovel cowering in the lee of the canal I knocked up the old lady and asked her how I could get to Duenas. She waved me towards the motorway.

'*Y con bici?*' I asked, pointing to my bicycle.

'Not possible.' She shrugged. 'Not possible.'

I knew then that Spain had won. I was giving up on the whole stupid expedition.

I pedalled off eastwards, leaving the confounded canal and its motorway to consort as often as they liked. I was furious. After a few minutes of blaspheming I admitted that I was more furious with myself for giving up than I was with Spain for being Spanish. Still fuelled by my anger I cycled blindly off the road onto a path because it led in the vague direction of Duenas. Along the edge of a field I puffed angrily, churning and cursing through the mud. Across a potato patch I went, through a gateway and weaved around a plantation of some sort. It was only when I came to the house that I realised that I was in somebody's garden. The dog barked. I shouted, 'shut up you stupid Spanish hound' and cycled past their Calor gas bottles and down their drive to the stony track at the bottom.

I turned again in the direction of Duenas. When I came to the farm blocking my way I cycled through it – farmyard, barns, slurry pit and all. I discovered a stretch of old tarmac with a yellow line peeling from it and I cycled provocatively along it. It was the remains of a section of the ploughed-up main road. Closed gates I brazenly opened. Imperious signs I laughed derisively at. The alleyway leading to the railway told me it was *'No Entry.'* I pedalled straight up it. I cycled alongside the railway track where it was strictly forbidden. Up the ramp onto the platform I went and out through the booking hall I wobbled, my muddy tyres weaving brown squidgy tracery on the tiled floor. I hoisted my bicycle onto my shoulders and carried it up the steps of the footbridge and over the canal which I still could not reach.

And then I cycled into Duenas town centre.

There I found a sign which directed me on the old main road towards Palencia. At last! I would stick to that now, no more canals. It crossed the canal again and I found myself hurtling down a slip road back towards their favourite motorway. What was wrong with this place?

I turned around and cycled back to the canal bridge. Here there was a towpath and I was going to follow it to Palencia come hell or high water. Once I was on the canal, Spain relented a little. The rain cleared up and weak sun filtered prettily through the leaves. It did not soften my heart. Driven by my unquenchable rage, I would go to Palencia whence I would take the train to Burgos and on to Bilbao. Alan and Raquel would be surprised to see me returning three days early. Suddenly I felt very guilty. I had not phoned to see how Alan was progressing. Here I was, mildly upset by a drop of rain and a new road and Alan had just had his chest sawn open and bits stuck onto his heart.

As I coasted down an avenue in Palencia, looking for a suitable hotel, a coach overtook me and then cut me up, forcing me into the kerb. My colourful and wide ranging vocabulary of Spanish oaths had been supplied by Mama who employs them much as a bricklayer uses mortar. I filled my lungs and let fly one of Mama's Specials, straight from the Extremadura. What I lacked in phonetic accuracy I compensated for in volume. It made me feel better and it did make about thirty people turn around.

Before stopping at the hotel I passed by the station and checked the train timetables. I was assured that there was a train to Bilbao via Burgos on the morrow, that it would accept my bicycle, but that it did not depart until half past four in the afternoon.

And I believed them.

'Alan is all right but he can't talk,' Raquel said.

'Do you mean he is not allowed to talk?'

'No, he can't talk. You know, where they put tubes down his throat?'

'He hasn't still got tubes down his throat has he?'

'No. But where they put the tubes down has altered his throat. He can't talk.'

'He has lost his voice?'

'Yes.'

'Will he get it back?'

'The doctor says he might or he might not.'

This was getting worse. I thought of an Englishman, unable to talk, stuck in a hospital full of Spanish people who were unable to stop talking. He would need some moral support. And some earplugs. All the more reason to abandon my stupid trip.

'I'm coming back. Probably tomorrow,' I said.

'But you don't have to.'

'I'm fed up with the rain.'

'What rain?'

'It's been raining solidly for five days.'

'Not here it hasn't. We've had sunshine every day.'

'I'll see you tomorrow then. Don't wait up, I've got my front door key.'

Before turning in to bed I went for a gentle evening stroll in the town. Palencia exuded the self satisfaction of a comfortable provincial capital. The main street was arcaded in stone and at nine o'clock in the evening, everybody was strolling under the arches. Couples, singles, children running, entire families – they were ambling along in the pleasantly mild evening air. The shops were doing a thriving trade; the restaurants, of course, were not yet open. The loudest noise in the street was the sound of voices and it was spoken conversation not uncouth shouting or drunken singing. The soft balminess of the town nearly tricked me into rescinding my decision but now, of course, I had an excuse. I was returning to help Alan; I was not abandoning my expedition in failure.

Having triumphed, Spain unleashed the sun on the following morning. It was not scorching but it was pleasant. As I had half a day to kill I set out to cycle a distance up the canal towards the next town and then turn around and return to Palencia to take my train. If you are working to a non-negotiable deadline it is always safer to ride out and back along the same route rather than take a circular ride. In the former manner you learn the character of the terrain on the outward leg and can make the turning point at the correct moment. If cycling in a loop, you could find yourself five miles from the station, cycling uphill into a headwind with only twenty minutes left before the train departs.

I had not seen boats of any sort on the water. In one respect this was understandable since the canal cannot be used to go anywhere – all the locks are in ruins – but this should not exclude pleasure boating on some lock-free stretches of considerable length. However, rather like Nelson, I saw no ships.

After a few miles I dropped from the canal to visit a decent sized village which I suspected of harbouring a shop. As you know, these village shops no longer fooled me. I knew how to winkle them out now. I cycled slowly up the main street, examining every house to see if it harboured an old lady and an extinguished strip light. I did not see one but when I got to the corner I saw a housewife walking along with a loaf of bread in her bag. Ah ha! I turned down the street and overtook a lady walking in the opposite direction, also carrying bread. I felt like an Excise man sniffing out an illicit still. I had not yet seen a sign of a shop so I took another slow turn around the block to try to catch them off guard. And I did.

Turning into the edge of a triangular square, if one can have such a trigonometrical oxymoron, I caught a woman with three loaves under her arm, bidding her adieus on the doorstep. The moment the customer was on the pavement, the old lady inside pushed the door closed and snapped off the fluorescent tube. But she had not been quick enough. Eagle Eye Martin, Village Shop Detector Extraordinaire had spotted her. With a pointless display of sardonic satisfaction (pointless since nobody was watching) I swaggered up to the door and leaned my bicycle against the wall. I could see the old lady watching me from inside but she had not been clever enough. Although the room was dark, I could see her head in front of the mirror on the wall. I tried the door. She had closed it. I rapped on it with the authority of somebody who would not be deterred by the suggestion that this village had no shop. I had caught them red handed. It was not one, but three loaves the woman had been carrying.

The old lady remained in the dark, watching me. I rapped again. Her face appeared at the door and she jerked her head upwards in a short nod of enquiry. I waved my hand at the door. For a moment I thought I had lost. We stood looking at one another, she, measuring me up and me, trying to look as if I would not be turned away. I won. She unbolted the door.

'*Si?*' she said. Her dark eyes glowed with suspicion in the crumpled brown paper bag of her face.

I waved my hand for her to open the door.

'I want some bread,' I said and without waiting to be invited I stepped past her. She was obviously not going to waste her electricity on me until I was inside.

'What?' she said.

I am never overly confident with my Spanish because I do not really speak it. I guess at it.

'Bread,' I said, glancing around. It looked more like her kitchen than a shop. There was a sink under the window and a set of cupboards fixed on the back wall.

'Bread?' She stood there with her hands on her hips, body bent backwards with her head thrown up to look at me. 'Bread? Well why don't you go to the *panaderia* then?' and she pushed me out of her kitchen and back into the street. Actually, I think she said a lot more than just, 'try the *panaderia*' but I lost the thread after the third reference to a bodily function. She would have got on well with Mama.

On the angle of the street was a flourishing bread shop. With an illuminated fascia sign. And a window display of cakes and pastries. And a small car park. And an A board advertising ice creams. Some villages have no shame.

I took my picnic back to the flight of locks that I had earlier earmarked as being sitdownuponable. The water thundered over the derelict sluices and raised a rainbow spray before me. I moved away and found a stone further back to rest on. I did not want a fine drizzle of typhus canal on my food.

The rattle of steel wheels drew my attention across the valley to where a locomotive was hauling a short train of blue coaches. That would be the local train to Burgos. Before it disappeared I put my spyglass on it and studied it. I felt uneasy about the configuration of the rake. So far, all the trains that I had been allowed to carry a bicycle on had been what is known as a 'multiple unit' type of train – one where each coach has a motor and they are all linked together. This train was a locomotive pulling ordinary coaches with narrow doors. I could see no baggage van. I did not see how I would get my bicycle onto a train such as that. It was nearly one o'clock and it would take me two hours to get back to the station at Palencia. That would give me an hour and a half to make further enquiries before my train to Bilbao. I just had a premonition.

I finished my lunch and cycled back. At ten past three I was at the station.

'The train to Bilbao via Burgos.'

'It leaves at half past four,' the ticket man said. 'You can buy your ticket in thirty minutes.'

'Can I take my bicycle on that train?'

'No.'

'I can't take my bicycle?'

'No. What made you think that you could?'

'You told me so, yesterday.'

'Not me. I wasn't here yesterday.'

'Well somebody else did.'

'Not me. I know you cannot take your bike on the train. Do you want a ticket to Bilbao?'

'Can I take my bike?'

'No you cannot take your bike. I have told you. Do you want a ticket?'

'No thank you.'

I sat down on a bench and reflected. Given that I had just wasted half the day waiting for a train which I could not take, I needed to do something quickly. Either I had to travel or I had to find myself an overnight stop. I knew that it was important that I take a decision quickly but despondency overcame me. I had tried my hardest with Spain, I really had. I sat there watching this race of Iberian midgets as they hurried about their business slowly. Why had this expedition gone so wrong? I gazed up at the 'departures' board. Burgos and Bilbao mocked me still. Santander. I remembered Santander and yet it seemed a century ago. That was the town where the two railway stations lay side by side, only a couple of hundred metres separating the narrow gauge from the broad. In my mind something clicked. I had got to Santander from Bilbao on the FEVE narrow gauge. If there was a train from Palencia which would take me and my bicycle to Santander I could get to Bilbao from there. I delved in my pouch and pulled out a miniature timetable. The train for Bilbao left Santander at 18.55. I returned to the ticket guichet.

'The train to Santander.'

'Leaves in ten minutes.'

'Yes. Does it take my bicycle?'

'Yes, but it doesn't go to Bilbao.'

'No but there is a train on the narrow gauge that does and it leaves Santander at 18.55. What time does the train from Palencia arrive in Santander?'

'A quarter to seven, but it is in a different station.'

'That's no problem. I can cycle between the two. It won't take two minutes.'

He obviously doubted my confidence.

'The train might be late.'

I recalled the train from Santander to Gijon.

'So might the other train.'

He shrugged.

'Do you want a ticket to Santander then?'

'Yes please.'

'Single?' he asked. I just looked at him. 'Single,' he said.

The journey was magnificent. It was another crossing of the coastal mountain range. I sat at the front next to the guard's section where I had attached my bicycle to a grab pole. As we neared Santander and I saw the clock ticking I began to make plans for a quick exit from the train and a smart sprint down the platform. I looked at my road map and pondered a different course of action. This main line train would be passing within a few miles of El Astillero, the station at which I had alighted in order to cycle my first Via Verde and had ended up crawling through a drain pipe. If I got off the train before Santander and cycled to El

Astillero I could catch the Bilbao train as it came through. Such a course of action might give me more time.

I took my map to the guard and asked his opinion.

'You want El Astillero?'

'Yes, but I want to go to Bilbao.'

'You want El Astillero? Quick, quick.' The train was already slowing down. 'Get your bike.'

I unwound my cord attaching my bike to the pole whilst the guard swung out on the step and opened the luggage van door. Then he pointed down the platform.

'Down there. Left, right then left. A FEVE station to El Astillero.'

I thanked him quickly and hurried along the platform. Down in the street, left, right, left, and I could see the station. The man in the ticket office could not make his directions understood to me as to where I should go to catch the train to El Astillero. He pulled down the blind and emerged from the door at the side and then walked me down a platform towards a train already approaching on the opposite line. We waited whilst it drew up and then we crossed the tracks behind it and he handed me over to the other guard. The moment I was on board, the train drew out. Three stops later I was at El Astillero. Fifteen minutes after that, the Bilbao train came through. I clambered on. It pulled in to Bilbao FEVE station at half past nine. I dragged my bicycle up those bloody steps at the back of Abando station, into the ticket hall, up in the lift to the concourse and walked onto a train to Putxeta. The doors closed as I boarded it. By half past ten I was sitting at Alan and Raquel's, drinking tea. In seven hours I had travelled three hundred and twenty kilometres on four trains and the total ticket disbursement had been less than ten pounds.

Spain was not so bad after all.

chapter fourteen

I do not know what somebody who has had a multiple heart bypass operation is supposed to look like afterwards but when Alan came back from the hospital I would say that he appeared tired. He still had no voice. This excluded him somewhat from the national occupation of talking; his participation being restricted to grimaces which were ignored or whispers which were not heard. All he needed now was peace and quiet, as was pointed out often and volubly and at great length with gesticulations and asides by every visitor in the never ending procession. They rang the doorbell; they dropped in unannounced; they phoned at eleven o'clock at night from far flung reaches of the Spanish colonial empire; they even called him to the balcony to wave at them in the street below. When they did that I used to sidle onto the balcony alongside him and pretend that I was the Pope's right hand man at St Peter's.

In the manner of sickbed visitors worldwide, they listened to the medical report on the patient just long enough to be able to use it to launch themselves off into a comparison with, and a swab-by-suture account of, every hospital operation that had been performed on the last three generations of their family. It was utterly gruesome. Particularly as it appeared that the greater proportion of these surgical interventions had either led to abstruse complications or the immediate expiry of the unfortunate ancestor. An examination of how the lineage had survived to the present generation would have required a redrafting of the laws of statistical probability.

This is a procedure that the Spanish heartily call 'convalescence'. It is the duty of the patient to make himself available at any time of night or day, to eat at least a sample of whatever titbit has been brought for him in defiance of his medically imposed diet and to furnish without demur all data requested concerning the functioning of his bowels and libido. The Spanish enjoy a complicated hospitalisation as others relish a decent apple crumble. And the ensuing convalescence is the ground nutmeg to be sprinkled on top.

I endeavoured to lighten his life by giving an account of my journeying. As he had selfishly shown no enthusiasm for it on the evening before he had gone into hospital I considered that it was simple courtesy that he should now listen to my exposé. I recounted crawling through the drainpipe and frightening the old lady in her bedroom. I mentioned the rain. Several times. Raquel found this amusing and unbelievable as they had enjoyed clear blue skies so we studied the weather reports printed in the last few days' newspapers. They showed that I had managed to make a circular tour of Northern Spain by unfailingly popping up underneath the only rain cloud on the daily weather map the moment it materialised, wherever that might have been. Raquel put her finger on one of the smiling cartoon suns grinning up from the map.

'So you never got to Burgos then?' she asked.

'No, the canal beat me.'

'Why did you want to go Burgos?'

'It was on the way back to Bilbao and anyway, I wanted to see if all the residents of Burgos had small feet.'

'Why should they have small feet?'

'Their feet are only 11.13 inches long. Ours are twelve.'

'What do you mean?'

'The old Spanish measures?' I prompted.

'Ah yes, *el pie de Burgos!* But Martin we don't use that anymore, not for hundreds of years. We have now the metric system.'

I think the metric system is daft. How can anybody envisage what a metre represents? You draw a line from the equator through Paris to the North Pole and one ten millionth of that distance is a metre. What relevance has that got to anything at the human scale? Until the French Revolution everybody used systems where the units of measure were related to human beings. Even the French used *pouces* and *pieds* – thumbs and feet – although their thumbs were a trifle bigger than our inches. So having discovered that the French had bigger thumbs than the English, I wanted to see if the Spanish of Burgos had smaller feet. But I reserved my venom for the guide book.

'You know, I've never read Cervantes or any other famous Spanish works but if ever I do, I shall always remember that I started my study of Spanish fiction with this guide book.'

'What do you mean?'

'It is a work of pure imagination. Look at this track here on the map. This is the one that was supposed to start in the hills inland from Gijon. The one where the husband and wife stood outside the old station. In the rain, I add parenthetically, and argued over whether I could get through the tunnel that I never found. Look! The route is clearly marked in a beautiful green line on the map.'

Raquel took the book.

'But it says that the track has not been cleared.'

'What? Where?'

'That is why the line is a different shade of green. It just shows the route of the railway line before it was abandoned. It does not mean that the Via Verde has been opened that far.'

'Well why doesn't it say so?' I was a little annoyed.

'It does. That's how I know.'

'Stupid book!'

'Yes but Martin, without the book you would not have found the good tracks would you? There were some good tracks?'

I conceded a little.

'Oh yes. The Senda del Oso. That was magnificent.'

'The Senda del Oso?'

'Near Oviedo.'

'Did you see any bears?'

I was astonished at her percipience.

'Yes, I did. How did you know?'

'*Senda del Oso.* 'The path of the bears'.' She looked at me as if I were one of her underachieving pupils. Then she nodded at me. 'You really ought to learn Spanish, you know.'

'Yes, I suppose I ought.'

But it was time for me to go. I had explained that I intended to do the reverse of my Pyrenean crossing of the first visit and Raquel had tried to lend me a mobile phone to take with me. I declined it, invoking as an excuse that it would almost certainly not work in the mountains. The real reason was that I had no idea how to operate one.

The article of technology that I was carrying with me was my camera. When I had recounted my crossing of the Pyrenees – the savageness of the scenery, the remoteness of the track – my audience had rejected Indian ink sketches and demanded photographs so that they could better visualise it. I thought that was a bit insulting. I had hoped that my description had evoked pictorially what I had been up against. Was there, in their demand for photographic substantiation, the smidgen of a suspicion that I might have exaggerated? Me? So to clear my name I was lugging my camera over a mountain range. Why was I making a fuss about that?

At a time when cameras were becoming electronic, automatic and lightweight, I had bought a brand-new mechanical Russian camera which proclaimed its thirty-year old technology like a banner headline on the front page of *Pravda*. It had been constructed from gas pipe and biscuit tin. It demanded roll film which had to be wound onto the empty spool in the back of the camera with a deft thumb in subdued light; it worked to a larger format than the more popular 35mm. so its accessories looked like Victorian plumbing and its size and weight compared unfavourably to those of a portable typewriter. It was the best example of the camera not to take on a bicycle ride. But it did produce superb colour slides, the intensity and lustre of which were greatly appreciated by the audiences attending my talks.

But I still had to cart the thing around for what, in total, would be only a few seconds' actual use. I suppose I was to be thankful that a camera does not get progressively heavier with every picture that it takes. This question of carrying unwanted weight on a bicycle is one which is difficult to explain to a non-cyclist but I can assure you that when your eyes are bulging and your lungs splitting as you cycle up a mountain pass, you mentally sort through your pannier bags and subject the contents to a vicious balloon debate. Do I really need a pair of nickel plated nail scissors? Could I get rid of my jumper and use a thermal vest instead? Do two pairs of thin socks weigh less than one pair of thick? Are sliced white bread sandwiches lighter than wholemeal?

Even Alan and Raquel do not really understand it. Mama made a fuss on my first visit when I took the fabulous sandwiches that she had made me for the return journey and sawed off the ends so that they would fit neatly into my pannier bags. With great affection and for all the right reasons, they still attempt to load me upon departure with presents of hardback books and kilo bags of tapioca. And I suppose I do not really help them to an understanding by phoning them before leaving the UK and asking if there is anything they want me to bring out. It all started before my second visit. Alan rang me to check on the final details.

'If it's no trouble, could you bring me over a couple of things?' he said.

'Sure, I'd be willing. What is it this time – postage stamps?'

'I need a couple of tins of baked beans,' he replied, 'the low salt variety.'

'Baked beans?' I confirmed in a pleasant voice as the smile set on my face. In order to lighten my bicycle and ensure an unstrenuous ride I had pared down my clothing and shaving kit to just below the essential minimum; with the aid of a micro-mapping pen I had transcribed all my relevant addresses and telephone numbers from my diary onto half a postcard, I had even put aereated water in my bike bottle on the basis that it must be lighter than flat water and now he wanted me to trundle down to Spain with two tins of baked beans in my bags.

I am sure you think I am obsessed. It is easy for you. If you wish to carry an entire case of baked beans home from the supermarket, you do. Your car does not make itself more arduous to drive. A slight pressure of the right foot is all that is required. On a bicycle, every ounce that is carried is propelled by the rider's legs and lungs.

'Low salt variety,' he had specified. I wondered if that made them lighter, I mean, salt is pretty heavy stuff. You've only got to compare the weights of the two pots in the cruet set and you know immediately that pepper is the airhead in the marriage. 'You can get them from Tesco's.' He was adding insult to injury. He wanted me to go into Tesco's? I had not been into Tesco's since they had stopped giving pink stamps.

'Yes, I can do that easily. I can put the tins in my front bags, one either side of the wheel. It will make it balance nicely. It's a good job you didn't want three tins.'

'Perhaps you should get three tins. An extra one to balance out the tin of golden syrup.'

I thought I would draw the line at golden syrup. Many years earlier I had worked in a supermarket warehouse. Thirty minutes before we were due to lock up for the Easter break, a lorry had turned up with a delivery of a half a ton of golden syrup, in one pound cans, twenty four to a case. An entire pallet load. Cursing and grumbling I had wriggled the pallet jack under the load and hauled it off the unloading dock to the goods lift. Arriving at the floor above, I had simply wheeled it out of the lift and dropped the jack, dumping the pallet at the top of the ramp which led into the warehouse. It was daft to leave goods in that position because it meant that any following load would be stuck in the lift until the space could be cleared to unload it but I knew that nothing else could come in that night so I took the risk. But then I noticed that there was one carton short. I hollered down the lift shaft and they sent it up on its own. It had been overlooked for it had fallen off the pallet into the blackness of the lorry. I plonked it on top of the stack as an extra cherry on the cake and then clocked out and went home.

Syrup has been bestowed with an entertaining quality of viscosity. I love the way that you can lift the spoon high above your porridge and the minute movements of your hand are magnified to create a sinuous, sweet snake to Charleston across the cereal. I adore the determination with which it fights any attempt to pile it up on the spoon; three quarters of what you start with finds its way back into the tin before the spoon has travelled six inches. It creates its own optical illusions – the syrup is in a falling column and the spoon, rising through it. And it has the elasticity of nylon thread. Indeed, I think all tins of golden syrup should be marked with a denier rating. I would have been in a very good position to provide the necessary data for, as I am sure you know, to calculate a denier rating it is necessary to stretch the yarn to a distance of four hundred and fifty metres, weigh it in grams and then multiply by 0.05.

When we started work on the Tuesday morning, it took us too long to notice that our shoes were sticking to the floor. By the time that we did, the damage had been done. My position in the hierarchy was such that I was given the mop and the bucket and told to clean the floor. I decided to investigate the cause and, sniffing up the trail like a sweet-toothed bloodhound, I arrived at the pallet of syrup. I clambered up to the top. The shock which had been administered to the case when it had fallen from the pallet in the back of the delivery truck must have dislodged the lid of one of the tins. And of course, I had put that box right on top of the stack. I now knew exactly how that tin had filled the uninterrupted time from four o'clock on Saturday afternoon until half past seven on Tuesday morning.

From the corner of the carton, a pure golden finger of syrup traced a dead straight line to the edge of the first layer. Neither gaining nor decreasing in gauge, it tipped over the edge and descended the vertical face of the stack, rippling over the uneven edges of the boxes below like a slow motion treacly version of the water feature at Chatsworth House. Arriving at the rough wood of the pallet it had insinuated itself between two slats and oozed down to the floor. Here, it had registered its gratitude to the architect by hurtling at a snail's pace down the ramp that he had provided and then crossing the warehouse along its length in a triumphal parade down the middle of the main alley. Arriving at the staircase at the far end, it had performed a limbo dance under the staff door which smugly declared itself to be fireproof but was patently not syrup proof, then it had done a Slinky Snake down the staircase and collected in a pool at the bottom whilst it regained its breath sufficiently to climb over the sill. It was at this point that we had interrupted its progress but, fortuitously, the sticky puddle was exactly where every employee was obliged to put his left foot in order to open the door. The syrup had been transported beyond its wildest dreams at speeds unheard of to the farthest flung reaches of the warehouse, the widest prairies of the sales floor and the most closetted corners of the clerk's office.

I did not consider carrying syrup in my cycle bags to be a sensible undertaking.

'Are you sure you can't you get syrup in Spain?' My charity knew its bounds.

'No, they don't use it. A one pound tin would suit me.'

There was no doubt that Alan was a car driver.

'What about crisps?' I suggested enticingly.

'Never eat them.'

'Paper tissues?'

'I use a hanky.'

'Wafer biscuits?'

'Don't like them.'

'Feather duster.'

'Mama wouldn't use it.'

'Expanded polystyrene?'

'What for?'

'Helium filled balloons. Now they are something you don't see in Spain.'

'Martin, do you–?'

I tried a different tack.

'Paving slabs. You were doing your garden path last time I was there. What do you want, pink or grey? Imitation Yorkstone looks nice. With a couple of half hundredweight bags of cement?'

Alan wilted under my outrageous onslaught.

'I don't want to put you to any trouble.'

'No, that's no trouble. Three tins of baked beans and a

tin of syrup. Is that the lot?'

'Yes thanks.'

In for a pennyweight, in for a pound. By the time I departed the shores of Albion I had also squeezed in a two pound Christmas pudding, a pint bottle of stout and some books for the Academia. A lot of fuss over nothing really.

So I stood there rather awkwardly trying to say my goodbyes to somebody who had no voice and did not know if he ever would have again.

'Which way are you going?' Raquel asked.

'Train into Bilbao then down those bloody steps at the Abando Station and cycle across the river to the Atchouri station.'

'But why do you always do that?'

'Do what?'

'Go up and down the steps at Abando station.'

'Because the train comes in at that station. I can't alter that.'

'But why use the steps?'

'Because the station is upstairs.'

She shrugged. 'I don't know why don't you go out of the other side of the station. It's flat.'

I looked at her. 'How long have you known that?'

'Everybody knows it. I thought you knew.'

'But did you think that for the last seven years I've been carrying my bicycle up and down those steps for fun?'

'Yes. You are always doing silly things.'

And she obviously believed it. But I did not make an issue of it. Raquel is not a cyclist.

The first leg of my return journey was simply the reverse of the last leg of the outward – it was the Euskotren to San Sebastian. Just to confuse me utterly, when I looked at the timetable in the ticket office I could find no mention of either San Sebastian or its Basque version, Donostia.

Nor did it appear on the route map yet here I was at the very station at which my train from San Sebastian had finished, albeit without me. Eventually I found that my destination was identified by the name of its station – Amara – rather as if London were St Pancras. I thought this a bit pretentious; after all, there are two stations in San Sebastian whereas there are about a dozen main line termini in London.

I was not sure what kind of negotiation the woman in front of me was making at the ticket guichet but then I realised that she was probably telling the man about her hysterectomy and enquiring after his warts. When she finally departed I moved up to the glass.

As I began my *'Amara, ida solo por favor'* the ticket man turned sideways and began a conversation with a colleague who was out of my sight. I waited. The exchange seemed heavily weighted to my ticket man with only an occasional grunt offstage left. It was clear that the initiation of the conversation had come from the ticket man who was now also supplying the momentum to keep it going. The thought that this man had found something far more interesting than talking to me would have been galling had I been wanting to buy a ticket to catch a train which was departing from, say, for the sake of argument, platform two in twenty one minutes time and my gall would have been even more finely distilled had I believed that the supply of the aforesaid ticket should have been his sole responsibility but, happily, it was apparent from his demeanour this was clearly not the case.

After several long pauses during which he had failed to evince even the most sibilant of grunts from his mate, it was obvious that the subject of discussion had been truly exhausted. The ticket man swivelled back to face me.

'Amara, ida so–' I began.

He continued turning through one hundred and eighty degrees to face stage right. He then leaned over and pulled an envelope towards him. He opened it and counted out pink ten-euro notes into the till drawer in front of him. He neatly folded over the top of the empty envelope, scored it with his finger nails and then tore it into four pieces and dropped it into an unseen but assumed receptacle under the counter.

'Por favor, un billete por–'

The next envelope contained twenty-euro notes. They were a sort of bluey grey colour. Every single one of them. I mention this fact because I had time to check them individually as he counted them into the drawer, failed in the tally, pulled them out and recounted them. They were still bluey grey at the second count.

The train was now due to leave in nineteen minutes.

'Por favor,' I said loudly, 'The train for Amara.'

He looked at me as he folded the empty envelope, scored it and then tore it into four pieces.

'Amara?'

'Amara, San Sebastian, Donostia.' I thought that covered it fairly comprehensively. He turned and looked at the clock.

'It's not yet.'

On the wall by the clock, three brightly coloured plastic snails crawled across the legend, 'Slow, Sure, Safe.' His arm reached off stage right and returned with a fistful of tight cardboard rolls containing coins. He opened the till drawer again and dropped them in but any suggestion that this concluded his housework was discounted as he pulled from the drawer a small plastic bag. He turned the top flap inside out and began to count euro coins into the tray. I dared not interrupt him. If he lost count he would only start again. When it was empty he did not try to tear up this bag but neatly turned it back the correct way and then pushed it onto the decorated handle of a cupboard door.

At last he looked up.

'Could I have a ticket for Amara?'

'Amara?'

I nodded confirmation as I saw with dismay his hand sneaking into the till drawer. He withdrew one of the cardboard rolls and smacked it sharply on the edge of the counter to snap it. He emptied the small bronze coins out and began to flick them one at a time into his cupped hand, counting as he did so. Every ten coins he emptied into a compartment in the drawer. The next tube contained five cent coins. He snapped it like its predecessor and counted them into his hand. They also rattled into the drawer.

'Could I have a ticket to Amara for the train which is there?' I pointed onto the platform where the two-tone blue rake had just pulled in.

'There is no train for Amara.' He pulled out a third cardboard roll and snapped it.

I looked at the train, at the destination board which clearly stated that departure was at a quarter to the hour and then back to the man.

'Yes there is.'

'No train for Amara today.'

'Yes there is. It goes at a quarter to. It's that one there.' I pointed provocatively at the weighty substantiation of my argument, as represented by several hundred tons of railway rolling stock.

'Oh that one. Single or return?'

His abrupt *volte-face* caught me off guard.

'Er... single.'

'Five euros.'

I slipped a pink ten euro note under the glass. He pulled a face at it.

'Hurr,' he sighed irritably, 'haven't you got any change?'

I looked at him. I shifted my glance to his drawer and then back to his face. I shook my head.

This bizarre wish of his to retain a complete set of change in his drawer, ready should he ever need it but never to be broken into when he did, reminded me of an incident in a modern hotel I once stayed in at Le Touquet. In those days, French hotels were proud to inform their clientele that a hair drier was available for the guests' use and could be borrowed from the reception upon request. At the same time in England, the equivalent hotel room came with a tea-making tray, kettle, biscuits, milk, coffee, a television, a fridge, a trouser press, a hair drier, barbecue and lawn mower. I was lodging at the hotel for five days, using the swimming pool and washing my hair every day. On the third day the girl at the reception desk grudgingly handed over the hair drier with the warning, 'You can't keep borrowing this you know.'

'Why not?'

'It's for the guests.'

'I am a guest.'

'But you keep using it.'

'That's because I keep needing it.'

'But other guests might want to use it.'

'Well, then they can ask for it.'

'But they can't use it if you're using it.'

'And I can't use it when they are using it.'

'But they don't use it.'

'So what's the problem?'

'I'm just warning you, that's all. You can't keep using this hair drier.'

'Thank you for the warning. And for the service.'

The hotel had eighty rooms and one hair drier. The receptionist probably held a hotel and catering diploma.

This drawer full of change was the ticket man's hair drier. It was there for my convenience but I must not use it. I take my ticket and change and proceed to the platforms. Here, have been installed mechanical barriers linked to automatic ticket-reading machines. I walk to the far end of the line to use the broad barrier which will allow me to push my bicycle through. I slip my ticket into the slot, it spews it out again. I try the barrier. It does not move. I put the ticket in again. Out it comes even more quickly. I turn it over and try it the other way around. No success. I lean forwards and rattle the barrier. I reinsert the ticket. It spits it out.

By now, I have attracted the attention of the ticket collector's offstage-left mate. He saunters up, tut-tutting loudly and puts his hand out for my ticket. I surrender it to him and he makes a great show of turning the ticket around in the air before my eyes into the orientation that I had started with originally and then inserting it in the machine. It spits it out. He tries again. The same thing happens. He turns the ticket around.

'That's not the good way,' I tell him with a leapfrog of raised eyebrows preceeded by a loud 'tut'.

He ignores me. The machine confirms my assertion with mechanical glee.

A door bangs open at the other end of the narrow concourse and out strides a man in a brown suit. When the door swings shut I can see that it bears an enamel sign, *'Jefe de Estación'*. The station master takes the ticket from his subordinate, turns it around in the air, 'tuts' and inserts it in the slot. We wait with baited breath. It is rejected. He turns it around.

'That's not the right way,' says the ticket office man's mate.

The station master glowers at him and pushes it into the machine. It comes straight out again. He hands me back my ticket, takes a key from his pocket, slips it into the lock and opens the gate for me.

Slow, Sure, Safe.

Off we go to San Sebastian, Donostia, Amara. The same tape is playing in the music machine. I settle down to watch the grooming of a teenaged girl wearing black trousers, a pilled jumper of shocking pink and nail varnish of a matching hue. She brushes and combs and trims and preens and buffs and polishes for over half an hour but however charitably I inspect her, I can honestly see no alteration, let alone, improvement.

The train picks its careful route amongst the white concrete giraffe legs of a new motorway and sidles timidly along the back of a main street which is dominated by the dirty bulk of a derelict sewing machine factory. Out in the country again and we pass by a school sports field. Three games of football are in progress. The eight-year olds are piled in a solid phalanx at one end of the pitch, hounding mercilessly the possessor of the ball; the twelve-year olds are positioned intelligently and are skilfully passing the ball from one to the other; the fifteen-year olds are gathered together in a group, deep in animated discussion whilst one of them lazily bounces the ball up and down on the hard turf.

I disembarked at San Sebastian, Donostia, Amara, railway station and started to look for a hotel. I like the town. It has a bit of something for everybody. The River Urumea, which at this point is really more an inlet of the sea than a river, divides the town with its broad channel. Across this are thrown three bridges. One of these, the Puente Maria Cristina, strikes a dramatic pose with its flamboyant spires and gilded decorations. On the eastern side of the river is the more modern and thus, more industrialised sector of the town. I know that I must eventually cross to this side for the main-line railway station is on the right bank, but for the moment I have time on my hands and so I cycle along the sea front, watching the last of the holidaymakers desporting themselves on the broad sandy beach which fringes the semi circular bay.

The cycle track runs from the foot of the rocky promontory of Mont Urgull with its wooded slopes and castle which forms the eastern edge of the bay, around the Playa de la Concha beach to the Playa de Ondaretta where the sand gives way to another rock outcrop which forms the western edge of the bay. Half way around the curve the track runs through a short tunnel of obvious railway parentage.

Although there is a charming 'old town' to be found near the port and the Mont Urgull, I would hesitate to ascribe any great age to it. Not a degree of antiquity in accord with its appearance at any rate. For the embarrassing truth is that we burned the town to the ground in 1813.

It was all to do with the Peninsular War. Napoleon Bonaparte had decided that it would be a jolly good wheeze if his brother Joseph could be made King of Spain as well as King of Naples so in 1808 he found a pretext and sent an army into Spain and proclaimed his brother king. This was not entirely to the liking of a proportion of the Spanish population who decided to resist. Any country who resisted Bonaparte was, by definition, a bosom pal of Britain and by redefining the Armada as an unfortunate naval excursion and the Inquisition as a misdirected excess of zeal, the British Government was able to send war materials and diplomatic encouragement to the Spanish with a clear conscience. One thing led to another and by 1813 the Duke of Wellington was in charge of an army composed of two hundred thousand English, Spanish and Portuguese troops which he deployed to chase the French out of Spain. San Sebastian, unluckily, got in the way of one of his generals.

But the town recovered and, with its later adoption by the Court of Spain as its summer residence, it went on to ensplendour itself with broad avenues and shady walks, imposing public buildings and comfortable hotels. It reminded me of Nice. It was full of the kind of people who commit themselves wholeheartedly to enjoyment. Instead of taking a siesta, they would come down to the beach, strip off and go sea bathing. But where had they all gone?

Suddenly the beach was empty. I had not noticed them going. It was as if they had evaporated.

And where was the sun?

The storm broke with a crash. Along the entire length of the promenade there were only three people. Somebody in white, a girl in turquoise and a cyclist. We all made for the only shelter that we could see – a sort of porch affair which had been installed to protect the beach chairs.

Frightened of sliding on the wet paving, I pedalled sedately up and slithered to a stop under the glass roof. We three looked at each other and shrugged. I was very wet. The girl in the turquoise dress was soaked through to the skin, which, to my eye produced a quite delightful effect and the man in the white anorak stood watching the water drip onto his bare legs and splash onto his flip-flops. We were obviously not acquainted with the customs of San Sebastian but we had just been indoctrinated into one of them – the daily afternoon storm.

The problem with pageantry is that it sometimes goes on for too long and this was certainly the case with the storm. I was beginning to shiver after forty minutes of watching torrential rain bounce in surprise from the glass roof of our thin shelter. Eventually the sound of the traffic began to make itself heard and I realised that the rain had stopped. I set off to find myself a hotel. I criss-crossed the town and discovered that all those people who had been on the beach were now safely tucked up snug in their hotels.

The cycle track that I was following left the path and became a contra-flow lane on the road, separated from the cars by a kerb and bollards. I continued around the corner, sweeping both sides of the street with my eyes for any hotel signs. I glanced ahead and hurriedly pulled on my brakes. They have a cruel sense of humour in San Sebastian. My contra-flow cycle lane stopped in ten metres. It did not lead anywhere, it just ceased to exist. It happily launched me head first into three lanes of approaching traffic. I turned around and invented the contra-contra-flow cycle lane.

I ended up at the hotel alongside the main line station.

This was useful. I would be on the doorstep to take the train in the morning.

I do not recall the number of my hotel room but it could quite easily have been identified as 'Platform 1' for my window gave out directly onto the station at exactly the position where the locomotives idled their diesels.

The bedroom floor was laid with large polished tiles. Every time I took a corner on the jute rug by the bathroom I found myself veering in a slow motion skid straight into the rickety wardrobe. It was like trying to walk on wet clay. I was pleased to climb into the solidity of the bed, yet, as I began to plan my route for the following day I became dimly aware of a strange sensation of slight dizziness or disorientation. The room was moving. No, my bed was moving. The headboard was attached to the wall and not to the bed so when I sat up and leaned against it to read the map, the bed began to creep stealthily across the slippery tiled floor.

It was quite late by the time that I had worked out my plan for the morrow. I would take the train towards Tolosa but get off at Andoain. From there, I would cycle a fifty kilometre out-and-back Via Verde and then board the train again at Andoain to continue on to Tolosa for the night.

I did not sleep well. The trains through my en-suite station ran late into the night and started early in the dawn and all the locomotives rattled their pistons under my window and never failed to hoot their klaxons before departing. At one moment during a period of nocturnal awakedness, I stood at the window and watched an overnight express trundle through. I noticed that several of the carriages had their doors wedged wide open to keep the train cool.

Health and Safety? That's for cissies.

chapter fifteen

I was probably a little bit grumpy when I came down to breakfast. I am not always pure sweetness and light in the morning. Behind the counter in the brasserie was an extraordinary looking machine. It could have come straight out of one of those 1950s science fiction films where the devilish contraption would be built out of futuristically finned shiny metal and suggestively bulbous glass and the death ray would be equipped with a large dial marked in bold letters *ON* and *OFF* so that the hideous intentions of the villain would be immediately apparent. But when the barman set it to work I realised that it was not *Invasion of the Martians* I was watching but *Tom and Jerry*. It was a composite of all those chopping, slicing, pulping machines which have ever threatened the life of the innocent rodent and skinned the tail of the hapless feline.

The barman was a heavy fifty years old at least. He climbed onto a short stepstool and, balancing a paper sack on his shoulder, he emptied its contents into the machine. Oranges. They bounced and jostled into a huge chrome wire hopper. He descended to earth and stowed the stool safely away. His hand wavered over the enamelled switch, just to make sure that we could all understand and quaver before the full dastardliness of his imminent action. I expected him to turn and leer nastily at us and was quite disappointed when he merely gave the knob a twist of the wrist as if breaking the neck of a hen. The ceiling lights flickered, the machine exploded into action and then oranges began to dance in all directions down spiralling glass tubes, jostling impatiently to be gutted, crushed, pummelled and juiced. It was now the *Hammer House of Horror* as, down below, the sinister blood of the oranges dripped into the waiting font.

At last he saw me and asked me what I wanted.

'*Desayunero,*' said I, having learned and practised the Spanish word for breakfast.

'*Desayunero?*' he quizzed me.

'*Si, desayunero,*' I insisted but it did not seem to be working. Perhaps it was the wrong word. Try adapting the French. '*Déjeunero?*' I ventured.

His face was a blank wall. I was making no headway. A young man at the other end of the counter had just paid his tab and, as he left, he threw helpfully over his shoulder,

'*Desayuno.*'

That was the word.

'*Desayuno,*' I repeated confidently.

'*Ah, desayuno!*' The barman's gruff face lit up with recognition. Now it obviously made sense although why my meaning had been so obscure earlier I could not understand. Surely he could have interpolated the correct word from my efforts?

'*No desayuno,*' the barman said.

What? No breakfast?

Oh, we are not starting all this again are we?

'*Comer?*' I said. Eat. I made a mime with my hand moving to my mouth.

'*No comer.*'

'*Si comer.*'

'*No comer,*' he said in block capitals and slid a plate of croissants across to me. '*Café?*'

I nodded. I had obviously crossed back over that invisible line on the map of Spain beyond which, you do not get breakfast. He slapped a thimble of coffee down onto the bartop. I pointed to a croissant. He pinched one in a pair of tongs and served it elaborately to me on a plate with a knife and a fork. I thought this action was bordering on insolence. I am tough. I can remember when bread came unsliced. I picked up the croissant in my bare fingers and contemptuously tore it apart. Ha!

I had forgotten that the Spanish lacquer their cakes with a clear sugar glaze. The dismembered halves of the pastry stuck to both my hands. I peeled one piece from my right hand and ended up with two on the left. I tore one off and shook my fingers irritably over the plate. Because of the way I am built I can never be certain where my fingers will end up when I make a movement like that. The portion of croissant departed but I clipped the knife handle and the utensil somersaulted into the air above me. Much to my astonishment, I succeeded in catching it in mid air with my sugary hand. I now had one piece of croissant glued to my left hand, a sticky knife blade on my right palm and the undivided attention of everybody in the bar. But something was missing. Where was the detached piece of croissant? As discreetly as I could, I looked around the bar. I dreaded that some bellicose Spaniard would propel his wife up to me, point at my half croissant welded to her left breast and drag me outside for a duel. I looked to my right and to my left. I looked down on the floor. It had disappeared.

Amongst the many spectators of this cabaret was the barman. He looked at me and tapped his hairy forearm.

Sure enough, I had half a croissant stuck to my left forearm, the other half still entwined lovingly around the fingers of my left hand.

'Silly me,' I said and lifted my left arm so that I could reach the morsel. But I still had a knife stuck in my right hand so I levered it against the counter and prised it off. It clattered onto the metal like the roll of a snare drum. If there had been any persons in the room not yet watching me, there were none thereafter. With my left forearm turned almost to my nose, I peered around my elbow and picked the croissant portion from my arm but, engaged in this ticklish operation, I did not pay sufficient attention to what my left hand was doing whilst it was waving about above my ear. So I now had the new section of croissant stuck to the fingers of my right hand and the other piece stuck in my hair. I then did what I should have done at the beginning. I transferred the piece of croissant from my hand to my mouth. This inspired action freed my right hand to assist my left in disentangling itself and the croissant from my scalp. After that, it was all quite easy. I've never had problems such as this with bacon and eggs. I blame it all on the Common Market.

A rustic looking man carrying an equally rustic bicycle climbed onto the train behind me. I asked him where he was going so as to know how to stack our bicycles. If he was getting off before me, his would need to be at the front of the pile. I could not understand a word of his reply. I shrugged, so he said the same phrase louder and more quickly. I pointed to myself and said, 'Andoain'. This, he understood and put his bicycle behind mine.

As a fellow cyclist, he obviously felt a responsibility of ensuring that the foreign tourist knew all that was going on around him, and so he gave me a running commentary, tapping my knee with a horny hand to make sure that my mind was focused on him. I still could not understand a syllable of what he said. This did not matter since I could mostly keep him going by nodding or raising my eyebrows or some such stratagem however, each time we arrived at a point where he considered that I should respond more fully, he would repeat the phrase, getting louder and louder and more and more demonstrative in his knee thumping until it was plain to everybody in the carriage that my IQ was not quite nudging double figures.

I found this quite chastening. Although, mercifully, I have never committed the sin myself, I have, on several occasions been present when monolingual Englishmen, finding that 'Johnny Foreigner' was just too stupid to understand the simplest of their English phrases, had shouted them hideously, accompanying them with a sub commentary on the intellectual shortcomings of the native. I had never bothered to wonder what it was like to be that native. I was him now. It is quite demeaning. And yet, unlike the Englishmen, this man in the train was not imputing any lack of intelligence to me, nor was he trying to exploit me. He was very kind and he believed that he was doing me a service. And, as it turned out, he was. When I arose to get off at Andoain, he held my arm to prevent me. He let me off at the next station which was nearer to the track I was looking for.

The sky was the grey that I had come to accept as uniform for Spain. I was not particularly surprised but as I was waiting in the supermarket for the lady in front of me to finish recounting what had happened on the previous evening's soap opera, I glanced at the newspaper on the rack. It showed that the only little yellow sun which would appear in the whole of this region today, would shine gloriously out over San Sebastian. Where I was no longer.

The beauty parlour owner's daughter who had had the illegitimate child fathered by the janitor of the apartment block where her mother regularly met, in secret, an Argentinian who had promised to take her away to

Buenos Aires to escape from her bullying husband as soon as he could raise the cash which was difficult for him, being an illegal entrant in Spain and thus suspected of political terrorism, had got a job in a fashion boutique in a posh part of town which was frequented by the famous film and rock stars and one of these such, Enrique by name, had brought in his present girlfriend to buy her a dress but had been struck by the dazzling, if discrete, pulchritude of the above daughter. The lady at the till, nodded, enraptured.

I turned the newspaper over. Now here was a challenge. This region was called 'Guipuzcoa.' How do you pronounce that? Whilst the raconteuse in front rambled on through the various cousins twice removed, the attempted suicide, the burglary and the plane crash, I twisted my lips and contorted my face in several silent attempts to pronounce 'Guipuzcoa'. The nearest I could guess at was something sounding like *'Weepers-coher.'* Yes, that must be it. For the pleasure of confirmation, I repeated it aloud and found a puzzled looking child inspecting me through the display of combs and hairbands. I smiled lopsidedly, hoping to reassure it that I was the harmless idiot that it thought me.

Up on the track, a strong draught was blowing down through the first tunnel, bringing with it, the sweet smell of sawdust from a sawmill. The tunnel was lit with sodium lamps and was obviously on a favourite walking route, being near the town. At this time of the morning it was deserted. The track would probably not wake up until the afternoon.

This railway had been built at the beginning of the twentieth century as a branch line to link the mines up in the hills of the Plazaola district with the main line station at Andoain. Its initial success in this context prompted some visionaries to extend the line further inland; over, around and through the hills to the important town of Pamplona. At last, Pamplona was linked to the sea. But nothing much came of this breakthrough. The line was not prosperous.

Like many of the small lines in Spain it suffered severe privations in stock and capital during the Civil War and finally, in 1953, a series of mountain freshets washed away a portion of the track and several bridges. That was the end. Pamplona still has no rail link northwards to the coast.

When I had shown the guide book's account of this track to Raquel she had made me promise not to try to go through the top tunnel of 2.6 kilometres. I had to admit that it did not sound too enticing. Unlit along all its length, it contained a dam and a dyke which retained several stretches of water within it; it was not recommended for those who, 'did not like to get themselves wet or who suffered from claustrophobia.' I assured her that I would not attempt it. I did not point out that I would have to go through thirty two tunnels before even reaching that one. Thirty two tunnels up and thirty two tunnels down.

I had soon left the town and civilisation behind. This ancient railway was the only line of communication travelling up the valley. The river was not navigable and no road had been built. Up and up I went, the track bursting through the outcrops in short tunnels which were never long enough to be dark. I stopped inside one of the larger tunnels and gawped for it had been used twice. They had obviously needed to build a line up a spur at right angles to the main valley to service a mine and so they had bored through the side walls of the first tunnel and crossed the track from left to right, opening up the hole in the middle into a cathedral of rough rock. I just hoped that they had used an efficient signalling system. The thought of two trains meeting at a crossroads in a tunnel left me aghast.

Outside in the overcast daylight, a persistent breeze was tugging and I welcomed it with glee for I would be coming back down again this afternoon and the wind would be blowing me downhill. The only noise I could hear was this wind hissing through the leaves of the trees and sometimes giving a sharp roar as it came down a side valley.

Another tunnel. I had lost count. I pedalled in. It must be on a curve for I could not yet see the other end. The effect of the daylight from behind me, reflecting on the rocky walls before me, suddenly gave out as I turned a corner into total black. I stopped and my dynamo light expired. Not that it had been much use. The light on my head was struggling bravely to illuminate something but the inside of a railway tunnel is usually black. This one was jagged dark grey in all directions. If it had not been for my semi-circular canals I would not have known which was up I was standing. A feeling of unease crept over me in the absolute silence. A silence impressed by the hundreds of tons of rock above me. I dismounted and started to walk but came to loose rocks piled up against the wall. I turned the other way, here the walls were solid. I shouted to hear an echo and my voice was swallowed up as if I had shouted into a curtain. By my dim lantern I wandered further and further into the mountain. I suppose this tunnel is open? I came to a curve leading the other way. Perhaps I would see daylight then. There was none. I decided that I had gone far enough and railway tunnels were very nice in their ones and twos and if you could see straight through them but I did not need actually to go to the end of this line. I could turn around now and nobody would know. It was rather sobering for me to admit that I was frightened. So, if I am going to be frightened, why not do it properly? I turned off my light and stood there in the absolute black, absolute silence. I felt as if somebody were smothering me. Even the air I was breathing felt black. In the modern Western world it is very rare that we ever see absolute nothingness. Many horizons are washed by the glow of some town; the sky is tacked in place by drawing pin stars.

To compensate for the deprivation, my brain began to make images for my eyes. It showed the track leading up here, the man on the train, the child in the shop; it would not accept that there was nothing to look at. It even showed a faint grey glow on the rocks ahead. Daylight. I stumbled forwards. The light became stronger and around the next corner was the end of the tunnel. I laughed. I had not really been scared, I was only kidding. I took a good look at the top entrance of the tunnel so that I would recognise it on the way down. Just to be ready.

After about an hour and a half and twenty or so tunnels, the sky became lighter. I would not say that the sun was shining but at least the dampness in the air had gone. I sat on the remains of a platform and ate some lunch. Nearby a great iron pipe brought the water down from a high level reservoir to the hydro electric station below me. I was now on part of my road map which was marked in empty white; up in hills of rock and trees, ravines and cascading water. The feat of engineering that had been necessary to carve and blast this railway track through such an inhospitable region was mind-boggling. Once again I was struck by the same feeling that I had experienced on other tracks which gave me privileged access to areas that I would not have been able to have reached otherwise; that although I enjoyed immensely the cycle ride, I regretted that the line was not functioning as a railway. I would have loved to have ridden that line in one of the trains of the era. The question of possession versus consumption of cake, I suppose.

The line now entered onto a series of curved tunnels linked directly by short viaducts thrown across the ravines which scored this valley wall. As I was about to exit the third tunnel in the set, something made me stop under the portal. I could not at first decide what it was and then I realised that I was looking at the silver birch trees which filled the ravine. They were bent hard over in the wind and hissing angrily like a Japanese tour group. I dismounted and pushed my bicycle onto the concrete deck of the bridge. What a sensible move! Had I cycled out of the portal the wind would have blown me straight over the edge, for the railing was quite insubstantial, and the wind was making me stagger in short steps. But it was only a local draught caused by the characteristics of the topography. After the next tunnel the air was quite calm once again.

I did my thirty two tunnels and stopped at a picnic site and ate some more lunch. Here the countryside was pasture land and settlements. I was back in civilisation. I did cycle up and look at the 2.6 kilometre tunnel. Just a look, you understand Raquel, but they had built a fence across it to deny entry even to me. Not that I would have gone in, of course. You know how sensible I am.

I think I sang all the way back. Can you imagine anything more delightful than being pushed downhill on a bicycle through some terrific scenery? Going faster through the tunnels made my dynamo light much brighter and the cycling more exciting and it was only when I had hurtled through a tricky one with a heart-stopping chicane in the middle that I realised that this was the dreaded tunnel that I was supposed to have been looking out for. Things often look different when seen from the other end.

chapter sixteen

I do not know where the time went, or rather, the daylight. Night had fallen by the time that I descended from the train in Tolosa. This was the town that I had cycled straight through on my first visit to Spain, so pressed had I been to reach Bilbao. Now I was only seeing it in the dark. Once again, the lighting provisions of my bicycle caused quite a stir. I was rather pleased. Sensitive and retiring though I am, I prefer motorists to pick holes in my appearance rather than pick bits of me out of their tyres.

I could find only one hotel in Tolosa and this one took itself rather seriously. My bicycle would not be propped up in the bar or wedged behind the reception desk overnight: it would be accommodated in the hotel's underground car park across the street.

The following morning, before setting off for the Pyrenees, I decided that I really ought to make a short tourist visit of Tolosa in the daylight. After all, everybody had heard of Tolosa and the Alcazar. Even I knew that it was an important city, and yet, I was disappointed with it. I could find nothing which could have been the famous mediaeval fortress – I was obviously in the wrong part of town. And the town itself looked so ordinary. It did not put on the airs and graces that one would expect. It behaved just like another flourishing industrial settlement of which there were several in this region. I was still mulling this over half an hour later as I slowly climbed the pass towards Lekumberri and as I entered a band of mist, paradoxically, things became clearer. I had not been in the wrong part of town. I had been in the wrong town altogether. Toledo: that was the name of the famous historical town, not Tolosa. Toledo had the Alcazar and stuff like that. And it was four hundred kilometres south of me. The sun was probably shining in Toledo.

And then I remembered something else, somewhat more pertinent. On my first journey I had come down this pass after meeting the two Dutch cyclists and I had remarked to myself with glee that I was doing it in the right direction because the gradient was one in five in places. Shortly I would be arriving at one of those places and I would be going in the wrong direction.

I cannot cycle up such a gradient. I am physically prevented from doing so by the configuration of my bicycle. When I had designed my bicycle frame I had insisted that it be constructed so that I could sit upright. I like to see where I am going. This means that if I attempt to climb a gradient steeper than one in six, when I apply the required pressure on the pedals and the corresponding contra-pull to the handlebars, the compound result as translated in mechanical terms is not to advance the machine up the slope but to lift the front wheel from the ground. The first time that this happened to me, the bicycle swivelled smartly through one hundred and eighty degrees on the rear wheel and my pedal push sent me hurtling back down the incline. It had taken me fifty yards to gain control and stop it. I mention this physical limitation of my bicycle in case you should be tempted to level at me the unfair accusation that I might not be sufficiently fit to cycle up a one in five gradient. The very thought! Any honest cyclist will tell you that it is far more tiring to walk a bicycle up a hill than to ride it.

The valley narrowed down to squares of pasture knitted together with barbed wire like a giant patchwork quilt. The mist turned to rain. The rain was not utterly committed to precipitation but it was heavy enough for me to wear waterproofs, and, such is the nature of waterproofs that I became as damp on the inside as I was on the outside.

I staggered up the final set of hairpins, pushing my bicycle in short bursts, my arms stretched straight out before me on the handlebars and my eyes fixed on the wet tarmac. I could hear the motorway traffic rumbling along the concrete pelmet that had been attached around the top edge of the valley, just below the crestline.

Once over the top, I zipped up everything to keep out the breeze that would be created by my descent. Allowing cold air to blow through a wet anorak is one of the quickest ways of getting a chill. After about a mile I came to the point where the construction of the motorway had removed a section of my road. I vaguely remembered wasting half an hour here on my first trip as I had tried all the side roads to bypass the check. As I stood there scratching my head and trying to recall exactly how I had solved the problem and what the reciprocal of the solution would be, a car bounced up. I tapped on the window.

'For Pamplona?'

The driver began to show me, then stopped.

'*Ah. Con bici,*' she said.

Yes, with a bicycle.

'Up to the petrol station. Turn left and cross over the motorway on the bridge. Straight on. Before the village turn right. Go back under the motorway and turn left.'

I reckon my Spanish comprehension is improving.

I reached the northern outskirts of Pamplona in the early afternoon. For the last hour I had seen it lying in the plain before me as I had swooped down the main road in a series of switchbacks where my speed at one point had touched forty miles per hour.

Decision time. Do I stop in Pamplona and look for a hotel or do I carry on for another twenty miles to Aoiz? The weather was dry this side of the pass and that decided me. I would continue to Aoiz. This would put me at the foot of the climb to the Pyrenees and my secret track. I was feeling quite excited in my own little way. Would I be able to find my way back? Would I, indeed, be able to find where my track started from the road? All those years ago I had paid no attention to what the entrance had looked like when I had wearily rolled out onto the tarmac. It would be just too silly to miss the turning after so many miles. The only identifying characteristic that I could recall was that there had been picnic benches but these would be useless as a landmark because they had been three hundred yards from the road. I would not be able to see them. I would have to trust to luck and my outstanding intellect.

I skirted around the north of Pamplona and set off eastwards. Although the sky now broke up into blue bits and white bits and the sun spasmodically warmed my thighs, those last twenty miles were not the most pleasant. I was tired. Perhaps I was getting too old for sixty five miles in one day. But I made it. By seven o'clock I was drifting past the boring factory blocks that lay along the road leading into the village. It is funny how you forget things like that. The road was not at all as I had remembered it but it was the same village. Half an hour later I was installed in my infamous inn. I had the same bedroom. The shutters were still jammed shut and the towel rail was still loose.

As I enjoyed an excellent dinner in the restaurant, I

wrote up my notes for the day. From curiosity, I flicked back through the tatty notebook, through various years of trips and excursions and came across a neat diagram executed in ballpoint pen, indicating how to get around the piece of missing main road near Lekumberri. I had even drawn in the signposts and what was written on them. I should have realised that a prudent man such as I would have immediately made a record of so convoluted a diversion for future reference What a pity that my memory had not proved itself as efficient as my prescience.

But I suspect that you are all wondering about breakfast, aren't you?

I shall not say a word about breakfast. That would be to trivialise my achievements. Something of monumental proportions was awaiting me just up the road and all you are interested in is breakfast. This was the day I was attempting a repeat of my agonised crossing of the Pyrenees but in the opposite direction. I did not intend a lung-busting marathon such as before. I would spread it over two days, breaking my journey in the middle. I had telephoned ahead and booked a bed in the chalet-hostel on top of the mountain pass in France. In one pannier I carried a sheet sleeping bag and a cache of stale croissants and chocolate, in the other, my camera: the tool with which I would finally nail the doubters. I was returning to the scene of my hard won triumph. I had braved flood, tempest and loose towel rails to get to this point and all you are interested in is whether or not I got breakfast. Pah! Nothing could stop me now. As I pushed off from the hotel I was aware, once again, of the sense of occasion; of the proximity of something of monumental proportions.

And around the corner I found it. In an undeniably concrete form. It was a dam. They had built a dam across my valley. It was two hundred feet high and, in the manner of dams, reached from one side to the other with no gaps.

A dam! It's a bit excessive. A ten foot wall across the road would have stopped me. A six foot wall with barbed wire stretched along it would have served just as well. You do not need five million cubic feet of rubble buried under thirty thousand tons of concrete to prevent me from passing. I'm not Hannibal. I'm not a Panzer division. It's just me, on my bicycle. In fact, you could probably stop me from going up here just by asking me nicely. I'm not that unreasonable.

The whole point about coming up this valley was that it led to my track. If they have blocked it, I might just as well turn around and go back to Bilbao. Except that I have to be in Toulouse on Thursday to meet the coach to take me home to the UK. I surveyed this unwanted feat of Spanish civil engineering and let fly a one word oath. And it was not 'damn'. I do so enjoy the English language. It can be satisfying to the point of catharsis at times.

When you are standing at the foot of a dam and looking up at it, the effect can be quite intimidating. But I noticed that my road had been diverted so I started upwards on it, climbing the valley wall to the level of the top of the barrage. Here I was given a choice. I could cross the dam eastwards and disappear into a series of hillocks which, according to my map, would eventually lead me nowhere, or I could take a road westwards to a junction where I would be able to turn northwards towards the Pyrenees. I stood there watching the concrete dust blow along the causeway and tried to make up my mind. On the upstream side of the dam, the valley was unchanged. The river was perhaps a little higher. I looked at the barrier which had been built across the site access road. It did not actually say that bicycles were forbidden. It just said that the road was closed. Well I cannot read Spanish can I?

I pulled the barrier apart, clambered through with my bicycle and closed it behind me. Quickly, before I could be challenged, I rattled down the other side of the dam onto the road that they were drowning. For the next hour I pedalled in spooky solitude up the valley of the Iraty. I recognised the village where the girl had been playing with the dog. It was empty. Abandoned. You do not meet much traffic when you are cycling on the closed road on the wrong side of a dam. As I recalled it, the road tended to hug the valley wall. If my memory were true, then I would be all right. What I could not afford was for the road to cross the river at a point where the rising level had flooded it.

As I gradually gained height, I looked down at the Iraty and realised that this was my farewell. I would not see this valley ever again. In fact, nobody would. These houses, the tracks and hedges. Those fields. The splendid trees. That outcrop of rock. They would all disappear for ever. When I got home I found that Michelin had jumped the gun and had already erased this road from the map and replaced it with the dotted blue outline of a reservoir. Unknown to me, I was already off the map.

I eventually found my way to the road junction and the road from which departed my track. I was now stopping every quarter mile to check that my location on the ground coincided with where I thought I was on the map. At half past twelve I was looking at a narrow lane. It had stinging nettles on one verge and a sign indicating that a campsite could be found further up. I was unsure. According to the map, this was the best bet. I ate a croissant and a piece of chocolate whilst I thought about it. Perhaps I should go further to see if this was the only lane leading off right.

I bit the bullet and turned up the lane. I tried to convince myself that I was recognising odd farm buildings and other paraphernalia on each side but I knew that in truth I was not. Eventually I came to the picnic benches. Now those I did remember. There was no doubt that this lane would soon lead me on its centuries-old surface through the wildest part of the forest to my secret border crossing. I tried not to be too smug about that but I was, just a little. It was a miracle that I had been able to find my

233

route from such a brief usage, so long ago. Obviously things are remembered differently, perspectives change. Those garish yellow portable toilets, for example, they were new and looked quite out of place for so remote a site. And I did not recall this little monument. I knitted my brows as I tried to conjure meaning from the Spanish text on the plaque. Commemorating what? Something to do with *pelegrinos,* which were pilgrims and *conquistadores* and an ancient pathway and the thirteenth century and now happily in 2000... I paused uneasily in my dog translation. I did not like the look of that word *recuperado.* I stared again at the portable toilets and injected some venom into my glance.

But it was my track so I swallowed another croissant in celebration, took a swig at my water and remounted my steed. The tarmac soon gave way, not to gravel or rock, but concrete. Again, this was not something that I remembered but I could see a farm gateway up ahead so it was quite understandable that the farmer should surface this end bit of track against the worst of the winter weather. That is progress. But you can take progress too far. The concrete did not stop at the farm gate, it continued off into the forest. Well, it would make the pedalling easier to start with. Fifteen minutes later I was still on concrete. I had been passed by six cars and now I was ankle deep in crisp packets and BMWs. Some busybody organisation had proudly *recuperadoed* my ancient track. A track which, by their own admission, had lasted maintenance-free as unworn rock for at least seven hundred years and they had covered it in concrete. Did they think that their concrete would last seven hundred years? In the meantime all the legless wonders in Iberia could drive their noisy vehicles right into the very heart of this tranquil, abandoned forest.

There are no words I could write that you would wish to read to describe my feelings as I pedalled further and further towards France, occasionally pulling over to allow another car to grind past. Eventually even the cars came to the end of their concession. At a broad turning point, a long chain had been suspended to block the road. Here the crisp packets were abundant and the concrete stopped to be replaced by a thick layer of gravel ballast. I ducked under the looping iron necklace and carried on, leaving the cars champing at the chain and their drivers chomping at their chips.

After another thirty minutes of cycling I had cooled down a bit and reluctantly accepted that the gravel was far easier to cycle along than the rock which I knew lay underneath. But what about the photographic evidence that I was supposed to be producing? I had forgotten all about it. Even if I took a photograph it would not be the jagged rock track about which I had told everybody. It would be painfully easy to portend the jeering disbelief of my detractors. Nevertheless, I had dragged this inanimate lump of Ukrainian metal half way up a mountain for the purpose of establishing the incontrovertible truth of my account and that was exactly what I would have to do.

Prior to leaving England I had found it necessary to go and see Adrian. This was the best way that I could think of to satisfy the demands of certain vocal members of my audiences. They come to my talks, goggle at my stupendous slides when I throw them up on the screen and then ask me why I am not in the picture. I remind them that I travel alone because nobody will cycle with me anymore, and thus there is no one to take a picture of me. For reasons utterly obscured from me, this explanation does not serve. 'But you were there,' they insist. 'Why aren't you on the photo?' By choosing my words as judiciously as my self control permits, I patiently explain that if I am on one side of the camera, taking the photograph, I cannot be on the other side, posing for it. When they persist in contradicting me I just have to smile sweetly and shrug my shoulders. Anything more precise would insult them.

And so I went to see Adrian. Adrian has a shop full of

cameras and he sold me a little gadget that will take a picture for me. I screw it into my camera, wind it up and fifteen seconds later, it takes a picture. Actually, he sold me two because the first one exploded in my bag – apparently this is a risk that one has to run when purchasing anything which is made in Russia and powered by a strong spring. At least now I was equipped to give my audiences what they wanted. Once I had achieved that, I could analyse at leisure their reasons for wanting a picture of me. It could hardly be the celebrity factor of my countenance; I hoped that it was not a desire for corroboration.

Idly fiddling with Adrian's gadget, I surveyed the site of my proposed picture. A photographic self portrait is not the work of a moment, it takes about half an hour. There is the difficulty of framing a picture without the subject being present within it. How does one focus on something that is not there? Another component not to be overlooked is the distance from the camera to the posing position. If it takes me more than fifteen seconds to get from one to the other then all I end up with is a photo of my back or some other less photogenic part of my anatomy which the camera snaps as I struggle astride my bicycle. But for this photograph, the problem would be where to site the camera. In one of my weight saving scourges I had returned my tripod to the cupboard. This meritorious act leaves me with the option of using a low brick wall or a bench or some other flat and regular surface to support my camera and this is exactly the style of surface that is in short supply in a wild Pyrenean forest. This was a pity since I had found a pretty part of the track with not too much sand and gravel in evidence and some fairly impressive outcrops of rock. I could stand with my bicycle *there,* with the backdrop of sunlight filtering through tree leaves behind me and the rocks to my right. But there was no bench, no wall and no tripod. Then I noticed a ledge about ten feet up the rock face. From where I stood it appeared to be fairly flat. If I shinned up and installed my camera there I would get a photograph taken from above which, in addition to being of an unusual slant, would accentuate all the angles relating to height and precipitiveness. This is an accepted artistic stratagem, I hasten to point out, should you have misled yourselves into believing that I would do such a thing in order to present my endeavours in a more rigorous light than was actual.

Being a man of great action and little reflection I slung the camera around my torso by its bandolero and stretched up to the ledge. The access was not too difficult for the rock was fairly soft and I found a couple of footholds in the strata. As the ledge was only about eight inches deep, I was unable to see through the viewfinder of the camera but I was able to align the camera on its almost certain axis by wedging a few angular stones under the lens. Satisfied with my work, I slithered down the rock face to the track, bringing some loose layers of shale cascading down with me. Quite dramatic it was. Pity there was nobody to see.

I walked over to my bicycle, picked it up, posed and then checked to see if I was looking into the camera lens. It was spot on. I was naturally pleased with this but I could not allow my contentment to run to complacency. I still had the tricky bit to do. I laid down my bicycle and walked across to the rock wall. Before climbing up again, I wound up Adrian's gadget and watched it click reliably after fifteen seconds. So that was OK. It would take me two seconds to get down from the ledge, another four to cross the track; that would leave me nine seconds to brush the dust from my clothes and get astride my bike. Child's play. All I had to do now was to pop up to the ledge, screw the gadget into the camera, wind it up and return the way I had come.

I put the gadget between my lips and reached up for my handholds. I could not find them. I felt a bit further to the left. The rock was smooth. I felt to the right. No luck there. This was silly. Now concentrate Martin. Where is the camera? Its black snout pointed uncompromisingly down at me as if it had caught me stuffing packs of supermarket prime steak down the front of my trousers. Right, so you must have climbed up that way. I looked at the obvious route. I tried it. I scrabbled and pulled but there was no way up. An awful suspicion nagged at me. On slithering down from the ledge in that spectacular shower of shale, had I brought down with me the rock that had provided my hand and footholds?

Yes I had.

I could already hear the hoots of derisive laughter when I tried to explain to my disbelievers that the reason why I had no photographs was because I had stuck my camera half way up a cliff and then had been unable to reach it. Who would ever believe that? I wouldn't for a start.

I looked up at the smug apparatus.

'Come right down here this minute!' I called to it. 'I'm waiting!'

It did not budge an inch. 'You come up and get me,' it said, in Russian. It always talks in Russian when it wants to annoy me.

'This is your last chance. I shall count to ten.'

'Count to a million for all I care. I'm not budging. I like it here. By the way, I've got a lovely view from up here.'

'Right, you've asked for it.'

I picked up a stone and then realised that I was allowing my emotions to dominate my reason. Knocking the camera from the ledge with a rock would deliver me a bent biscuit tin and some interesting shapes of glass. I needed to use my stupendous brain. This was the same brain, alas, that had encouraged me to put the confounded camera up there in the first place.

If there were no footholds, then I would make some. I laid out my tool kit. Selecting a metal tyre lever for a chisel and a heavy adjustable wrench for a hammer, I proceeded to chisel finger and toe grips out of the soft rock. How fortuitous it was that I had not lightened my tool kit.

Wedging my toes precariously into the grooves and scrabbling finger tips into the rock I lunged up and grabbed the camera. As I did this, in a burst of trans Caucasian insolence, it snapped a close up picture of me.

Back on terra firma, I pushed the unspeakable object into my cycle bag and packed up. There would be no photographic proof. I had spent thirty five minutes clambering up and down a rock face all to no purpose. Deprived of its hour of glory, my camera plotted a hateful, hateful revenge.

By now I was beginning to question the worth and purpose of continuing. The valley had been dammed and the track, part-concreted and part-gravelled. This was not a dramatic re-run of my earlier expedition; it was a rather poor farce. There was now no archival or sentimental reason for me to go on. I chose to continue for purely procedural considerations – I had a room reserved in the chalet and a coach return ticket to the UK from Toulouse.

When I got to the frontier stream it was an innocent little sparkling rill tumbling between sturdy stepping stones which projected a good height clear of the water. Under the circumstances I would have expected nothing less. With the nonchalance of an habitué, I wheeled my bicycle into the water and, not allowing my familiarity to lull me into carelessness, picked my route across the stream. On the French side, a small group of French holidaymakers had gathered to watch my progress. As I stepped onto the bank an elderly lady in a flowered print dress twittered,

'We thought you were going to fall in.'

What she meant was that they had hoped that I was going to fall in.

'Oh no, not me,' I replied gaily. 'I'm used to it. I always come this way.'

'The challenge I suppose,' the man in the beret said. Then he announced to the others. 'Some people just like the challenge.'

'It's more prosaic than that,' I said as I straddled my bicycle. 'I have just come from Spain. That is the way across the frontier.'

'Spain?' the flowered dress twittered.

'That forest is in Spain.' I pointed back to the trees.

'Oh, we've been to Spain, Gérard. Fancy that!' she said to her husband.

I looked at the stepping stones and then at her. She was seventy if she was a day. She caught the direction of my glance.

'*Mais non*, young man, we didn't cross on the stones of course,' she laughed. 'We went across the concrete bridge up there.' She pointed towards the heavy foliage behind her.

I did not even deign to look. By then, I would not have been surprised to hear that they had come by Métro.

Dammed valleys, concreted roads, gravel paths, portable toilets, sturdy bridges; I formed the plaint into a string of pounding expletives as I puffed up the mountain climbs to the chalet.

The warden gave me the key and a token for the shower. Three hundred yards up the hill, the bar restaurant was perched on the edge of the drop and awaiting me. I was fed up with chewing croissants and sucking chocolate. Perhaps it was because I was tired and hungry, but the dinner in that restaurant was to be one of the best I had ever eaten.

Whilst I was awaiting the meal I was entertained by a group of about fourteen men who were seated around a settlement of bottles which had grown up in the middle of one enormous table. Carved, chiselled faces and flabby, adipose faces; thin ascetic heads and angry, voluptuous eyebrows; this group had them all. The men came in all shapes and sizes but one factor bound them sturdily together. They were all countrymen, that was obvious from their healthy faces and tawny clothes. They were cheerful drinkers all, as witnessed by the collection of bottles and the laughter and chivvying but the one thing that drew them together was that they were all speaking Basque. The ancient language that unified the separationists across the unrecognised Franco-Spanish border.

Their noisy linguistics had attracted the attention of a man in a dark coat who had come in from the night road to have a drink at the bar. He wandered over to them in a strange mixture of eager diffidence. He stood nearby, grinning and laughing with them and then he put in an observation of his own. They accorded him the reluctant politeness that one would to a status-seeking gate-crasher. He repeated his phrase and they threw it back and forth amongst themselves until one of them came up with a different version. Then they all nodded. The stranger, obviously encouraged by this, pronounced several more sentences. Two or three of the group now began to lose interest in this exercise and started chatting amongst themselves, but a few of the others considered his statements and then launched a riposte. This floored the man. He had to ask for clarification but the very process of doing so, served to further obfuscate his enquiry. Soon they were enmired in a stuttering slurry of misunderstanding and broken communication. That was when I realised what was happening. I was observing a group of Basque-speaking Frenchmen failing to comprehend a Basque-speaking Spaniard. Not only could the two factions not understand each other in their supposedly common language, but when the Spaniard explained proudly that he came from Donostia, it became embarrassingly apparent that I, an Englishman who lived nine hundred miles away, was the only other person in the room who not only knew where he meant but had also been there. Donostia could have been the meat counter in Harrod's as far as the French Basques were concerned.

An enormous tureen of vegetable soup arrived on my table: I refilled my bowl three times. Then came the French version of the Spanish *lomo* – the pork. I finished with an almond cake and a good strong coffee. If I had done nothing else worthy of note today, then I had at least found a good restaurant and enjoyed a superb meal.

And now, as I stand out on the porch, I gaze up at the night sky and see the stars in their correct setting. No squinting against sodium street lights, no peering through a haze of pollution. Just clear, sparkling points of white, blue, and pink, twinkling from generations away.

I had left my survival pouch in the chalet which was a mistake for it contained a small torch. No matter. I knew the way back which was just as well for I found that on top of that mountain at ten o'clock at night, it was black.

Unafraid of the dark, I turned to my right and strode confidently out into the obscurity. My foot stepped into space. There was nothing there.

I started to go down.

chapter seventeen

There is an awful lot of tripe written about people whose lives flash before them in bright outline whilst they plunge down the precipice. And I can assure you that it is tripe. Had the highlights of my drab existence been paraded before my world weary orbs I am certain that I would have died of boredom before I had contacted the ground. As it was, I registered a sort of puzzled surprise that my foot had encountered the kind of support that ramblers expect from arable farmers and then entered into what seemed at the time to be a prolonged period of detached wonderment at how far I would fall which gradually metamorphosed into a speculation on what exactly my injuries were likely to be when I stopped.

Then, of course, there was the purely physical reflex of my body tensing up to receive a shock. And that is another thing which annoys me. The experts in falling over always maintain that they reduce their injuries to near zero by relaxing and letting themselves just go. Jockeys can be nauseatingly smug about this. 'Oh yes, came off at the third fence doing about forty miles per hour, don't yer know. Just relaxed and rolled up into a ball, of course. Chipped a finger nail, dashed nuisance.' But then when you read their biographies you discover that they have broken more bones in their bodies than they actually possess. The execution of a fall from start to finish takes a remarkably short span of time – mere seconds. The body's natural defence is to tense up. Are we saying that Mother Nature does not know what she is doing? How do horsemen manage to overcome this reflex in time to be soaking in a spiritual jacuzzi before hitting the deck? They must decide pretty early on that they are going to give in. 'Oh dear, the gee-gee has sneezed. I think I'll let go and fall off.' Wheeh thud! Does it never occur to them that if, instead of giving up immediately, they actually tried to recoup the situation, then they might not have to go into curly-hedgehog mode quite so often?

I have occasionally fallen from my bicycle and on all occasions bar one, I had fought to reverse the situation all the way down. The one exception was on an icy lane near Lingfield where I went down so quickly that I had felt the pain of hitting the ground before I had realised what had happened. And boy did it hurt! As I had lain there entangled in my bicycle I had heard a car approaching from around the corner behind me. In my precariously prone position I had frantically waved my arm out so that the driver would see me. 'Are you all riiiiiiiiight?' the front seat passenger enquired solicitously of me as the car span deftly through half a circle and slid backwards out of sight around the next corner. The driver was probably a jockey.

So immediately I realised that I had no visible means of support, I tried to turn around in mid air and step back to where I had started from. It was the kind of manoeuvre whose success could only realistically be expected within the context of the animated cartoon film but I thought it was worth trying since events in my life had occasionally aped that particular cinematographic genre. The result was that when I hit the car park five feet below me, I rolled onto my back. Good. No expensive dentistry involved then. The first task in a situation such as this is to lie still and take a serious stock of one's position before moving so, naturally, I leaped up in the air to prove that everything was working and then gasped in pain at the stinging burn coming from my grazed hip and forearm.

When I had regained my composure sufficiently to consider trying to get to a place of safety, I came up against the difficulty of choosing a direction for although I knew with a brutal certainty that I had reached my destination, I did not yet know what that destination was. It was not until the following morning that I discovered that I had merely stepped off the top of a five foot wall into a car park. I ask you to mark the restrained use of the word, 'merely'.

I set to crawling with my hand sweeping the ground before me. It was painful. I eventually found my way to the road and hauled myself shakily upright. I hung on to the bank for a while and then gingerly edged sideways down what I hoped was the road. It took me another ten minutes just to totter the three hundred yards back to the chalet.

Once inside, I inspected my wounds. My forearm was a bloody mass of graze and gravel, my hip was bruised and sore. Enough of this self obsession! I washed at the sink, took two aspirins, went to bed and cried myself to sleep.

Next morning I hobbled into the communal kitchen and waited whilst a couple of ramblers bickered at the gas hob.

'You've put far too much water in the saucepan.'

'Do you want coffee or don't you?'

'Of course I do, but that will take all day to heat.'

'You have to put in sufficient water to cover the bottom or it'll burn the pan.'

'But we don't need that much water.'

'Well find a smaller pan then.'

'There isn't one.'

'So that is why I am having to use this one.'

'They should have a smaller pan.'

'You find one then.'

I also only wanted to heat up a beaker's worth of water. I intended to pour it on a sachet of instant coffee that I had found wedged in the skirting board by my bed. Never pass up a free breakfast. At this rate I would not get away before midday. I edged into the kitchen area. The two ramblers glanced suspiciously at me and closed ranks around the hob. They continued their warfare in hisses.

'Why isn't there a kettle?'

'I don't know why there isn't a kettle.'

'It would be quicker in a kettle.'

I took down a beaker from the rack. They stopped to watch me.

'I know it would be quicker in a kettle.'

'Have you looked for one?'

'Of course I've looked.'

Pardon,' I said pleasantly. They froze as I squeezed past to get to the sink, then they continued.

'I shall give the warden a piece of my mind when we hand in the key.'

'He told us to drop it back through the letter box. He won't be there.'

'Well somebody will be there.'

They stopped and watched whilst I filled my beaker with cold water from the tap. They were feeling threatened. They had the only saucepan and we all knew that they were heating up too much water for themselves to use. What were they intending do with the surplus?

'No, he won't be there.'

'But the office will be open. Someone will be there.'

'No they won't. The office does not open till after lunch. Not till three.'

'But that's scandalous.'

They stopped again as I walked past to the other end of the kitchen but they were too engrossed in their own conflict and too worried that I might try to negotiate for their surplus water to pay any heed to what I was doing.

'I told you yesterday that they did not open until the afternoon.'

'But yesterday, I didn't know that they only had one saucepan, did I?'

'Neither did I.'

Ping!

I opened the microwave oven door and removed my beaker of steaming water. I shook in my coffee powder and stirred it vigorously. They were staring at me.

'Bon appetit!' I said and walked to the table where the last two of my Spanish croissants were lurking crustily in a paper bag. The ramblers turned back to the hob.

'Why didn't you tell me about the microwave oven?'

'I didn't know. You could have used it if you had seen it.'

'Get me two beakers. We can pour some of this water in. It'll be quicker.'

'You idiot. You've used a saucepan with no lip. How are you going to pour from that.'

'I used the only saucepan that was there...'

They went on like this for another three minutes.

My key clunked safely from the letter slot to the floor inside the office. I had walked my bicycle up the short distance from the chalet. This exercise allowed me to assess how my body was working after my fall. It was not brilliant. My arm was still stinging even though the accident had been twelve hours earlier. At least nothing was broken as far as I could tell. It seemed that the Pyrenees were destined always to try to damage me in some way or another, as if demanding respect.

From the corner of the road, where my old shale track would lead me back over cow-haunted summits to Mauléon

Licharre, the view was magnificent and restful. Magnificent, for the splendid diorama of raw peaks and misted summits and restful, if one did not think too hard about cycling up them. There could be no argument that this would make a stunning photograph. My Russian camera, however, begged to differ.

I dragged it squealing from its slumbers in my cosy cycle bag and prepared to wind on the film. My camera weighs three and a half pounds so this is a two handed job. I have to point the camera downwards, grip it firmly with my left hand and with my right thumb twist a ratchet lever through one hundred and eighty degrees and then allow it to spring back. This advances the film by one frame and cocks the shutter ready for a photograph. And I knew that twisting my right wrist would pull at my grazed forearm. I gritted my teeth and did it.

Kerchunk.

That sounded as if I had fired the shutter. I looked through the viewfinder and sure enough, a photograph had been taken. Counting the insolent snapshot of yesterday, that left me with ten frames remaining. Taking great care to keep my errant wiggly fingers as far as possible away from the shutter button, I twisted the lever again.

Kerchunk.

It had taken another picture. Now I did not think that my fingers had been anywhere near the shutter button this time so how had that happened?

I wound on the film again.

Kerchunk.

That means I have eight left now. So I take great care and do it properly.

Kerchunk.

Seven left.

I tried two in a row to fool it.

Kerchunk.

Kerchunk.

It was not fooled. Five left.

There was apparently a malfunction somewhere. I had modestly thought that it had been mine. I now realised that it was the camera's. This was its hateful revenge. I tried moving the lever smartly to its full extent in one sharp movement.

Kerchunk.

I tried softly. It stuck halfway. That was no earthly use. It needed to go the full distance to cock the shutter. I nudged it to the end of its arc. It wedged itself there. I delicately peered through the viewfinder. I focused on the mountains and pressed the shutter button. Nothing happened. The shutter was not fully cocked. I lowered the camera and gently eased the lever.

Kerchunk.

Three left.

Those last three were consumed in an angry frenzy of lever wrenching and teeth gnashing. I had wound a complete film through the camera without managing to frame a single shot. Why?

'Why?' was probably also the word which formed in the mind of the chemist when he returned the processed film to me some weeks later. Why should anybody want one close-up photograph of his left nostril and eleven blurred pictures of his groin? I did not bother to elucidate. Some things are best left unexplained.

I thrust my camera back into the bag and launched myself off onto the shale track. It was not shale any more, of course, it now wore a coat of beautifully smooth tarmac.

I think this was the point at which I gave in and admitted that the trip had not quite been the resounding success that I had hoped for. Certain minor aspects had, perhaps, not been fully researched. Indeed, upon honest reflection, the expedition had been an unmitigated failure but, quite frankly, I did not care anymore. If people did not want to believe my account then that was their privilege. I should not need their acclaim just as they should not need my photographs.

I had got five days left to get myself to Toulouse. By unashamedly using trains for hilly bits and the bike for the flat bits, I did it in three. Cathy and Freddy in Toulouse, I had not seen for a quarter of a century yet they opened their house to me. I evoke this as an illustration of their unconditional hospitality and not as an irrefragable proof of my irresistible charm.

Toulouse was nice. The sun shone. Nobody harried me. The roads were flat. The food was good. It did not occur to me that my old enemy France was baiting a trap. What a simple minded fellow I am.

Thursday morning came and I bade goodbye and many thanks to my hosts and set off for the rendezvous with my coach. This was to be in an industrial estate on the outskirts of the city. The reason for this was operational. The coach had several pick up points on its return to Calais and in order to reduce the delay to the minimum, each stop was chosen to be as close to a motorway junction as possible. My seat was already reserved. I had the ticket in my pouch but I could not afford to be late because the coach would only wait at the pick up point from two o'clock until half past. After that, it would have to continue.

I had only ten miles to cover. The road was flat and the wind was slight. I could do it in an hour without effort. I allowed myself two. The sun beat down on the avenues of the Toulousain *banlieue* which were refreshingly empty of traffic for I was travelling in the lunch hour. I had dawdled a bit on the country part of the route just to savour the quiet and the warmth. It was now half past one and I was twenty minutes away from my coach. As I entered a roundabout, tufted in the middle with barren brown grass, I gave a kick on my pedals just to clear myself ahead of the proposed trajectory of one of the rare vehicles joining. My back wheel locked solid and I slithered to a halt askew the road.

I was jerked from the saddle and staggered sideways, trying to convince my damaged hip that it could support me. Thankfully, the driver was awake. In a screech of tyres the car stood on its nose, changed gear and then slalomed around me.

Huffing and wincing, I dragged my bicycle to the verge. The jammed tyre marked a black liquorice lace on the soft tarmac. That last kick of the pedals had pulled the wheel forwards on the chainwheel side and wedged it crookedly between the rear forks. The effect it produced was similar to locking the brakes full on. I started to unscrew the fiddly gnurled bolt which would allow me to remove the gear changing mechanism from my axle end and thus give me the access to the wheel nut necessary to redress the situation. I could not shift it. By ten to two, the thumb and forefingers of both hands were red and blistered and the bicycle was ruddy and blasted. And a few other epithets which I would blush to divulge.

By five past two, I was wondering whether I should try to walk to the coach but I knew that my arms and hips would not allow me to drag a loaded bicycle three miles and I would have to drag it because the wheel would not turn and I could not carry it all that way. I sat on the hot, bald grass alongside my bicycle and asked it if it thought that it was really being fair to me and it replied that any prudent rider would have checked the tightness of his wheelnuts several times on a journey which involved shaking along bumpy tracks. All right then, said I, allowing it to be my fault, what do you suggest? I might point out that I can walk to the bus without you. I could leave you here. Ah, but you wouldn't, the bike replied, not after the twenty odd thousand miles we have done together. Why don't you slacken off the wheel nut on the opposite side to straighten my wheel? If you promise to cycle gently I will try to keep my chain on the sprockets.

So that is what I did.

I rolled precariously into the car park at twenty five minutes past two.

'You for us?' one of the crew shouted.

'Yup, that's me,' I replied and another of the coach drivers jumped up onto the double deck trailer, ready to load my bike.

The passengers from the bus who had been loafing in the car park now reboarded in a businesslike manner.

'You were lucky. Another five minutes and we would have gone without you.'

I looked at him. He had straggly fair hair and a beaky nose. From his scrawny shoulders hung a short sleeved shirt with two breast pockets and from his baggy khaki shorts protruded whitish spindly legs, blobbed with knobbly knees.

'I had a breakdown just up the road.'

I did not feel like justifying myself to this twerp. I had taken an instant dislike to his busybodying manner. What an ambassador for British cycling! He looked like a half drawn cartoon character. Big goofy eyes behind circular spectacles, gawky limbs, and that know-all, nosiness; that wish to revel in another's misfortune. I bet he used to hang around at the back of the school playground and kick people when they had fallen over.

'We were going without you.' He poked his head irritatingly into my face again as I handed up my bags to the driver on the coach.

'The coach is not due to depart for another five minutes,' I said evenly. I felt more like poking him in the eye with a dirty stick.

His strutting head was now jutting over my left shoulder.

'Another two minutes and we'd have gone. You'd have been stuck.'

The drivers jumped down and tied the tarpaulin.

'OK' he said, 'let's go.'

'You were lucky,' said the twerp. His tongue flicked over

his lips like a lizard's. 'Nearly went without you.'

I drew myself up and looked at the specimen. In my best imitation of a rich, lazy, drawl I assured him with utter nonchalance, 'Oh they wouldn't have gone without me. You see,' I stared brazenly into his goggling eyes, 'THEY know who I am.'

I swept past him and up the stairs to my seat.

'Wha? Wha?' I heard him choking behind me as the driver ushered him onto the coach. Then he whispered urgently, 'Who is he? Who's that?'

'Oh I can't tell you that sir,' the driver replied with a scrupulous honesty that the twerp naturally interpreted as a security clamp down.

I busied myself with my food bag on the floor between my feet. I could feel his rabidly curious stare burning into the top of my head as he squeezed down the aisle to his seat at the front, his baggy shorts flapping against the seats like an elephant's ears at a coffee morning. He stopped a couple of times and quizzed other passengers but they could not see whom he was talking about. For the next few hours of daylight, every time I looked forwards I saw his periscope neck straining to identify the celebrity that was me.

My house was probably pleased to see me but it had a funny way of showing it. I had no hot water. And I mean, no hot water. No moisture of any sort emerged from any of the hot water taps in the house. This was because three weeks earlier, I had turned on the hot water tap on my washbasin and then got on my bicycle and departed for Spain. I had remembered to lock my doors but not to turn off the tap so for three carefree weeks, the water had thundered down the plug hole, cheerily warmed by the glowing boiler that I had also omitted to extinguish. Our street must have had the cosiest drains in the city. They now probably support a flourishing community of tropical algae.

Perhaps they will name it after me.
Martinus Fagottenaturnoffatapus.

Two days later I was listening to the French news on the radio as I shaved in cold water and I learned that the roundabout where my bicycle had seized up had been singed to a cinder by the gigantic industrial explosion that had wrecked that portion of the city. It raised the unworthy suspicion in me that France really did not want me back.

But I would have to go back to Spain.

If only to disprove Keith's ju-ju assertion that it would rain on me every time that I visited. Who knows? I might even make an attempt to learn a bit of the lingo.

Yes I would have to go back.

The people were worth it. And in any case...

Spain still owes me a breakfast.

Illustrations

Thumbnail faces

Spaniards who stopped talking long enough for me to sketch them

The Trouble with France

Martin Lloyd's new international number one blockbusting bestseller

"...makes Baedeker's look like a guidebook..."

When Martin Lloyd set out on his holiday to Suffolk why did he end up in Boulogne? What caused Max the Mad Alsatian to steal his map and what did the knitted grandma really think of his display of hot plate juggling? The answers to these and many more mysteries are to be found in THE TROUBLE WITH FRANCE

THE TROUBLE WITH FRANCE contains no recipes and no hand drawn maps. It does not recount how somebody richer than you went to a part of France that you have never heard of, bought a stone ruin for a song and converted it into a luxurious retreat which they expect you to finance by buying their book.

Nor is it the self satisfied account of another ultra fit expedition cyclist abseiling down Everest on a penny farthing but Martin Lloyd attempting an uneventful ride on a mundane bicycle through an uninteresting part of France... and failing with outstanding success.

THE TROUBLE WITH FRANCE is destined to be a worldwide success now that Margaret's Mum has been down the road and told her friend Pat about it.

Published by Queen Anne's Fan ISBN: 9780 9547 15007

Martin Lloyd has recorded THE TROUBLE WITH FRANCE as a talking book for the blind. RNIB catalogue no: TB 15323

Hunting
the
Golden Lion

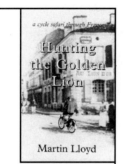

a cycle safari through France

Having recklessly declared in a previous book that it
must be possible to cross all of France staying only
in hotels called the HOTEL DU LION D'OR,
Martin Lloyd is challenged by his critics to prove
his assertion in the only way possible – by doing it.

Surely it will be a straightforward and leisurely ride
through France? As long as the hotels are no more than
a day's cycle ride apart, of course. And if your bicycle
has been constructed this century, and if you remember
to take with you all that you need... and if your name isn't
Martin Lloyd.

Is this why, on the the first day of his safari,
he is standing in his pyjamas on a pavement
a thousand miles from home,
clutching a broken bicycle
with a bleeding hand?

Published by Queen Anne's Fan ISBN: 9780 9547 1506 9

The
Chinese
Transfer

Martin Lloyd

The
Chinese Transfer

a thriller romance that you will
not want to put down

'...this is storytelling as it used to be...'

Paris in the 1970s – student demonstrations, union
strikes and oppressive heat. Coach driver Simon
Laperche is sent to Orly Airport to pick up a Chinese
group and take them to their hotel in the city. A run
of the mill job. He could do it with his eyes shut.
It was a pity about the guide, but then, he could
not expect to please everybody.

Abruptly, things go wrong. The plane is diverted to
Lyons and Laperche is ordered to drive his coach
south to meet it... and he has to take that infuriating
guide with him. Unknown to them both,
a terrorist unit has targeted their group and
is intent upon its destruction.

Stalked by the terrorists, the driver and guide continue
to bicker as they struggle to bring their group safely to
Paris. Will the mutual respect which eventually begins
to grow between them prove strong enough
when the test comes?

Published by Queen Anne's Fan ISBN: 9780 9547 15021

Rue Amélie

Rue Amélie

Martin Lloyd

another fast-paced thriller from Martin Lloyd.

Following the success of *The Chinese Transfer*, Martin Lloyd takes us back to the seedy side of Paris in the 1970s. Joel LeBatard, a driver for a small-time crook, loses his boss's car and his position. With no job and soon to be thrown out of his bedsit, he accepts a commission from a woman he meets at a funeral, to find out where her father had invested his secret pension.

LeBatard discovers that others are on the same trail – a ruthless big-time gangster whom he has already been stupid enough to upset, and an ex-colleague from his army days who now heads an undercover squad in the Ministry of Defence. They will stop at nothing to get their hands on the very thing that he is looking for, but nobody can tell him what it is.

The hectic action takes them to the four corners of Paris. Whilst pursuing his relentless search, LeBatard struggles with two difficulties: is his new employer telling him the truth and how, in the face of such energy and charm, can he uphold his vow never to get mixed up with another woman?

Published by Queen Anne's Fan ISBN: 9780 9547 1507 6

Every
Picture

Martin Lloyd

Every

Picture

'... a tender and engaging love story...'

When the son of an earl meets the daughter of
a coal miner in the doorway of the art college he
does not tell her that he is a viscount.

Why should he?

How was he to know that their paths would cross
and recross and that he would fall in
love with her?

And once that has happened, he finds it impossible to
tell her the truth for fear of losing her. At the very
moment that they finally admit their feelings for one
another, the relationship is wrenched asunder as their
lives take a violent and unpredictable turn, casting their
two destinies onto divergent courses.

Will they ever meet again?

Published by Queen Anne's Fan ISBN: 9780 9547 1505 2

The Impetus Turn

...Western prejudice meets Eastern corruption...

His Boss: 'You must have misunderstood me Mr. Wrighton... there is nothing here to say that you were special and were to be paid to be ready to serve abroad without acutally having to pack your bags.'

His Wife: 'You want to go don't you? You can't wait to get away from your wife and family for six months, can you?

In the 1980s, a civil engineer is sent to work in Bangladesh and is thrown into a world of stark contrasts; of poverty and disease, of diplomatic parties, corporate power and corruption.

With a naivety aggravated by his stubbornness, he begins to uncover a fraud which threatens to cause devastating repercussions in the political arena and exert a disastrous influence upon his career. Should he continue?

Published by Queen Anne's Fan ISBN: 9780 9573 639 5 3

THE PASSPORT

The History of Man's Most Travelled Document

THIRD EDITION, REVISED AND ENLARGED

Hardback with 294 pages
and 83 illustrations

The passport is a document familiar to many, used and recognised worldwide and yet it has no basis in law: one country cannot oblige another to admit its subjects simply by issuing a document. But the state, by insisting on the requirement to hold a passport, provides for itself a neat, self-financing data collection and surveillance system.

This well illustrated book tells for the first time the story of the passport from its earliest origins to its latest high-tech developments. Handwritten documents adorned with wax seals, modern versions in plastic covers, diplomatic passports and wartime safe conducts, all drawn from the author's collection, complement the exciting exploits of spies and criminals and the tragic real life experiences of refugees.

Whether recounting the birth of the British blue passport of the 1920s or divulging the secrets of today's machine readable passport, Martin Lloyd has written an informative and engrossing history book which is accessible to everyone.

"...a lively and thoughtful book..."
SUNDAY TELEGRAPH

Published by Queen Anne's Fan   ISBN: 9780 9547 1503 8

Neither Civil nor Servant

Twenty-four years in the
Immigration Service

Hardback 442 pp.
sixty b&w illustrations.

Neither
Civil
nor
Servant

Twenty-four years in the
Immigration Service.

Martin Lloyd.

When Britain joined the Common Market, Martin Lloyd joined the UK Immigration Service. For the next twenty-four years he rubbed shoulders with royalty and rascals while stamping passports in the company of scholars, schemers and scatterbrains.

This colourful narrative traces Martin Lloyd's progress from Heathrow's Terminal Three, when Concorde was a novelty, through the first waves of political asylum refugees to the complexities of manning the United Kingdom's first real international land border – the Channel tunnel.

His dealings with the dangerous, the illegal, the lunatic and the famous are recounted within the framework of the politics and the social issues of the time. This is no high treatise on the international right of the movement of labour; it is a down-to-earth account of how the Immigration Service functioned at the human level and of the challenges faced by those employed to police the borders of the United Kingdom.

Martin Lloyd is an amusing and entertaining public speaker and brings to this work the wit, humour and sharply focused observation for which he is well known.

Published by Queen Anne's Fan ISBN: 9780 9573 6390 8

Fire Smoke and Iron

Fuego, Humo y Hierro

Spanish artists and the Bilbao iron industry.

95 full colour illustrations and 35 black & white.

Bilbao in Spain has been producing iron for centuries, drawing in workers from all over the country. Its rapid industrialisation in the nineteenth century was helped in no little measure by British capital and entrepreneurship. Ships carried Welsh coal to Spain and brought back Spanish iron ore for the steelworks of South Wales.

By 1985, it was all over. But the rise, heyday and demise of the Bilbaoan iron industry has been forever fixed in oils, water colours and bronze.

This book tells how iron is made into steel; showing the machinery involved and explaining the processes used. It then presents the evocative artworks which have recorded this industry in its various stages and explains and interprets the activities depicted therein.

Published by Queen Anne's Fan ISBN: 9780 9573 639-3-9

No Harm in Looking

A beautifully bound hardback with
nine colour plates.

being a collection of

TALES OF EROTIC FANTASY

for the delectation of

LADIES AND GENTLEMEN ALIKE

*especially illustrated
and published in this edition
for the author's friends
by*

K. T. Yalta

Published by Queen Anne's Fan ISBN: 9780 9547 1508 3